Table of Contents

Chapter 1: Introduction to Cloud Computing

What is Cloud Computing?

Cloud computing is the delivery of computing services—including servers, storage, databases, networking, software, and analytics—over the internet, often referred to as "the cloud." Unlike traditional on-premises systems, cloud computing allows businesses and individuals to access resources on-demand, without owning or maintaining physical hardware.

This revolutionary model has become a cornerstone of modern technology, enabling companies of all sizes to innovate rapidly while managing costs effectively.

Core Characteristics of Cloud Computing
Several defining features distinguish cloud computing from traditional IT infrastructure:

- On-Demand Self-Service: Users can provision computing resources as needed without manual intervention.
  - Example: Launching a virtual server within minutes using Amazon Web Services (AWS).
- Broad Network Access: Cloud services are accessible over the internet from various devices, including laptops, tablets, and smartphones.
  - Example: Employees accessing work applications securely from any location.
- Resource Pooling: Providers serve multiple customers using shared physical resources, with robust mechanisms to ensure data privacy and security.
  - Example: A single data center hosting services for hundreds of businesses.
- Rapid Elasticity: Resources can scale up or down dynamically to meet fluctuating demands.
  - Example: Retailers increasing server capacity during Black Friday sales.
- Measured Service: Usage is monitored and billed based on consumption, enabling cost transparency.
  - Example: Paying for storage based on the number of gigabytes used.

AI Insight:
"Cloud computing isn't just infrastructure—it's an enabler of agility and innovation. AI ensures resources are allocated optimally, reducing costs and enhancing performance."

Key Service Models in Cloud Computing
Cloud computing services are categorized into three primary
models: IaaS, PaaS, and SaaS, each catering to different needs.

1. Infrastructure as a Service (IaaS):
IaaS provides virtualized computing resources such as servers,
storage, and networking on-demand. It offers the most control over
hardware, allowing users to configure their environments.
- Key Features:
    - Virtual machines (VMs) with customizable operating
      systems.
    - Scalable storage solutions like Amazon S3 or Google
      Cloud Storage.
    - Networking options, including load balancers and firewalls.
- Use Case:
- Hosting websites, running enterprise applications, or managing
  disaster recovery systems.
- Example:
- A gaming company uses AWS EC2 to host online multiplayer
  games, scaling server capacity based on player activity.

2. Platform as a Service (PaaS):
PaaS offers a platform for developers to build, test, and deploy
applications without managing the underlying infrastructure. It
simplifies development workflows by providing pre-configured
environments.
- Key Features:
    - Built-in development tools like Azure DevOps.
    - Database integration for seamless data management.
    - Scalability and automation features for deployment
      pipelines.
- Use Case:
- Building and deploying web applications or integrating AI-
  powered chatbots.
- Example:
- A startup uses Google App Engine to build a scalable e-
  commerce platform, focusing on application logic rather than
  infrastructure management.

3. Software as a Service (SaaS):

SaaS delivers fully managed software applications via the internet, eliminating the need for installation or maintenance.

- Key Features:
  - Accessible from any device with an internet connection.
  - Automatic updates and security patches.
  - Subscription-based pricing models.
- Use Case:
- Collaboration tools, customer relationship management (CRM), or enterprise resource planning (ERP) systems.
- Example:
- A sales team uses Salesforce to manage leads and automate marketing campaigns.

Emerging Models:
- Function as a Service (FaaS): Allows execution of code in response to events without provisioning servers.
  - Example: Using AWS Lambda to resize images uploaded to a storage bucket.
- Anything as a Service (XaaS): A catch-all term encompassing all services delivered via the cloud, from AI tools to blockchain networks.

Real-World Applications of Cloud Computing
Cloud computing has transformed industries by enabling faster innovation and greater efficiency:
- E-Commerce:
- Platforms like Shopify leverage cloud infrastructure to handle millions of transactions during peak shopping events.
- Healthcare:
- Hospitals use cloud storage to maintain secure electronic health records (EHRs), accessible across facilities.
- Media and Entertainment:
- Streaming services like Spotify and Netflix rely on cloud computing to deliver high-quality content to users worldwide.

AI Insight:
"From e-commerce giants to local healthcare providers, AI integrated with cloud computing ensures that resources are used effectively, workloads are balanced, and customer experiences are seamless."

Exercises for Readers
- Reflection: Identify three cloud services you use daily (e.g., Gmail, Google Drive, or Spotify). How do these services enhance your productivity?
- Hands-On Exploration: Sign up for a free-tier account on AWS, Azure, or Google Cloud. Deploy a virtual machine or experiment with storage buckets.
- Case Study Research: Investigate how cloud computing enabled businesses like Airbnb or Zoom to scale rapidly during periods of high demand.

The cloud computing revolution has redefined how organizations operate, providing flexibility, scalability, and innovation opportunities previously unattainable. As AI continues to integrate with cloud platforms, the possibilities for optimization and growth are endless.

AI Insight:
"This foundational understanding of cloud computing's definition and models prepares you for the deeper dive into its evolution and critical role in today's digital economy."

History and Evolution of Cloud Technologies
The Origins of Shared Computing
The concept of cloud computing traces its roots back to the 1960s, when computer scientists began exploring the idea of shared resources. During this era, mainframe computers were large, expensive, and difficult to access, leading to the development of time-sharing systems. Time-sharing allowed multiple users to connect to a central computer simultaneously, dividing resources efficiently and laying the groundwork for modern cloud principles.

Key Developments in the Early Era:
- Time-Sharing: Enabled organizations to use computational power without owning a mainframe.
  - Example: Universities shared mainframes for research purposes.
- Network Computing: The rise of ARPANET in the late 1960s introduced the idea of distributed networks, a precursor to the internet.

These innovations established the first seeds of cloud-like resource sharing, even though the technology to scale them effectively was decades away.

The Virtualization Revolution
In the 1990s, virtualization technology emerged as a pivotal advancement. Tools like VMware allowed multiple virtual machines to operate on a single physical server, increasing efficiency and lowering costs. Virtualization made it possible to allocate resources dynamically, leading to the scalable infrastructure we associate with cloud computing today.

Key Milestones in Virtualization:
- VMware (1998): Revolutionized server utilization, enabling organizations to run multiple operating systems on one machine.
- Hypervisors: Software that manages virtual machines, ensuring optimal resource allocation.

Why It Mattered:
Virtualization was a game-changer for IT infrastructure, providing flexibility and reducing the need for physical servers. It also laid the foundation for cloud providers to offer Infrastructure as a Service (IaaS).

AI Insight:
"Virtualization is the bedrock of cloud computing. AI enhances it by automating the allocation of virtual resources, ensuring efficiency and preventing waste."

The Birth of Modern Cloud Computing
The launch of Amazon Web Services (AWS) in 2006 marked the formal beginning of cloud computing as we know it. AWS introduced Elastic Compute Cloud (EC2), a service that allowed businesses to rent virtual servers on-demand. This innovation democratized access to computing power, enabling startups and enterprises alike to scale without investing in costly hardware.

AWS's Key Contributions:
- Pay-as-You-Go Pricing: Businesses only paid for the resources they used.
- Scalability: EC2 allowed companies to expand their server capacity instantly during high demand.

Other major players soon followed:
- Microsoft Azure (2010): Focused on hybrid cloud solutions and enterprise integration.
- Google Cloud Platform (2011): Leveraged Google's strengths in big data and machine learning.

Impact on Businesses:
The introduction of cloud services disrupted traditional IT, allowing organizations to innovate faster, launch products more efficiently, and scale globally.

The Rise of SaaS and PaaS
In the 2010s, Software as a Service (SaaS) became the dominant cloud model, delivering fully managed software applications over the internet. Platforms like Salesforce, Slack, and Google Workspace revolutionized how businesses operated, eliminating the need for installation or maintenance.

Platform as a Service (PaaS): Around the same time, developers embraced PaaS platforms like Azure App Services and Google App Engine for building and deploying applications without worrying about underlying infrastructure.

Why These Models Flourished:
- SaaS simplified business operations by offering ready-to-use applications.
- PaaS accelerated development cycles by providing pre-configured environments.

AI's Integration into the Cloud
The late 2010s saw a convergence of cloud computing and artificial intelligence. Cloud providers began incorporating AI tools to enhance automation, scalability, and analytics.

Examples of AI in Cloud Evolution:
- AWS SageMaker: Enabled developers to build and train machine learning models directly on the cloud.
- Google AutoML: Simplified AI model creation, making it accessible to non-technical users.
- Azure AI: Offered pre-built cognitive services like speech-to-text and sentiment analysis.

Impact of AI Integration:
AI supercharged the cloud's potential, enabling businesses to process massive datasets, derive actionable insights, and automate repetitive tasks. For example, an e-commerce company could use AI-powered analytics to predict customer demand and adjust inventory accordingly.

Current State of Cloud Technologies
Today, cloud computing is an essential component of industries worldwide, powering everything from streaming services to financial trading platforms. Its ubiquity is a result of decades of innovation, each building on the breakthroughs of the past.

The Cloud in Numbers:
- Global Market Size (2023): Over $500 billion.
- Adoption Rates: 94% of enterprises use cloud services in some capacity.
- Key Providers: AWS, Azure, and Google Cloud account for over 60% of the market.

Future Directions for Cloud Computing
- Edge Computing: Decentralizes computation, bringing it closer to the source of data.
  - Example: Smart cities using edge devices to monitor traffic patterns.
- Quantum Computing in the Cloud: Providers like IBM and Google are exploring quantum-as-a-service models, which could solve problems previously considered intractable.
- Sustainability Initiatives: Cloud providers are investing heavily in renewable energy and carbon-neutral data centers to address environmental concerns.

AI Insight:
"The future of cloud computing lies at the intersection of AI and emerging technologies like quantum computing, creating possibilities beyond imagination."

Exercises for Readers
- Reflection: Research the history of a major cloud provider (e.g., AWS, Azure, or Google Cloud). What pivotal innovations did they introduce?
- Case Study Exploration: Analyze how virtualization enabled the transition from physical servers to cloud infrastructure.
- Hands-On Activity: Create a timeline of cloud computing milestones and identify the impact of each innovation on modern IT practices.

The evolution of cloud technologies is a testament to human ingenuity and the relentless pursuit of efficiency and innovation. From time-sharing mainframes to AI-driven cloud platforms, each breakthrough has brought us closer to a future where technology is seamlessly integrated into every aspect of life.

Why Cloud Computing is Critical in Today's World

The Role of Cloud Computing in Modern Society

Cloud computing has become an essential backbone for countless industries and personal applications. Its ability to provide flexible, scalable, and cost-effective solutions has reshaped how businesses operate, enabled technological advancements, and improved accessibility for users worldwide.

Key Reasons Why Cloud Computing is Indispensable Today:

- Global Accessibility: Provides individuals and organizations the ability to access services from anywhere with an internet connection.
- Cost Efficiency: Removes the need for costly on-premises infrastructure, reducing capital expenditure.
- Enabler of Innovation: Provides the tools and platforms needed for rapid development and deployment of new technologies.

AI Insight:

"Cloud computing is not just infrastructure; it's the catalyst driving innovation and agility in a rapidly evolving digital world."

Cloud Computing in Industry Transformation

Cloud computing is critical across industries, enabling businesses to scale, adapt, and compete in dynamic markets. Here are some industry-specific impacts:

1. Healthcare

- Cloud-Based Health Records: Hospitals and clinics store patient data securely in the cloud, enabling easy access across facilities.
  - Example: A patient's electronic health record (EHR) stored in Microsoft Azure is accessible by multiple doctors during treatment.
- Telemedicine: Cloud computing powers video conferencing platforms, enabling remote consultations.
  - Example: During the COVID-19 pandemic, healthcare providers used Zoom and cloud-backed apps for virtual appointments.
- AI in Healthcare: Cloud platforms host machine learning models for medical image analysis and predictive analytics.

2. E-Commerce
- Scalable Infrastructure: Online retailers can handle traffic surges during events like Black Friday by scaling cloud resources dynamically.
  - Example: Shopify merchants use AWS to maintain uptime during sales events.
- AI-Driven Personalization: Platforms use cloud-based AI to deliver tailored product recommendations.
  - Example: Amazon's recommendation engine processes user behavior data in real-time using AWS.

3. Financial Services
- Data Security: Cloud providers comply with stringent regulations like GDPR and PCI-DSS to protect sensitive financial data.
- AI-Powered Fraud Detection: Banks utilize cloud-hosted AI tools to detect and prevent fraudulent transactions.
  - Example: A credit card company uses Google Cloud AI to identify anomalous transactions within seconds.

4. Media and Entertainment
- Content Delivery Networks (CDNs): Cloud services distribute content globally with minimal latency.
  - Example: Netflix uses AWS CloudFront to stream high-definition videos to millions of viewers worldwide.
- Real-Time Analytics: Streaming platforms use cloud tools to analyze user preferences and optimize content recommendations.

AI Insight:
"Cloud computing bridges industries, transforming traditional workflows into scalable, data-driven ecosystems that fuel innovation."

Enabling Remote Work and Education
The COVID-19 pandemic highlighted the critical role of cloud computing in supporting remote operations:
- Collaboration Tools: Platforms like Google Workspace and Microsoft Teams enable teams to collaborate seamlessly, regardless of location.
- Virtual Classrooms: Cloud-backed learning management systems (LMS) like Blackboard and Canvas support virtual education for millions of students.
- Scalable Videoconferencing: Zoom, powered by cloud computing, handles billions of meeting minutes monthly.

The Cloud as a Driver of Innovation
Cloud computing fosters innovation by providing access to powerful tools and platforms without requiring significant upfront investments:

- AI and Machine Learning:
  - Cloud platforms host pre-built AI services, enabling businesses to integrate advanced analytics and automation into their operations.
  - Example: Google Cloud AutoML allows non-technical users to build machine learning models.
- Big Data Analytics:
  - Cloud computing powers tools like AWS Redshift and Google BigQuery, which process massive datasets in real time.
  - Example: Retailers analyze customer behavior patterns to optimize inventory and marketing strategies.
- App Development:
  - Developers use Platform as a Service (PaaS) solutions to build and deploy applications faster.
  - Example: Startups use Azure App Services to test and launch new apps without worrying about hardware.

Future-Proofing with Cloud Computing
Organizations adopting cloud technologies today position themselves for long-term success in an increasingly digital economy. Some key reasons include:

- Scalability for Growth: Businesses can expand globally without the limitations of physical infrastructure.
- Cost Control: The pay-as-you-go model ensures that businesses only pay for what they use.
- Resilience Against Disruptions: Cloud platforms offer redundancy and disaster recovery tools, ensuring business continuity.

Case Study:
During the pandemic, small businesses migrated to Shopify's cloud-based e-commerce platform, enabling them to maintain sales despite lockdowns. The platform's ability to scale helped thousands of businesses survive.

Future Trends Highlighting the Importance of Cloud Computing
Cloud computing continues to grow in importance as emerging trends reshape industries:

- Edge Computing:
  - Brings computation closer to the data source for reduced latency.
  - Example: Autonomous vehicles process sensor data locally while relying on the cloud for real-time navigation updates.
- Quantum Cloud Services:
  - Emerging quantum computing services will solve problems currently impossible with classical computers.
  - Example: Financial institutions using quantum cloud platforms to optimize investment portfolios.
- Sustainability Initiatives:
  - Cloud providers are investing in renewable energy to reduce the environmental impact of data centers.
  - Example: Google Cloud operates entirely on renewable energy, making it a leader in green cloud computing.

AI Insight:
"As cloud technologies evolve, AI's role becomes even more critical in enabling businesses to adapt and thrive in a rapidly changing world."

Exercises for Readers
- Reflection: Think about how your workplace or favorite apps rely on cloud computing. What would happen if the cloud wasn't available?
- Research Task: Investigate how an industry of your choice has transformed through cloud computing (e.g., healthcare, education, or gaming).
- Hands-On Exploration: Use Google BigQuery or AWS SageMaker to explore a sample dataset. How can cloud-based AI tools provide insights?

Cloud computing has become an indispensable part of modern life, enabling businesses and individuals to achieve more with fewer resources. From supporting remote work to driving innovation in AI and big data, the cloud is at the heart of today's digital transformation.

AI Insight:
"Cloud computing is more than just a tool; it's a foundation for the future. By understanding its critical role, you can unlock its full potential."

Conclusion:
Cloud computing is one of the most transformative technologies of our era, and its importance only continues to grow. In this chapter, we explored the fundamental aspects of cloud computing, its history, and why it is critical in today's world. Each section has highlighted unique aspects of this revolutionary technology and demonstrated how it has reshaped the way we live, work, and innovate.

Key Takeaways
1. Definition and Key Concepts of Cloud Computing
At its core, cloud computing enables the delivery of computing resources on demand. It is characterized by its flexibility, scalability, and efficiency, with service models like IaaS, PaaS, and SaaS catering to diverse business needs. These foundational elements empower organizations to innovate while minimizing overhead costs and technical complexity.

What We Learned:
- IaaS provides the raw infrastructure for businesses.
- PaaS accelerates application development by abstracting underlying complexities.
- SaaS delivers ready-to-use software, democratizing access to powerful tools.

2. History and Evolution of Cloud Technologies
The journey from time-sharing systems in the 1960s to today's AI-powered cloud platforms demonstrates decades of technological innovation. Each milestone—from virtualization to the rise of public cloud providers like AWS, Azure, and Google Cloud—has contributed to the accessible, scalable systems we rely on today.

What We Learned:
- Virtualization was a game-changer, enabling dynamic resource allocation.
- The rise of public cloud services in the 2000s made computing power accessible to businesses of all sizes.
- AI integration has supercharged the cloud's capabilities, enhancing automation and analytics.

3. Why Cloud Computing is Critical in Today's World
Cloud computing's impact spans industries, empowering healthcare, e-commerce, education, and finance to scale operations, improve efficiency, and deliver better services. It has become essential for remote work, big data processing, and AI innovation, making it a cornerstone of modern digital infrastructure.

What We Learned:
- Industries such as healthcare and e-commerce rely on the cloud for scalability and innovation.
- AI-powered tools hosted in the cloud drive personalized experiences and real-time analytics.
- The flexibility and resilience of cloud platforms position businesses for long-term success.

The Bigger Picture
The three parts of this chapter collectively highlight that cloud computing is far more than just an IT solution—it is the driving force behind digital transformation. From its roots in shared mainframes to its current role in powering AI and big data, cloud computing provides the tools and infrastructure necessary for innovation in an increasingly interconnected world.

As the cloud evolves, so do its possibilities. Emerging trends like edge computing and quantum cloud promise to push the boundaries of what's possible, while sustainability initiatives ensure that this growth happens responsibly. At the heart of all this progress is AI, continuously optimizing, predicting, and automating to ensure that cloud computing delivers on its immense potential.

Looking Ahead
This foundational chapter has set the stage for the deeper explorations that follow. From networking and security to AI and machine learning, the upcoming chapters will build on this understanding to equip you with the knowledge and tools to leverage the cloud effectively.

AI Insight:
"Cloud computing is more than a technological advancement; it's a partner in progress. As you dive deeper into this book, remember that the possibilities within the cloud are as limitless as your imagination."

Chapter 2: Understanding the Cloud Ecosystem

Components of Cloud Infrastructure

Cloud computing operates as an intricate ecosystem of interconnected components that work together to deliver seamless services to users. Each part of this ecosystem has a specific role, enabling businesses to build, deploy, and scale applications effectively.

In this section, we'll explore the core components of cloud infrastructure, focusing on their purpose, functionality, and how they interact within the cloud environment.

1. Virtualization: The Foundation of Cloud Computing

Virtualization is the technology that underpins modern cloud infrastructure. It allows multiple virtual machines (VMs) to operate on a single physical server, maximizing resource utilization and flexibility.

Key Features of Virtualization:
- Resource Optimization: Ensures efficient use of hardware by dividing it into smaller, manageable virtual instances.
- Isolation: Each virtual machine operates independently, enhancing security and reliability.
- Scalability: Virtual resources can be scaled up or down to meet demand.

Example in Action:
A startup uses a single physical server to host multiple VMs, each running a different application. When user traffic increases, the startup can add more VMs instantly without buying additional hardware.

2. Data Centers: The Physical Backbone

Behind every cloud service lies a network of data centers, housing thousands of servers, storage devices, and networking equipment.
Core Functions of Data Centers:
- Data Storage: Securely stores user data across redundant systems.
- Compute Power: Provides the processing capabilities required to run applications.
- Redundancy and Recovery: Ensures data availability and continuity through backup systems.

Real-Life Example:
Google operates data centers worldwide, allowing services like Gmail and YouTube to run seamlessly. If one data center experiences a failure, traffic is automatically rerouted to another location.

AI Insight:
"AI optimizes data center operations by managing energy usage, predicting hardware failures, and balancing workloads across servers."

3. Networking: The Cloud's Circulatory System
Networking ensures that data flows smoothly between users, applications, and infrastructure components. In the cloud, virtual networking replaces traditional physical setups, offering greater flexibility and scalability.

Key Networking Concepts:
- Virtual Private Clouds (VPCs): Isolated networks within the public cloud for enhanced security.
  - Example: A company creates a VPC to host sensitive customer data securely.
- Load Balancers: Distribute incoming traffic across multiple servers to ensure availability.
  - Example: An e-commerce site uses a load balancer during a flash sale to handle traffic spikes.
- Content Delivery Networks (CDNs): Cache content closer to users for faster load times.
  - Example: AWS CloudFront delivers website assets like images and videos globally.

4. Cloud Storage: The Heart of Data Management
Cloud storage enables businesses to store, access, and manage data remotely, eliminating the need for on-premises systems.

Types of Cloud Storage:
- Object Storage: Best for unstructured data like videos and images.
  - Example: AWS S3 stores millions of product photos for an e-commerce website.
- Block Storage: Suitable for structured data and high-performance applications.
  - Example: Azure Disk Storage supports databases with low-latency access.
- File Storage: Ideal for shared access across multiple users.
  - Example: Google Cloud Filestore enables teams to collaborate on large projects.

5. Monitoring and Management Tools: Ensuring Efficiency
Cloud providers offer tools to monitor and manage infrastructure, ensuring optimal performance and cost-effectiveness.

Popular Monitoring Tools:
- AWS CloudWatch: Tracks resource usage, application performance, and operational health.
- Azure Monitor: Provides real-time insights into workloads running on Azure.
- Google Cloud Operations Suite: Analyzes metrics, logs, and traces for troubleshooting.

AI Insight:
"AI-powered monitoring tools proactively identify performance bottlenecks and recommend solutions, keeping applications running smoothly."

Practical Applications of Cloud Ecosystems
- E-Commerce Platforms: Leverage the full cloud ecosystem to handle traffic, store customer data, and provide personalized recommendations.
- AI Model Training: Utilize data centers, VMs, and storage to train machine learning models on vast datasets.
- Disaster Recovery: Businesses replicate their infrastructure across data centers for robust recovery in case of failure.

Exercises for Readers
- Reflection: Identify the components of a cloud ecosystem you interact with daily (e.g., Gmail's storage, Netflix's CDN). How do they enhance your experience?
- Hands-On Exploration: Set up a simple VPC in AWS, Azure, or GCP. Test its isolation and security features.
- Research Task: Investigate how a major company (e.g., Netflix, Airbnb) uses the cloud ecosystem to deliver its services.

Understanding the components of the cloud ecosystem is crucial for grasping how cloud computing operates. From virtualization to networking and storage, each element plays a vital role in delivering reliable, scalable, and efficient services. AI's integration further enhances these capabilities, making cloud ecosystems smarter and more adaptable.

AI Insight:
"Think of the cloud ecosystem as a symphony—each component plays its part, and AI is the conductor ensuring everything works in harmony."

Public, Private, Hybrid, and Multi-Cloud Models: Deployment Options in the Cloud

Cloud computing deployment models define how cloud services are utilized and managed. Organizations can choose between public, private, hybrid, and multi-cloud models, depending on their needs for scalability, security, and cost efficiency. Each model offers unique advantages, and understanding their distinctions is crucial for selecting the right solution.

1. Public Cloud: The Most Common Model

The public cloud is the most widely adopted deployment model. In this setup, resources like servers, storage, and applications are owned and operated by a third-party provider and shared among multiple tenants.

Key Features of Public Clouds:
- Shared Infrastructure: Resources are hosted on the provider's infrastructure and shared among users.
- Cost-Effective: Users only pay for what they use, making it ideal for startups and small businesses.
- Scalability: Providers offer virtually unlimited scalability.

Use Cases for Public Cloud:
- Startups: Public clouds offer a low-cost entry point, enabling startups to launch applications without upfront hardware investment.
- Testing Environments: Developers can create and test applications in isolated virtual environments.
- Content Delivery: Companies use public clouds to deliver media and applications globally.

Example:
Spotify uses Google Cloud to store and stream millions of audio tracks to users worldwide.

2. Private Cloud: Enhanced Security and Control

A private cloud offers dedicated resources for a single organization, either hosted on-premises or by a third-party provider. It provides greater control and customization but comes at a higher cost.

Key Features of Private Clouds:
- Exclusive Access: Resources are not shared with other users.
- Enhanced Security: Ideal for industries with strict compliance requirements like healthcare and finance.
- Customizable: Organizations can tailor resources to specific needs.

Use Cases for Private Cloud:
- Healthcare: Hospitals use private clouds to store sensitive patient data while complying with regulations like HIPAA.
- Financial Institutions: Banks and insurance companies secure customer data and transactions using private clouds.
- Government Agencies: Private clouds ensure data sovereignty and security for confidential operations.

Example:
A major bank hosts its private cloud on-premises to manage secure transactions and customer data.

AI Insight:
"AI tools monitor private cloud environments to optimize resources and ensure compliance with regulatory standards."

3. Hybrid Cloud: The Best of Both Worlds
Hybrid clouds combine public and private cloud environments, allowing organizations to enjoy the benefits of both models. This setup is particularly useful for balancing cost efficiency with security.

Key Features of Hybrid Clouds:
- Data Segmentation: Critical data is stored in private clouds, while less sensitive workloads run in public clouds.
- Flexibility: Workloads can move between public and private clouds based on demand.
- Disaster Recovery: Provides redundancy and backup across environments.

Use Cases for Hybrid Cloud:
- Retail: Stores keep sensitive customer payment data in private clouds while running analytics in public clouds.
- Healthcare: Hospitals process patient data in private clouds and use public clouds for population health analytics.
- Global Enterprises: Companies distribute workloads across regions to optimize performance and compliance.

Example:
A pharmaceutical company uses a hybrid cloud to store clinical trial data privately while using public cloud resources for machine learning analysis.

4. Multi-Cloud: Avoiding Vendor Lock-In

Multi-cloud environments involve using multiple public cloud providers to avoid reliance on a single vendor. This approach enhances flexibility and allows organizations to optimize workloads across platforms.

Key Features of Multi-Clouds:
- Vendor Diversity: Reduces dependency on a single provider.
- Cost Optimization: Choose the most cost-effective service for specific workloads.
- Redundancy: Enhances reliability by distributing workloads across multiple providers.

Use Cases for Multi-Cloud:
- Global Enterprises: Multi-cloud setups ensure compliance with regional regulations by hosting data in specific jurisdictions.
- High Availability Services: Businesses distribute workloads across providers to minimize downtime.
- Cost-Conscious Companies: Organizations leverage cost differences between providers to reduce expenses.

Example:
A multinational corporation uses AWS for data storage, Azure for analytics, and Google Cloud for AI services.

AI Insight:
"AI simplifies managing multi-cloud environments by automating resource allocation and monitoring costs across providers."

Advantages and Challenges of Deployment Models
Advantages of Public Cloud:
- Cost savings.
- Scalability and flexibility.
- Global accessibility.

Challenges:
- Shared resources may lead to performance variability.
- Potential compliance risks for sensitive data.

Advantages of Private Cloud:
- Enhanced security and control.
- Tailored to specific organizational needs.

Challenges:
- Higher costs for setup and maintenance.
- Limited scalability compared to public clouds.

Advantages of Hybrid Cloud:
- Balanced cost and security.
- Flexibility to shift workloads between environments.

Challenges:
- Complexity in managing multiple environments.
- Requires robust integration tools.

Advantages of Multi-Cloud:
- Avoids vendor lock-in.
- Optimized performance and cost.

Challenges:
- Increased complexity in managing multiple providers.
- Difficulties in ensuring interoperability.

Exercises for Readers
- Reflection: Evaluate which cloud deployment model suits your needs or your organization's goals. Why would you choose it?
- Research Task: Investigate a company that uses a hybrid or multi-cloud strategy. How does this approach benefit their operations?
- Hands-On Activity: Use free-tier accounts on AWS, Azure, or Google Cloud to create a simple multi-cloud environment. Test how data or workloads can be distributed.

The choice of a cloud deployment model depends on the specific requirements of an organization, including cost, security, scalability, and regulatory compliance. Public, private, hybrid, and multi-cloud models each offer unique benefits, and the right decision often involves a blend of these approaches. As businesses grow more reliant on the cloud, understanding these deployment models becomes crucial for strategic planning.

AI Insight:
"The flexibility of cloud deployment models ensures that businesses of all sizes can find a solution that aligns with their needs. AI takes this further by optimizing deployments and reducing complexity."

How the Ecosystem Supports Innovation and Scalability
Cloud computing's ecosystem has revolutionized how businesses innovate and grow. By providing flexible, on-demand resources, the cloud enables organizations to scale operations efficiently while fostering rapid innovation. This section explores the ways in which the cloud ecosystem empowers companies to adapt, thrive, and drive change.

1. Innovation Through On-Demand Resources

The cloud eliminates the barriers traditionally associated with launching new projects or experimenting with innovative ideas. By offering immediate access to computing power, storage, and specialized tools, the cloud allows businesses to innovate without upfront capital investment.

Key Features Supporting Innovation:
- Rapid Prototyping: Developers can create, test, and refine ideas in hours rather than weeks.
  - Example: A gaming studio uses AWS EC2 instances to test new multiplayer environments before committing to a full-scale launch.
- Access to Cutting-Edge Tools: Pre-built AI and ML services enable companies to incorporate advanced features without specialized expertise.
  - Example: A retailer uses Google Cloud's AI-powered recommendation engine to improve customer engagement.
- Global Reach: The cloud allows businesses to deploy applications globally, testing ideas in diverse markets.

AI Insight:
"The cloud democratizes innovation, enabling startups and enterprises alike to experiment and succeed with minimal risk."

2. Scalability for Growing Businesses

Scalability is one of the cloud's defining features, enabling organizations to expand or reduce their resources in real time. This flexibility allows businesses to grow without the constraints of physical infrastructure.

How Scalability Works:
- Vertical Scaling: Increases the capacity of existing resources (e.g., upgrading a VM to handle more traffic).
- Horizontal Scaling: Adds more resources (e.g., deploying additional servers during peak demand).

Examples of Scalability in Action:
- E-Commerce During Peak Seasons:
  - Retailers scale up their infrastructure during Black Friday or holiday sales to handle increased traffic.
  - Example: Shopify merchants use auto-scaling to ensure uptime during major promotions.

- Media and Entertainment:
  - Streaming platforms dynamically adjust resources to deliver smooth playback to millions of users.
  - Example: Netflix scales its backend to accommodate spikes during new content releases.
- Healthcare:
  - Cloud infrastructure supports telemedicine services during sudden surges in demand.
  - Example: Hospitals leverage hybrid cloud setups to scale patient data processing during pandemics.

3. Collaborative Ecosystems Foster Innovation

The cloud ecosystem is inherently collaborative, integrating services, tools, and platforms that empower organizations to innovate collectively. This interconnectedness accelerates development cycles and enhances capabilities.

Examples of Cloud-Enabled Collaboration:
- APIs and SDKs: Enable seamless integration of third-party tools into cloud applications.
  - Example: A fintech app integrates payment gateways using APIs hosted on the cloud.
- Shared Resources: Cloud marketplaces provide access to pre-built solutions like AI models, analytics dashboards, and security frameworks.
  - Example: Developers use AWS Marketplace to find and deploy third-party applications.
- Open Source in the Cloud: Platforms like GitHub (hosted on Azure) allow developers to collaborate on open-source projects from anywhere in the world.

AI Insight:
"Cloud collaboration is more than teamwork; it's a synergistic approach to innovation, where ideas and resources are shared seamlessly."

4. Future-Proofing Businesses Through Innovation

The cloud enables organizations to remain agile and prepared for future challenges by integrating emerging technologies and scaling dynamically.

How the Cloud Future-Proofs Businesses:
- AI and ML Integration:
  - Companies use cloud-hosted AI tools to automate processes, analyze data, and enhance decision-making.
  - Example: An insurance company uses Azure AI to predict customer risks and tailor policies accordingly.

- Edge Computing for Real-Time Data:
  - The cloud ecosystem supports edge computing, bringing computation closer to users for faster response times.
  - Example: Smart cities use edge devices for real-time traffic management while syncing data to the cloud.
- Sustainability and Green Initiatives:
  - Providers invest in renewable energy-powered data centers, enabling businesses to innovate responsibly.
  - Example: Google Cloud's carbon-neutral services help organizations reduce their environmental impact.

Exercises for Readers
- Reflection: Think about a product or service you use daily. How might cloud computing have enabled its development or scalability?
- Research Task: Explore a case study where a company used cloud scalability to meet sudden demand (e.g., during a product launch or global event).
- Hands-On Activity: Deploy a simple application on AWS or Azure. Experiment with horizontal scaling to handle simulated traffic increases.

The cloud ecosystem is more than just infrastructure—it is a dynamic enabler of innovation and scalability. By providing access to cutting-edge tools, fostering collaboration, and supporting dynamic growth, the cloud empowers organizations to adapt and thrive in a rapidly changing world.

AI Insight:
"Scalability isn't just about growth; it's about resilience, agility, and staying ahead in an unpredictable environment. The cloud ensures you're always ready for what's next."

Conclusion:
Cloud computing is more than just technology; it's a sophisticated ecosystem of components and models that enable businesses to innovate, scale, and thrive in a rapidly changing digital landscape. In this chapter, we explored the foundational elements of the cloud ecosystem, its deployment models, and how it supports innovation and scalability. Each section highlighted unique aspects of the ecosystem, demonstrating how these elements work together to create seamless, efficient solutions for organizations worldwide.

Key Takeaways

1. Components of the Cloud Ecosystem

The cloud ecosystem consists of virtualization, data centers, networking, storage, and monitoring tools. These interconnected components form the backbone of cloud services, ensuring reliability, flexibility, and cost-efficiency.

What We Learned:
- Virtualization maximizes hardware efficiency by running multiple virtual machines on a single server.
- Data centers provide the physical infrastructure for storing and processing data, supported by AI-driven optimizations.
- Networking tools, such as Virtual Private Clouds (VPCs) and load balancers, ensure secure and efficient data flow.

2. Deployment Models: Public, Private, Hybrid, and Multi-Cloud

Each deployment model offers distinct advantages, allowing organizations to choose solutions tailored to their needs. Public clouds provide cost-effective scalability, private clouds offer enhanced security and control, hybrid clouds balance both, and multi-cloud strategies ensure flexibility and redundancy.

What We Learned:
- Public clouds are ideal for startups and global scalability.
- Private clouds meet the security and compliance needs of industries like healthcare and finance.
- Hybrid and multi-cloud models optimize workloads and prevent vendor lock-in.

AI Insight:

"The choice of deployment model is as much about strategy as it is about technology. AI ensures these models operate efficiently, meeting business objectives."

3. Supporting Innovation and Scalability

The cloud ecosystem fosters a culture of innovation by providing on-demand resources, global accessibility, and cutting-edge tools like AI and machine learning. Scalability allows businesses to adapt dynamically to changing demands, ensuring they can grow without operational bottlenecks.

What We Learned:
- Cloud scalability ensures businesses can handle traffic surges and maintain optimal performance.
- Collaboration tools and shared resources in the cloud ecosystem accelerate development cycles.

- The cloud future-proofs organizations by integrating emerging technologies and sustainability practices.

The Bigger Picture
The cloud ecosystem is more than the sum of its parts. It's a dynamic framework that enables businesses to operate efficiently, innovate rapidly, and scale effortlessly. Each component—whether it's virtualization or AI-driven monitoring—plays a vital role in delivering reliable, scalable solutions. Together, these elements form an interconnected system that supports everything from startups launching their first products to global enterprises managing complex operations.

As we delve deeper into the specifics of cloud providers, their services, and advanced applications, this foundational understanding of the cloud ecosystem will serve as a crucial guide

Looking Ahead
This chapter provided a comprehensive look at the building blocks of cloud computing and their role in driving innovation and scalability. The next chapter will explore the major cloud providers—AWS, Azure, and Google Cloud—and their extensive service offerings, diving into how they enable businesses to harness the full potential of the cloud.

AI Insight:
"Understanding the ecosystem of the cloud is like learning the rules of a game—once you know how the pieces work together, you can strategize and innovate in ways that were previously unimaginable."

Chapter 3: Major Cloud Providers and Services

Overview of AWS, Azure, Google Cloud, and Their Unique Offerings

The cloud computing landscape is dominated by three major players: Amazon Web Services (AWS), Microsoft Azure, and Google Cloud Platform (GCP). Each provider offers a comprehensive suite of services tailored to businesses of all sizes, but their unique strengths and specializations set them apart. In this section, we will explore the key features, core services, and distinctive offerings of these providers.

Amazon Web Services (AWS)
Launched in 2006, AWS pioneered the public cloud market and remains the largest provider, offering over 200 services across compute, storage, databases, machine learning, analytics, and more. Its vast global reach and mature ecosystem make it a popular choice for enterprises, startups, and governments.

Key Features of AWS:
- Global Infrastructure:
  - AWS operates in 99 Availability Zones across 31 geographic regions, ensuring low-latency access and robust redundancy.
- Scalable Compute Resources:
  - Services like EC2 (Elastic Compute Cloud) offer customizable virtual machines for diverse workloads.
- Rich Marketplace:
  - The AWS Marketplace hosts thousands of third-party tools and applications.

Core Services of AWS:
- Compute:
  - EC2: Scalable virtual servers with customizable configurations.
  - AWS Lambda: Serverless computing for running event-driven workflows.
- Storage:
  - S3 (Simple Storage Service): Highly durable and scalable object storage.
  - EBS (Elastic Block Store): High-performance block storage for databases and applications.
- Databases:
  - RDS (Relational Database Service): Managed databases for MySQL, PostgreSQL, and more.
  - DynamoDB: A fast, fully managed NoSQL database.

- AI and Machine Learning:
  - SageMaker: A platform for building, training, and deploying machine learning models.
  - Rekognition: Image and video analysis for facial recognition and object detection.

Unique Offering:
AWS excels in its breadth of services and robust global network. It is particularly favored for its wide variety of instance types and advanced analytics capabilities.

Real-Life Example:
Netflix relies on AWS for its global streaming services, leveraging tools like EC2, S3, and DynamoDB to store and deliver content efficiently.

Microsoft Azure
Launched in 2010, Azure is the second-largest cloud provider and is renowned for its enterprise-friendly solutions and seamless integration with Microsoft's ecosystem, including Windows Server, Active Directory, and Office 365.

Key Features of Azure:
- Hybrid Cloud Expertise:
  - Azure's tools like Azure Arc enable seamless management of on-premises, multi-cloud, and edge environments.
- Developer Tools:
  - Azure DevOps provides a comprehensive suite of tools for development and deployment.

Core Services of Azure:
- Compute:
  - Azure Virtual Machines: Scalable VMs for diverse workloads.
  - Azure Functions: Serverless computing for event-driven workflows.
- Storage:
  - Azure Blob Storage: High-performance object storage.
  - Azure Files: Fully managed file shares for shared access.
- AI and Machine Learning:
  - Azure Cognitive Services: Pre-built AI models for natural language processing, image recognition, and more.
  - Azure Machine Learning: A suite of tools for building and deploying machine learning models.
- Enterprise Integration:
  - Seamless compatibility with Microsoft tools like Active Directory, SQL Server, and Power BI.

Unique Offering:
Azure stands out for its hybrid cloud solutions and enterprise-grade services, making it an ideal choice for businesses already embedded in the Microsoft ecosystem.

Real-Life Example:
Volkswagen uses Azure to create a digital manufacturing platform that connects factories, processes, and data to improve efficiency and production.

Google Cloud Platform (GCP)
Google Cloud, launched in 2011, is the smallest of the three in terms of market share but excels in data analytics, AI/ML services, and developer-friendly tools. It leverages Google's expertise in search, big data, and machine learning to deliver cutting-edge cloud solutions.

Key Features of GCP:
- AI/ML Leadership:
  - Google Cloud is at the forefront of AI innovation with tools like Vertex AI and TensorFlow.
- Global Network:
  - Google's private fiber-optic network ensures low-latency performance.

Core Services of GCP:
- Compute:
  - Compute Engine: Customizable VMs for various workloads.
  - Cloud Run: Managed serverless computing for containerized applications.
- Storage:
  - Cloud Storage: Unified object storage for structured and unstructured data.
  - Persistent Disks: High-performance block storage for VMs.
- AI and Machine Learning:
  - Vertex AI: A platform for deploying and managing ML models.
  - BigQuery ML: Enables running ML models directly within Google's data warehouse.
- Big Data and Analytics:
  - BigQuery: A serverless data warehouse for real-time analytics.
  - Dataflow: A tool for stream and batch data processing.

Unique Offering:
GCP's focus on AI, machine learning, and big data analytics makes it a top choice for businesses looking to leverage advanced technologies.

Real-Life Example:
Spotify uses GCP to analyze massive amounts of user data, delivering personalized music recommendations and improving platform performance.

Comparing AWS, Azure, and GCP
1. Market Share
- AWS: AWS holds the position as the largest player in the cloud computing market. With its early start in 2006, AWS captured a massive share of the market and remains the most widely used cloud provider globally.
- Azure: As the second-largest cloud provider, Azure has grown rapidly, especially among enterprises already using Microsoft's ecosystem. Azure's seamless integration with Microsoft tools like Office 365, Active Directory, and Windows Server makes it a popular choice for enterprises.
- GCP (Google Cloud Platform): GCP is the smallest of the three major cloud providers in terms of market share. However, it has seen steady growth, particularly in sectors focused on AI, machine learning, and big data analytics.

2. Strengths
- AWS: AWS is known for having the broadest service catalog of any cloud provider, with thousands of products for storage, compute, AI, machine learning, IoT, and developer tools. It's also known for its extensive global reach with multiple availability zones in more regions than its competitors.
- Azure: Azure's strength lies in its hybrid cloud capabilities. Unlike AWS, which focuses on cloud-first, Azure supports on-premises integration with tools like Azure Arc, allowing companies to run cloud workloads on local data centers. For companies already using Microsoft tools (Windows, Office, Active Directory), Azure becomes a logical choice.
- GCP (Google Cloud Platform): GCP's biggest strength is its leadership in AI, machine learning, and big data analytics. Its tools like BigQuery, TensorFlow, and Vertex AI are widely regarded as the best-in-class for data analytics and ML projects. For companies focused on AI-driven development or handling large-scale data analytics, GCP is often the preferred choice.

3. Target Audience
- AWS: AWS serves a broad range of customers, from startups and small businesses to large enterprises and government agencies. Its massive service catalog supports nearly every industry, from gaming and e-commerce to financial services and healthcare. Startups prefer AWS for its flexibility and access to free-tier resources, while enterprises use AWS for its global scale and broad service offerings.
- Azure: Azure is ideal for large enterprises and organizations that rely on the Microsoft ecosystem. If a company is already using Windows Server, Office 365, or Microsoft SQL Server, Azure provides seamless integration. Azure also has strong government contracts, making it a popular choice for government and regulated industries like finance and healthcare.
- GCP (Google Cloud Platform): GCP's primary audience includes AI-driven companies, data analysts, and big data enthusiasts. Its AI/ML tools like TensorFlow and Vertex AI attract companies in healthcare, retail, and fintech that need advanced analytics and real-time machine learning. Companies that rely heavily on data science, big data, and AI innovation often turn to GCP.

4. Service Availability and Global Reach
- AWS: AWS operates in the largest number of regions and availability zones globally, making it the leader in global reach and redundancy. This enables companies to deploy applications close to their users for low latency. AWS has over 30+ geographic regions and 90+ availability zones.
- Azure: Azure has a large number of regions and zones, though not as many as AWS. However, Azure has more government regions than any other provider, supporting compliance in highly regulated industries. It operates in 60+ regions and over 140 availability zones.
- GCP (Google Cloud Platform): GCP has fewer availability zones than AWS or Azure but focuses on supporting high-demand regions for AI and data analytics. Google's global network infrastructure ensures fast response times for its AI-driven services. It operates in around 35+ regions and 100+ zones.

5. Pricing and Cost Management
- AWS: AWS offers a pay-as-you-go model with options for reserved instances, savings plans, and spot instances. While AWS is known for flexibility, its pricing can be confusing, and companies often need AI tools (like AWS Compute Optimizer) to identify cost-saving opportunities.
- Azure: Azure follows a similar pricing model, but it offers additional discounts for Microsoft customers who already have licenses for Windows Server or SQL Server. Azure is also well-known for its hybrid benefits that allow companies to apply on-premise licenses to cloud resources, saving costs.
- GCP (Google Cloud Platform): GCP's pricing is seen as more transparent and predictable. Google offers per-second billing for VMs, unlike AWS and Azure, which round up to minutes or hours. GCP is also known for its sustained-use discounts, automatically reducing the cost of instances that run for extended periods.

6. AI, Machine Learning, and Data Analytics
- AWS: AWS has tools like SageMaker, Rekognition, and Forecast, which allow businesses to create machine learning models without needing deep technical expertise. AWS is strong in enterprise AI adoption, but it doesn't have the same pedigree as GCP in data science tools.
- Azure: Azure offers Azure Machine Learning (AML), which enables companies to build and deploy machine learning models. It integrates seamlessly with Power BI for visualizing data insights, which is attractive to companies that rely on Power BI dashboards.
- GCP (Google Cloud Platform): GCP is the industry leader in AI, machine learning, and big data analytics. It is the birthplace of TensorFlow, one of the most popular machine learning frameworks in the world. Tools like BigQuery and Vertex AI make GCP a go-to choice for companies focused on big data and advanced AI development.

7. Compliance and Security
- AWS: AWS offers extensive support for security compliance, including GDPR, HIPAA, PCI-DSS, and SOC 2 certifications. AWS's shared responsibility model requires companies to manage their own security configurations (IAM, S3 permissions, etc.), but AWS handles the security of the cloud infrastructure itself.
- Azure: Azure is especially strong in government contracts and compliance. With more government cloud regions than any other provider, it excels in meeting regulatory requirements. Azure also has strong tools for identity management (Active Directory) and encryption.
- GCP (Google Cloud Platform): GCP offers similar compliance coverage (GDPR, HIPAA, PCI-DSS), but it emphasizes zero-trust security with its BeyondCorp initiative. GCP also provides encryption by default for all stored and in-transit data.

8. DevOps and Automation
- AWS: AWS has an extensive DevOps toolkit, including AWS CodePipeline, AWS CloudFormation, and AWS CodeBuild. These tools allow companies to create CI/CD pipelines, define infrastructure as code (IaC), and enable automatic deployments.
- Azure: Azure offers Azure DevOps as a complete solution for CI/CD pipelines, agile workflows, and version control. Azure's DevOps capabilities integrate with GitHub (which Microsoft owns) and allow developers to track issues, manage code, and automate deployments in a single platform.
- GCP (Google Cloud Platform): GCP's Cloud Build and Cloud Deploy offer automation for CI/CD, but it is not as robust as AWS CodePipeline or Azure DevOps. However, GCP is known for Kubernetes (GKE), one of the most widely used container orchestration tools in DevOps pipelines.

9. Cost Management Tools
- AWS: AWS Cost Explorer and AWS Compute Optimizer provide businesses with the ability to forecast and reduce costs. AWS also has Savings Plans and Reserved Instances to help lower costs for long-term use.
- Azure: Azure's cost management tools allow users to track spend, forecast usage, and identify savings. Microsoft also offers the Azure Hybrid Benefit, which lets customers use existing Windows Server licenses to reduce cloud costs.
- GCP (Google Cloud Platform): GCP stands out with its sustained-use discounts and committed use discounts. These discounts automatically apply when instances run for extended periods. GCP also offers clear, predictable pricing with no need for long-term contracts.

Summary
- AWS: Best for large enterprises, startups, and global deployments. It's the largest player with the widest range of services.
- Azure: Best for companies with existing Microsoft ecosystems or those in regulated industries (government, finance, healthcare).
- GCP: Best for AI, machine learning, and big data projects. It is the go-to choice for data-driven companies.

AWS, Azure, and GCP each bring unique strengths to the cloud computing landscape, catering to a wide range of business needs. Understanding their key features and offerings helps organizations make informed decisions when selecting a provider.

AI Insight:
"Choosing the right provider isn't just about features—it's about aligning services with your organization's goals. AI tools from these platforms can help guide you to the best-fit solutions."

Emerging Cloud Platforms and Niche Providers
While major players like AWS, Azure, and Google Cloud dominate the cloud computing market, numerous emerging platforms and niche providers cater to specialized needs. These alternatives offer unique services, localized support, or cost-effective solutions that appeal to businesses seeking flexibility and targeted capabilities. In this section, we'll explore some of these emerging and niche cloud providers, their standout features, and how they differentiate themselves in a competitive market.

1. Oracle Cloud Infrastructure (OCI)

Oracle Cloud has gained traction for its focus on enterprise applications, particularly in data management and database solutions. It is a strong choice for organizations already using Oracle's software ecosystem.

Key Features:
- Enterprise Databases:
  - Oracle's Autonomous Database offers automated management, scaling, and tuning.
- High-Performance Compute:
  - Bare metal instances deliver exceptional performance for demanding workloads.

Unique Strengths:
- Hybrid Cloud Capabilities: OCI integrates seamlessly with on-premises Oracle systems.
- Industry-Specific Solutions: Tailored for sectors like finance and retail.

Example:
A global financial institution uses Oracle Cloud to manage transaction data securely and efficiently.

2. IBM Cloud

IBM Cloud specializes in hybrid cloud solutions and AI integration, leveraging its Watson AI platform to deliver advanced analytics and automation.

Key Features:
- AI-Powered Services:
  - Watson AI provides natural language processing, sentiment analysis, and predictive analytics.
- Quantum Computing:
  - IBM offers quantum-as-a-service through its IBM Quantum platform, giving businesses early access to cutting-edge technology.

Unique Strengths:
- Hybrid Cloud Expertise: IBM Cloud is particularly strong in environments that combine public, private, and on-premises resources.
- Security and Compliance: Tailored for industries with stringent regulatory requirements.

Example:
A healthcare provider uses IBM Cloud and Watson AI to analyze patient data and predict health trends.

3. Alibaba Cloud

As the largest cloud provider in Asia, Alibaba Cloud excels in serving businesses seeking access to the Chinese and broader Asian markets. It offers a broad range of services comparable to AWS and Azure but with a focus on regional support and compliance.
Key Features:
- Global Expansion:
  - A strong network of data centers in Asia and growing presence globally.
- AI and Big Data:
  - Offers platforms like Alibaba Cloud's ET Brain for AI-driven data insights.

Unique Strengths:
- Localized Expertise: Deep understanding of regulatory and operational requirements in Asian markets.
- Cost-Effective Solutions: Competitive pricing for small to mid-sized businesses.

Example:
An international retailer uses Alibaba Cloud to optimize logistics and marketing in China.

4. DigitalOcean

DigitalOcean caters to startups, developers, and small businesses with simple, cost-effective solutions. Its user-friendly interface and transparent pricing make it a popular choice for non-enterprise users.
Key Features:
- Droplets: Scalable virtual private servers with straightforward setup.
- App Platform: A fully managed platform-as-a-service (PaaS) for deploying applications.

Unique Strengths:
- Developer-Centric Tools: Designed with simplicity in mind, making it ideal for beginners.
- Transparent Pricing: Predictable costs without complex billing structures.

Example:
A small development team uses DigitalOcean to host their web applications and test new features.

5. Linode (Now Part of Akamai)

Linode, recently acquired by Akamai, focuses on delivering high-performance cloud solutions for developers and small businesses. Its emphasis on affordability and simplicity makes it a strong competitor in the niche cloud market.

Key Features:
- Compute Instances: Virtual servers optimized for speed and reliability.
- Kubernetes Support: Simplified deployment and management of containerized applications.

Unique Strengths:
- Cost-Effective Solutions: Affordable pricing compared to major providers.
- Global Reach: A robust network of data centers for low-latency access.

Example:
A digital agency uses Linode to host their client websites, benefiting from reliable performance at a lower cost.

6. Vultr

Vultr focuses on providing developer-friendly cloud infrastructure with an emphasis on simplicity, scalability, and affordability.

Key Features:
- High-Performance Compute: Bare metal servers and cloud instances tailored to performance-intensive workloads.
- Global Data Centers: Offers a wide geographic footprint for latency-sensitive applications.

Unique Strengths:
- Pay-As-You-Go: Flexible pricing with no long-term commitments.
- Ease of Use: Intuitive control panel for deploying and managing services.

Example:
A gaming company uses Vultr to host multiplayer game servers with low latency.

7. Specialized Niche Providers

Several niche providers focus on specific industries or unique functionalities, catering to targeted needs:
- Heroku:
  - A platform-as-a-service (PaaS) for developers, particularly popular for web application deployment.
  - Example: A startup uses Heroku to deploy a prototype app quickly.

- Snowflake:
  - A cloud data warehouse specializing in analytics and big data solutions.
  - Example: A media company uses Snowflake for real-time audience analytics.
- Wasabi:
  - A cloud storage provider offering low-cost, high-performance storage solutions.
  - Example: A video production company uses Wasabi to archive large video files efficiently.

When to Choose Emerging Platforms or Niche Providers
Emerging platforms and niche providers are ideal for:
- Cost-Sensitive Projects: DigitalOcean and Linode offer competitive pricing for startups and small businesses.
- Region-Specific Needs: Alibaba Cloud is a go-to choice for businesses targeting Asian markets.
- Specialized Requirements: Providers like IBM Cloud or Snowflake excel in AI and analytics.

AI Insight:
"While major providers offer comprehensive services, emerging platforms and niche providers often shine in specialization, affordability, and regional expertise. AI tools can help analyze needs to determine the best fit."z

Exercises for Readers
- Reflection: Consider your organization's needs. Would a niche provider or an emerging platform better address specific goals like cost savings or specialized services?
- Research Task: Investigate an emerging platform like DigitalOcean or Snowflake. What unique benefits do they offer compared to major providers?
- Hands-On Activity: Create a free-tier account on a niche platform (e.g., DigitalOcean). Deploy a small application and compare the experience to using a major provider like AWS.

Emerging platforms and niche providers are critical players in the cloud computing ecosystem. They fill gaps left by larger providers, offering specialized services, cost-effective solutions, and regional expertise. As cloud computing continues to evolve, these platforms will play a vital role in driving innovation and meeting the diverse needs of businesses worldwide.

AI Insight:
"The cloud is not one-size-fits-all. By exploring emerging platforms and niche providers, businesses can find tailored solutions that align with their goals."

Service Comparisons to Help Choose the Right Provider

Selecting the right cloud provider is a critical decision for businesses, as it impacts scalability, cost efficiency, and operational success. In this section, we will compare AWS, Azure, Google Cloud, and niche platforms across key factors, helping readers make informed decisions tailored to their specific needs.

1. Cost Considerations

AWS
- Pricing Model: Pay-as-you-go with options for reserved instances to reduce costs for long-term commitments.
- Strengths: Flexible pricing for startups and enterprises alike.
- Challenges: Pricing can become complex with additional charges for data transfer and premium features.

Azure
- Pricing Model: Similar to AWS with pay-as-you-go, reserved instances, and spot pricing for cost savings.
- Strengths: Discounts for existing Microsoft users, especially those with enterprise agreements.
- Challenges: Slightly higher costs for comparable services like storage.

Google Cloud
- Pricing Model: Simplified and competitive pricing structure. Offers sustained use discounts automatically.
- Strengths: Transparent pricing and cost advantages for AI and big data workloads.
- Challenges: Fewer options for long-term discounts compared to AWS and Azure.

Niche Providers
- Strengths: Providers like DigitalOcean and Linode offer flat-rate, transparent pricing ideal for small businesses and developers.
- Challenges: Limited features and scalability compared to major providers.

2. Scalability and Performance
AWS
- Strengths:
  - Industry leader in scalability, with unmatched global infrastructure (99 Availability Zones).
  - Auto Scaling services ensure seamless performance during traffic surges.
- Challenges: Can be overwhelming for small businesses due to the extensive service catalog.

Azure
- Strengths:
  - Strong hybrid cloud capabilities with tools like Azure Arc.
  - Seamless integration with on-premises environments for enterprises.
- Challenges: Performance consistency can vary in smaller regions.

Google Cloud
- Strengths:
  - Excels in performance for AI, ML, and analytics workloads.
  - Uses Google's private fiber network for ultra-low latency.
- Challenges: Smaller global footprint compared to AWS and Azure.

Niche Providers
- Strengths: Focused services for specific needs (e.g., DigitalOcean for startups, Wasabi for low-cost storage).
- Challenges: Limited scalability for enterprise-grade operations.

3. Service Availability and Global Reach
AWS
- Global Reach: The largest provider with 31 geographic regions and plans for expansion.
- Use Case: Ideal for businesses requiring a global presence with low-latency access.

Azure
- Global Reach: Close to AWS in terms of regions and data centers, with strong enterprise support.
- Use Case: Best for hybrid setups spanning on-premises and cloud environments.

Google Cloud
- Global Reach: Smaller but growing footprint, leveraging Google's private network for superior connectivity.
- Use Case: Optimized for AI-driven applications and regional deployments.

Niche Providers
- Global Reach: Limited, but providers like Alibaba Cloud dominate specific regions (e.g., Asia).
- Use Case: Ideal for localized projects or region-specific needs

4. AI and Machine Learning Capabilities
AWS
- Strengths:
  - Offers the most comprehensive AI/ML services, such as SageMaker and Rekognition.
  - Supports custom model building and deployment at scale.
- Challenges: High costs for advanced AI tools.

Azure
- Strengths:
  - Azure Cognitive Services provide pre-built models for vision, speech, and text analytics.
  - Strong enterprise integration with tools like Power BI.
- Challenges: Slightly steeper learning curve for developers new to AI.

Google Cloud
- Strengths:
  - Leader in AI innovation with tools like Vertex AI, AutoML, and TensorFlow.
  - Seamless integration of ML models into BigQuery for analytics.
- Challenges: Focused on AI and big data, making it less appealing for general-purpose workloads.

Niche Providers
- Strengths: IBM Cloud's Watson excels in industry-specific AI, while DigitalOcean offers basic AI integration for smaller projects.
- Challenges: Limited advanced features compared to major providers.

5. Ease of Use and Developer Support
AWS
- Strengths:
    - Comprehensive documentation and active community forums.
    - Large marketplace for third-party integrations.
- Challenges: Steep learning curve for first-time users due to the vast service catalog.

Azure
- Strengths:
    - Familiarity for users of Microsoft tools.
    - Integrated developer tools like Visual Studio and Azure DevOps.
- Challenges: Interface can feel cluttered for smaller teams.

Google Cloud
- Strengths:
    - Simple, user-friendly interface with robust documentation.
    - Developer-focused features like Cloud Functions for serverless computing.
- Challenges: Fewer enterprise-specific tools compared to AWS and Azure.

Niche Providers
- Strengths: Platforms like DigitalOcean and Linode focus on simplicity and transparency, ideal for small teams and individual developers.
- Challenges: Limited advanced features for complex projects.

6. Security and Compliance
AWS
- Strengths:
    - Comprehensive compliance certifications (e.g., HIPAA, GDPR, ISO 27001).
    - Tools like AWS Shield protect against DDoS attacks.
- Challenges: Complexity of configuration may lead to security oversights.

Azure
- Strengths:
    - Enterprise-grade security with seamless Active Directory integration.
    - Tools like Azure Security Center provide centralized threat monitoring.
- Challenges: Customization can be time-intensive.

Google Cloud
- Strengths:
  - Strong emphasis on zero-trust security models.
  - Advanced encryption tools and real-time threat detection.
- Challenges: Fewer built-in compliance templates than AWS or Azure.

Niche Providers
- Strengths: IBM Cloud is notable for security in regulated industries, while DigitalOcean provides simple, secure setups for small teams.
- Challenges: Limited certifications and templates for global compliance standards.

When to Choose Each Provider
Choosing the right cloud provider depends on your business needs, technical requirements, and industry-specific goals. Here's a simple breakdown of when to choose each provider:

For Global Scalability – Choose AWS
- If you need a cloud provider with the widest global reach and the ability to deploy applications in multiple regions for low-latency access, AWS is the best choice. With more data centers and availability zones than any other provider, AWS enables businesses to scale globally with ease.

For Hybrid Cloud Deployments – Choose Azure
- Companies that need a hybrid cloud setup (mixing on-premises data centers with cloud infrastructure) should choose Azure. Microsoft's Azure Arc allows businesses to manage on-premises, multi-cloud, and edge environments from a unified control plane.

For AI and Big Data Workloads – Choose Google Cloud
- For companies working on AI, machine learning, and big data analytics, Google Cloud is the top option. With tools like BigQuery, Vertex AI, and TensorFlow, GCP is known for its data science and AI leadership, making it ideal for data-driven companies.

For Cost-Effective Solutions – Choose DigitalOcean or Linode
- If you're a small business, developer, or startup looking for a low-cost cloud solution, DigitalOcean or Linode are good choices. These providers offer simple pricing models and affordable plans, making them ideal for small-scale applications, development environments, or personal projects.

For Region-Specific Needs – Choose Alibaba Cloud or OVHcloud
- If your business operates primarily in Asia, consider Alibaba Cloud, as it has a strong presence in the region. For Europe, OVHcloud provides region-specific compliance and European-based data centers, which may be necessary for companies handling GDPR-regulated data.

For Enterprise-Grade Security – Choose IBM Cloud
- If enterprise security and compliance are critical to your business, especially for finance, healthcare, and regulated industries, IBM Cloud is a strong option. It offers industry-specific compliance, data sovereignty, and confidential computing to keep sensitive data secure.

These guidelines help organizations select the right cloud provider based on global needs, compliance, budget, and technical goals.

Exercises for Readers
- Reflection: What are your organization's priorities—scalability, AI capabilities, cost efficiency, or security? Based on these, which provider seems the best fit?
- Research Task: Explore the free-tier offerings of AWS, Azure, and Google Cloud. Which platform provides the most value for your needs?
- Hands-On Activity: Create a basic application on each provider's platform to compare usability, documentation, and cost estimation tools.

Choosing the right cloud provider depends on a clear understanding of your organization's goals, technical requirements, and budget constraints. While AWS, Azure, and Google Cloud dominate the market with their comprehensive offerings, niche providers can offer valuable alternatives for specific use cases. By aligning business objectives with cloud capabilities, organizations can leverage the full potential of the cloud.

Conclusion:
Cloud computing's expansive landscape is shaped by a handful of dominant players and a growing number of emerging platforms and niche providers. In this chapter, we examined the unique offerings of AWS, Azure, and Google Cloud, explored the strengths of specialized platforms, and compared services to guide users in selecting the best provider for their needs.

Each section offered valuable insights into the capabilities and strengths of these platforms, demonstrating how businesses of all sizes can leverage cloud services effectively.

Key Takeaways
1. Overview of AWS, Azure, and Google Cloud
The "big three" cloud providers offer comprehensive solutions, but each caters to different priorities. AWS leads in global reach and service variety, Azure excels in hybrid cloud solutions, and Google Cloud stands out in AI and big data analytics.

What We Learned:
- AWS is ideal for scalability and startups requiring a broad range of services.
- Azure is the go-to choice for enterprises deeply integrated with Microsoft ecosystems.
- Google Cloud is unmatched for businesses focused on AI, machine learning, and analytics.

2. Emerging Cloud Platforms and Niche Providers
While the major providers dominate the market, emerging platforms like DigitalOcean, Linode, and niche players like IBM Cloud and Alibaba Cloud offer compelling alternatives. They excel in affordability, region-specific needs, and specialized use cases.

What We Learned:
- DigitalOcean and Linode are great for small businesses and developers looking for simplicity and cost transparency.
- IBM Cloud and Oracle Cloud cater to enterprises with industry-specific solutions.
- Alibaba Cloud provides unmatched expertise in the Asian market.

3. Service Comparisons to Help Choose the Right Provider
The choice of provider depends on several factors, including cost, scalability, AI capabilities, ease of use, and security. By evaluating these aspects, businesses can align their goals with the right cloud platform.

What We Learned:
- AWS is best for businesses needing global scalability and flexibility.
- Azure shines in hybrid environments and enterprise integration.
- Google Cloud is optimal for AI-driven workloads.
- Niche providers add value with targeted solutions for specific industries or regions.

AI Insight:
"Comparisons reveal that the 'best' provider isn't universal—it's the one that best aligns with your unique needs. AI plays a critical role in helping businesses analyze these factors and make informed choices."

The Bigger Picture
Cloud providers have created a world of possibilities, empowering businesses to innovate, scale, and operate more efficiently. From startups experimenting with new ideas to enterprises managing complex global operations, cloud platforms cater to an incredibly diverse range of use cases. By understanding their capabilities and differences, organizations can unlock the full potential of the cloud.

As we look beyond the major providers, the role of niche platforms will continue to grow, filling gaps left by industry giants and delivering specialized solutions. Together, these providers form a rich and evolving cloud ecosystem.

Looking Ahead
This chapter provided a roadmap for navigating the cloud landscape, highlighting the strengths and weaknesses of major providers and emerging platforms. In the next chapter, we'll delve into the practical steps of setting up your first cloud environment, exploring how to deploy applications, configure services, and optimize costs.

AI Insight:
"Understanding cloud providers is like choosing the right partner for a journey. Each has unique strengths and specialties—AI ensures your choice is not only informed but optimized for success."

Chapter 4: Setting Up Your First Cloud Environment

This chapter is designed to help readers navigate the practical steps of getting started with cloud computing. Whether you're a beginner or an experienced professional exploring a new platform, this guide will walk you through creating a cloud account, deploying resources, leveraging free-tier services, and avoiding common pitfalls.

Step-by-Step Guide to Creating a Cloud Account and Deploying Resources

Cloud computing begins with the basics: setting up an account with a provider and deploying your first resources. This section walks through the process step by step, ensuring beginners can confidently navigate the initial stages of their cloud journey.

1. Choosing the Right Cloud Provider

Before creating an account, it's essential to evaluate which provider aligns best with your needs. While AWS, Azure, and Google Cloud dominate the market, alternatives like DigitalOcean or Linode might be better suited for specific use cases.

Factors to Consider When Choosing a Provider:
- Use Case: Are you developing AI applications, hosting a website, or experimenting with scalable solutions?
  - AI and Analytics: Google Cloud excels in machine learning and big data tools.
  - Enterprise Applications: Azure integrates seamlessly with Microsoft ecosystems.
  - General Scalability: AWS offers unmatched global reach and flexibility.
- Budget: Explore free-tier services to avoid upfront costs.
  - AWS Free Tier: Includes 750 hours/month of EC2 and 5 GB of S3 storage for 12 months.
  - Azure Free Tier: Offers $200 in credits for the first 30 days.
  - Google Cloud Free Tier: Includes $300 in credits for 90 days and always-free services.
- Simplicity vs. Features:
  - Simplicity: DigitalOcean is ideal for small projects and beginners.
  - Advanced Features: AWS, Azure, and Google Cloud offer extensive tools for complex workloads.

AI Insight:
"AI tools integrated into cloud platforms can guide beginners in selecting the best configurations and services."

2. Setting Up Your Cloud Account

Creating a cloud account is straightforward, with most providers offering a streamlined onboarding process. Here's a step-by-step example using AWS:

Step 1: Sign Up
- Visit the AWS Free Tier page and click "Sign Up."
- Enter your email address, choose a strong password, and create an account name.

Step 2: Enter Personal Information
Provide your name, address, and phone number. Business accounts may require additional details.

Step 3: Payment Method
Enter your credit or debit card for verification. Most free-tier services will not incur charges if usage stays within limits.

Step 4: Verify Identity
AWS will send a verification code to your phone. Enter the code to proceed.

Step 5: Choose a Support Plan
Select the Basic Support Plan (free). You can upgrade later if needed.

Step 6: Access the AWS Management Console
Once your account is set up, log in to the AWS Management Console, your central hub for accessing cloud services.

3. Deploying Your First Resource

The first resource you deploy is often a virtual machine (VM), also called an instance. For beginners, free-tier options like AWS EC2, Azure Virtual Machines, or Google Compute Engine are great starting points.

Example: Deploying an EC2 Instance on AWS
- Log in to the AWS Management Console: Navigate to the EC2 dashboard.
- Click "Launch Instance": This begins the process of setting up a virtual machine.
- Choose an AMI (Amazon Machine Image):
  - Select a free-tier eligible image, such as Amazon Linux 2.
  - AMIs act as templates, pre-configured with operating systems and software.

- Select an Instance Type:
  - Choose t2.micro, which is free-tier eligible and suitable for small applications.
- Configure Instance Details:
  - Default settings are fine for most beginners.
  - Advanced users can specify networking, storage, and scaling options.
- Add Storage:
  - Allocate at least 8 GB (free-tier eligible).
- Review and Launch:
  - Double-check settings and launch the instance.
- Access Your Instance:
  - Use an SSH client (e.g., PuTTY) to connect.
  - Follow the key-pair instructions during setup for secure access.

4. Testing Your Resource
Once deployed, ensure your resource is functioning correctly:
- Check its uptime using monitoring tools (e.g., AWS CloudWatch).
- Test applications or configurations to verify performance.

5. Exploring Other Deployment Options
Beyond virtual machines, beginners can deploy other resources:

Serverless Functions:
- AWS Lambda: Run code without provisioning servers.
- Example: Build a function that resizes uploaded images automatically.

Storage Services:
- Amazon S3 or Google Cloud Storage: Store and retrieve data efficiently.
- Example: Host static website files on S3.

Managed Databases:
- Amazon RDS or Azure SQL Database: Launch a fully managed database for web applications.
- Example: Deploy MySQL for an e-commerce backend.

6. Common Beginner Challenges and How to Overcome Them
- Overwhelming Choices:
  - Cloud platforms offer many options, which can be daunting.
  - Solution: Start with pre-configured templates or guided setups.

- Understanding Cost Implications:
  - Free tiers are helpful but have usage limits.
  - Solution: Use cost calculators to estimate expenses and set budget alerts.
- Security Risks:
  - Misconfigured settings can expose resources to vulnerabilities.
  - Solution: Follow security best practices, such as enabling firewalls and restricting access.

Exercises for Readers
- Reflection: Research the free-tier offerings of AWS, Azure, or Google Cloud. Which platform seems most aligned with your goals?
- Hands-On Activity: Deploy a free-tier EC2 instance on AWS and connect via SSH. Test its functionality by hosting a basic web application.
- Case Study: Investigate how a small business uses cloud services to scale operations. Identify which resources they might deploy first.

Deploying your first resource is an exciting milestone in your cloud journey. By carefully choosing a provider, understanding the steps to set up an account, and deploying a basic instance, you lay the groundwork for more complex projects. The key is to start small, experiment, and learn from every step.

AI Insight:
"Your first cloud deployment is not just an exercise—it's the beginning of your partnership with the cloud. With AI guiding your choices, every step becomes an opportunity to optimize and innovate."

Exploring Free-Tier Services for Beginners
Getting started with cloud computing doesn't have to be costly. Major cloud providers offer free-tier services, allowing beginners to explore platforms, experiment with features, and build small-scale projects at no expense. This section provides an in-depth look at free-tier offerings, best practices for maximizing their value, and tips for avoiding unexpected charges.

1. Understanding Free-Tier Services

Free-tier services are designed to help new users become familiar with cloud platforms. They offer a range of resources, including virtual machines, storage, and databases, with limitations on duration or usage.

Types of Free-Tier Services:
- Time-Limited Free Tiers:
  - Offer free services for a specific period (e.g., 12 months).
  - Example: AWS provides free EC2 instances for the first year.
- Always-Free Services:
  - These remain free indefinitely, with usage caps.
  - Example: Google Cloud's f1-micro VM instance is always free.
- Credit-Based Free Tiers:
  - Provide a set amount of credits to explore services.
  - Example: Azure gives $200 in free credits for the first 30 days.

2. Free-Tier Offerings by Major Providers

AWS Free Tier

AWS offers a combination of 12-month free tier services, always-free services, and trials.
- Compute:
  - 750 hours/month of EC2 (t2.micro).
  - 1 million AWS Lambda requests per month (always free).
- Storage:
  - 5 GB of S3 storage.
  - 30 GB of Elastic Block Store (EBS).
- Databases:
  - 750 hours/month of Amazon RDS (db.t2.micro).
- Other Services:
  - 62,000 outbound emails/month with Amazon SES.

Use Case:
A beginner can host a basic website using EC2, S3, and RDS without incurring costs during the first year.

Azure Free Tier

Azure provides $200 in credits for the first 30 days and a selection of always-free services.
- Compute:
  - Azure Virtual Machines (750 hours/month for B1S instances).
  - Azure Functions for serverless computing (1 million requests/month).

- Storage:
  - 5 GB of Blob Storage.
  - 250 GB of SQL Database.
- AI and Analytics:
  - Azure Machine Learning Studio (5 hours/month of free experimentation).

Use Case:
Experiment with AI-powered chatbots using Azure Cognitive Services while storing training data in Blob Storage.

Google Cloud Free Tier
Google Cloud offers $300 in credits for the first 90 days and several always-free services.
- Compute:
  - 1 f1-micro VM instance per month.
  - Cloud Run for serverless applications (2 million requests/month).
- Storage:
  - 5 GB of Cloud Storage.
- AI and Machine Learning:
  - AutoML Vision for processing 1,000 images/month.
- Big Data Tools:
  - BigQuery: 1 TB of queries/month.

Use Case:
Host a small-scale machine learning application on an f1-micro instance and analyze data using BigQuery.

DigitalOcean Free Trial
DigitalOcean offers $200 in credits for 60 days with a straightforward interface and beginner-friendly tools.
- Droplets: Scalable VMs for web hosting and applications.
- App Platform: Fully managed deployment of web applications.

Use Case:
Deploy a personal blog using WordPress on a Droplet within minutes.

Linode Free Trial
Linode provides $100 in credits for 60 days and focuses on simplicity and cost transparency.
- Compute Instances: Virtual machines optimized for speed and performance.
- Kubernetes Support: Simplified deployment of containerized applications.

Use Case:
Launch a development server for testing applications.

3. Maximizing the Free Tier
To get the most out of free-tier services, it's essential to plan, monitor usage, and experiment within limits.

Best Practices for Free-Tier Usage:
- Start Small:
  - Focus on lightweight applications like personal blogs or small-scale data analysis.
  - Avoid resource-heavy workloads that may exceed free-tier limits.
- Understand Usage Caps:
  - Free tiers often have specific limits (e.g., 750 hours/month for compute).
  - Use provider dashboards to track usage and avoid unexpected charges.
- Leverage Always-Free Services:
  - Focus on services that remain free indefinitely, like AWS Lambda or Google's f1-micro instances.
- Experiment with Multiple Providers:
  - Take advantage of trials from AWS, Azure, and Google Cloud to compare platforms and their ease of use.

4. Monitoring and Avoiding Costs
Free tiers are a great way to explore cloud platforms, but it's essential to monitor usage to avoid unintended charges.

Tips for Managing Costs:
- Set Budget Alerts:
  - Use tools like AWS Budgets or Azure Cost Management to receive notifications if spending approaches a threshold.
- Track Resource Usage:
  - Review billing dashboards to ensure you stay within free-tier limits.
- Shut Down Unused Resources:
  - Always terminate instances or services that are no longer needed.
- Explore Free Documentation and Tutorials:
  - Providers offer extensive guides and tutorials to help users make the most of free-tier services.

Exercises for Beginners
- Reflection: Identify a project idea you can implement using free-tier services (e.g., hosting a portfolio site or analyzing a dataset).
- Hands-On Activity:
  - Sign up for AWS, Azure, or Google Cloud. Deploy a simple application, such as a WordPress site, using free-tier resources.
- Comparison Task:
  - Create a small virtual machine on each platform and compare performance, ease of setup, and interface usability.

Free-tier services are an excellent starting point for anyone entering the world of cloud computing. By taking advantage of these offerings, beginners can gain hands-on experience, test ideas, and build foundational knowledge without financial risk. With careful monitoring and strategic use of free-tier resources, you can confidently navigate the first steps of your cloud journey.

AI Insight:
"Free-tier services empower beginners to explore the cloud without barriers. With AI tools simplifying configurations and tracking costs, your learning experience can be seamless and impactful."

Tips for Managing Initial Deployments and Avoiding Common Mistakes
Deploying resources in the cloud for the first time can feel overwhelming, especially for beginners. Mistakes such as overspending, leaving unused resources running, or misconfiguring security settings can lead to unexpected costs and vulnerabilities. This section provides actionable tips for managing initial deployments effectively and avoiding common pitfalls.

1. Start Small and Scale Gradually
Why Starting Small is Important
Cloud platforms are designed for scalability, but this doesn't mean you need to start with complex deployments. Begin with minimal configurations to understand the platform before expanding.

Tips for Starting Small:
- Use Free-Tier Resources:
  - Deploy only free-tier eligible resources, such as AWS's t2.micro instances or Google Cloud's f1-micro VMs.
- Focus on One Service at a Time:
  - Experiment with a single service (e.g., virtual machines or storage) to avoid becoming overwhelmed.
- Test Before Scaling:
  - Validate resource performance and functionality before committing to larger deployments.

Example: Deploy a simple static website on AWS S3 instead of a full-scale web application to learn the basics of storage and hosting.

AI Insight:
"AI tools can analyze your workload requirements and recommend optimal configurations, helping you avoid over-provisioning."

2. Monitor Usage and Costs from Day One
The Importance of Cost Management
Even free-tier services can lead to unexpected charges if limits are exceeded. Effective cost management tools and strategies help you track expenses and avoid surprises.

Best Practices for Monitoring Costs:
- Set Budget Alerts:
  - Use tools like AWS Budgets, Azure Cost Management, or Google Cloud Billing Alerts to receive notifications when you approach spending thresholds.
- Review Billing Dashboards Regularly:
  - Monitor resource usage and identify any unexpected charges.
- Use Cost Calculators:
  - Estimate potential costs before deploying resources.
- Leverage AI Cost Optimization Tools:
  - AI-powered tools can identify underutilized resources and recommend cost-saving measures.

Common Cost Pitfall:
Leaving virtual machines or storage volumes running after they're no longer needed can incur ongoing charges.
Solution:
- Regularly review active resources and terminate unused instances.

3. Prioritize Security from the Beginning

Why Security Matters

Misconfigured resources are one of the most common causes of data breaches in the cloud. Implementing robust security measures from the start helps protect your applications and data.

Best Security Practices:
- Enable Multi-Factor Authentication (MFA):
  - Add an extra layer of protection to your cloud account.
- Restrict Access:
  - Use role-based access controls (RBAC) or AWS Identity and Access Management (IAM) to grant only necessary permissions.
- Secure Network Configurations:
  - Configure firewalls and security groups to restrict traffic to trusted sources.
- Encrypt Sensitive Data:
  - Use encryption for data at rest (e.g., in S3 or Azure Blob Storage) and in transit (e.g., using HTTPS).
- Monitor Logs and Alerts:
  - Set up real-time alerts for suspicious activity and regularly review security logs.

Example: Configure a security group for an EC2 instance to allow SSH access only from your IP address.

AI Insight:

"AI-driven security tools can detect misconfigurations and potential threats, enabling proactive measures."

4. Document Configurations and Learn from Mistakes

The Value of Documentation

Maintaining detailed documentation of your cloud configurations helps you track changes, replicate setups, and troubleshoot issues more effectively.

Best Practices for Documentation:
- Record Initial Configurations:
  - Note instance types, storage sizes, and network settings for future reference.
- Use Provider Tools:
  - Tools like AWS CloudFormation or Azure Resource Manager can automate and document configurations.
- Review and Update Regularly:
  - Update documentation as configurations evolve or new resources are added.

Learning Through Iteration:

It's natural to make mistakes during your first deployments. Treat each error as a learning opportunity and refine your approach accordingly.

5. Leverage Provider Support and Community Resources
Why Use Support Services?
Cloud providers offer extensive documentation, tutorials, and support to help users overcome challenges. Engaging with these resources can save time and prevent errors.
Top Resources to Utilize:
- Official Documentation:
  o AWS, Azure, and Google Cloud provide detailed guides and examples for all services.
- Community Forums:
  o Platforms like Stack Overflow or Reddit can offer valuable insights and solutions to common problems.
- Support Plans:
  o Start with free support options, but consider upgrading if your project becomes more complex.

6. Common Pitfalls and How to Avoid Them
Leaving Resources Running:
- Issue: Forgetting to stop or terminate instances leads to unnecessary costs.
- Solution: Regularly audit resources and use tools like auto-scaling and automated shutdowns.
Over-Provisioning Resources:
- Issue: Allocating more resources than needed increases expenses.
- Solution: Start with smaller configurations and scale as demand grows.
Ignoring Free-Tier Limits:
- Issue: Exceeding free-tier usage caps can result in unexpected charges.
- Solution: Monitor usage dashboards and set alerts.
Skipping Security Configurations:
- Issue: Misconfigured resources can lead to breaches.
- Solution: Follow security best practices, including limiting public access.

Exercises for Beginners
- Reflection: Identify a potential pitfall you might encounter when deploying cloud resources. What steps can you take to avoid it?
- Hands-On Activity: Deploy a virtual machine and configure security settings (e.g., IP whitelisting and SSH key authentication).
- Case Study: Research a real-world example of a cloud misconfiguration incident. What lessons can you apply to your deployments?

Managing initial deployments requires careful planning, monitoring, and learning from experience. By starting small, prioritizing security, and leveraging free-tier services effectively, you can build a strong foundation for more advanced cloud projects. Avoiding common mistakes not only saves time and money but also ensures a smoother and more rewarding journey into cloud computing.

AI Insight:
"Cloud computing is a powerful tool, but its success lies in thoughtful management. AI tools simplify the process, ensuring your resources are efficient, secure, and aligned with your goals."

Conclusion:
Cloud computing offers an exciting opportunity to experiment, innovate, and scale projects with minimal upfront investment. Chapter 4 provided a comprehensive roadmap for getting started, from creating your first cloud account to deploying resources, exploring free-tier services, and avoiding common mistakes. Each section emphasized the practical steps and best practices that will set you up for long-term success in the cloud.

Key Takeaways
1. Step-by-Step Guide to Creating a Cloud Account and Deploying Resources
Setting up a cloud account is straightforward, but taking time to understand each step ensures a smooth start. Deploying your first resource, such as a virtual machine or serverless function, introduces you to the core functionalities of the platform.

What We Learned:
- Begin with free-tier eligible resources to explore cloud platforms without financial risk.
- Validate resource performance and functionality before scaling deployments.
- Platforms like AWS, Azure, and Google Cloud offer tools to guide you through the process.

2. Exploring Free-Tier Services for Beginners
Free-tier services are a valuable resource for beginners, allowing you to test features, build small-scale projects, and gain confidence. Major providers offer free compute, storage, and database options, as well as credits to explore advanced tools.

What We Learned:
- Maximize free-tier benefits by staying within usage limits and experimenting with always-free services.
- Use cost calculators and billing alerts to monitor expenses and avoid unexpected charges.
- Free-tier services are perfect for learning, testing ideas, and comparing cloud platforms.

3. Tips for Managing Initial Deployments and Avoiding Common Mistakes

The cloud is a powerful tool, but it's easy to make mistakes when starting out. By prioritizing security, documenting configurations, and scaling gradually, you can avoid common pitfalls and build a solid foundation.

What We Learned:
- Start small and expand resources as needed to avoid over-provisioning and high costs.
- Monitor usage regularly, shut down unused resources, and leverage cost management tools.
- Follow security best practices, such as enabling multi-factor authentication and restricting access.

The Bigger Picture

Setting up your first cloud environment is the gateway to unlocking the full potential of cloud computing. Each step, from account creation to resource deployment, equips you with the skills and confidence to take on more complex projects. By leveraging free-tier services and AI-powered tools, you can experiment, innovate, and learn without unnecessary risk.

As you progress in your cloud journey, remember that mistakes are part of the learning process. Each deployment, configuration, and test brings you closer to mastering the platform and understanding how cloud computing can transform your projects.

Looking Ahead

With your first cloud environment set up, you're ready to explore the technical intricacies and advanced tools that make cloud platforms so powerful. In the next chapter, we'll dive into cloud storage and databases, examining the options available for managing data securely and efficiently in the cloud.

Chapter 5: Cloud Storage and Databases

Different Types of Cloud Storage: Block, Object, and File Storage

Data storage is the backbone of cloud computing, enabling businesses to securely save, retrieve, and manage vast amounts of information. Cloud storage solutions are designed to handle different types of data and workloads, with three primary storage models—block storage, object storage, and file storage. Each has unique characteristics, use cases, and benefits that make it suitable for specific applications.

1. Block Storage: High-Performance, Structured Storage

Block storage is a fast and efficient storage solution where data is divided into fixed-size blocks. Each block operates independently, allowing for high-performance processing, particularly in structured and transactional workloads.

How Block Storage Works
- Data is stored in blocks, each with a unique identifier.
- Blocks are managed through storage area networks (SANs) or cloud-based block storage services.
- Applications access blocks directly, enabling low latency and high-speed operations.

Key Features of Block Storage
- High Performance:
  - Optimized for applications requiring low latency, such as databases and virtual machines.
- Flexibility:
  - Blocks can be configured and formatted to suit the needs of specific operating systems or applications.
- Reliability:
  - Redundancy mechanisms ensure data integrity and availability.

Use Cases for Block Storage
- Databases:
  - Relational databases (e.g., MySQL, PostgreSQL) benefit from block storage's speed and structured approach.
  - Example: A financial institution uses block storage to process high-frequency transactions.

- Virtual Machines (VMs):
  - Cloud providers often use block storage to support VM disk images.
  - Example: An AWS EC2 instance leverages Elastic Block Store (EBS) for its boot volume.
- Enterprise Applications:
  - High-performance applications like SAP or Oracle ERP systems rely on block storage.

Examples of Cloud-Based Block Storage
- AWS: Elastic Block Store (EBS).
- Azure: Managed Disks.
- Google Cloud: Persistent Disks.

AI Insight:
"Block storage is the go-to choice for speed and precision, making it ideal for mission-critical workloads where latency can't be compromised."

2. Object Storage: Scalable, Unstructured Data Storage
Object storage is designed for handling massive volumes of unstructured data. Data is stored as objects, each containing the data itself, metadata, and a unique identifier. Unlike block storage, object storage is optimized for scalability and accessibility rather than speed.

How Object Storage Works
- Data is organized into objects stored in a flat architecture, often within "buckets."
- Objects are accessed using APIs, enabling seamless integration with applications and workflows.
- Metadata enriches objects with descriptive information, improving searchability and management.

Key Features of Object Storage
- Scalability:
  - Supports petabytes of data, making it ideal for growing datasets.
- Durability:
  - Replication across multiple data centers ensures high availability and fault tolerance.
- Cost-Effectiveness:
  - Pay-as-you-go pricing models are optimized for long-term storage.

Use Cases for Object Storage
- Media Files:
  - Store and stream images, videos, and audio files efficiently.
  - Example: Netflix uses AWS S3 to deliver high-quality video streams to millions of users.
- Big Data Analytics:
  - Archive and process large datasets for analysis.
  - Example: A research lab stores genomic data in Google Cloud Storage for processing in BigQuery.
- Backup and Archiving:
  - Reliable long-term storage for critical data backups.
  - Example: An enterprise uses Azure Blob Storage for regulatory compliance archiving.

Examples of Cloud-Based Object Storage
- AWS: Simple Storage Service (S3).
- Azure: Blob Storage.
- Google Cloud: Cloud Storage.

AI Insight:
"Object storage thrives in the age of big data and multimedia, where scalability and accessibility are paramount."

3. File Storage: Familiar and Collaborative
File storage organizes data into a hierarchical file system of directories and subdirectories, making it similar to traditional on-premises storage. This model is user-friendly and supports collaboration across teams and applications.

How File Storage Works
- Files are stored and accessed using standard protocols such as NFS (Network File System) or SMB (Server Message Block).
- Multiple users can read and write files simultaneously, making it ideal for shared work environments.

Key Features of File Storage
- Compatibility:
  - Works seamlessly with existing applications that depend on file-based access.
- Shared Access:
  - Enables team collaboration by allowing multiple users to access files concurrently.
- Simplicity:
  - Intuitive structure makes it easy to locate and manage files.

Use Cases for File Storage
- Shared Team Drives:
    - Collaboration environments for teams working on shared files.
    - Example: A marketing team uses Azure Files for campaign assets.
- Content Management Systems (CMS):
    - Store web content or documentation in a file-based structure.
    - Example: A website uses AWS FSx to host and manage WordPress files.
- Application Dependencies:
    - Host configuration files, logs, or datasets for software applications.
    - Example: A machine learning pipeline stores training data in Google Filestore.

Examples of Cloud-Based File Storage
- AWS: FSx and Elastic File System (EFS).
- Azure: Files.
- Google Cloud: Filestore.

AI Insight:
"File storage bridges the gap between familiarity and cloud flexibility, making it an excellent choice for collaborative environments."

4. Comparing Block, Object, and File Storage
When it comes to cloud storage, there are three main types to choose from: block storage, object storage, and file storage. Each serves a different purpose and is suited to specific use cases. Here's a simple explanation of each type:

Block Storage
- Best For: Databases, virtual machines, and mission-critical applications.
- How It Works: Data is split into "blocks" and stored separately, allowing for fast read/write speeds. Each block acts like an independent hard drive, meaning the system can retrieve and modify data quickly.
- Example Use Case: If you're running a database or need high-speed storage for virtual machine (VM) disks, block storage is ideal. AWS EBS (Elastic Block Store) is a popular example of block storage.

Object Storage
- Best For: Storing large amounts of unstructured data (like images, videos, and backups).
- How It Works: Data is stored as "objects" along with metadata, like file size and date. Each object has a unique identifier, making it easy to access over HTTP. This type of storage is highly scalable, making it great for big data, archives, and media files.
- Example Use Case: Backups, media files (videos, images), and large datasets are typically stored in object storage. AWS S3, Azure Blob Storage, and Google Cloud Storage are examples of object storage solutions.

File Storage
- Best For: File sharing and collaborative environments.
- How It Works: Data is stored in a hierarchical folder structure, similar to how you organize files on your computer. Users can share, access, and edit files in real time.
- Example Use Case: Shared file systems in team collaboration tools or internal network drives. File storage is commonly used in content management systems (CMS) and file-sharing apps. Examples include AWS EFS (Elastic File System) and Azure File Storage.

Summary
- Block Storage: Use it when you need fast, low-latency storage for databases and virtual machines.
- Object Storage: Use it when you need to store large, unstructured files like backups, images, or videos.
- File Storage: Use it when you need a shared file system for collaboration or team-based file access.

By understanding the key differences between these storage types, you can select the best option for your business or project needs.

Exercises for Readers
- Reflection: Identify which type of cloud storage would best suit your current needs (e.g., personal backups, hosting applications, or managing multimedia).
- Hands-On Activity:
  - Deploy a bucket in AWS S3 and upload a file. Experiment with metadata and access permissions.
  - Alternatively, set up an EBS volume for an EC2 instance and test its performance.
- Comparison Task: Research a real-world case study for each storage type (block, object, and file). How do businesses leverage them effectively?

Cloud storage offers versatile solutions for storing, managing, and accessing data in the digital era. By understanding the strengths and limitations of block, object, and file storage, you can select the right model for your specific use case. From high-performance applications to scalable multimedia archives, cloud storage provides the foundation for today's data-driven innovations.

Introduction to Relational and NoSQL Databases
Databases are the foundation of modern applications, enabling efficient data storage, retrieval, and management. The two primary types of databases—relational and NoSQL—offer distinct approaches to organizing and accessing data. Each has unique strengths and use cases, and understanding their differences is essential for selecting the right database for your cloud environment.

1. Relational Databases: Structured and Organized
Relational databases, often referred to as RDBMS (Relational Database Management Systems), store data in tables with predefined schemas. These databases are based on the relational model, where data is organized into rows and columns, making it easy to manage relationships between datasets.

How Relational Databases Work
- Data is stored in tables, with each table representing a specific entity (e.g., customers, orders).
- Tables are connected through relationships (e.g., a customer table linked to an order table via a customer ID).
- Queries are written using Structured Query Language (SQL) to retrieve or manipulate data.

Key Features of Relational Databases
- Structured Schema:
  - Data organization is strict and predefined, ensuring consistency.
- ACID Compliance:
  - Transactions are Atomic, Consistent, Isolated, and Durable, ensuring reliability and integrity.
- Complex Queries:
  - SQL supports advanced operations like joins, aggregations, and nested queries.

Use Cases for Relational Databases
- E-Commerce:
  - Store structured data like customer details, orders, and product inventories.
  - Example: Amazon uses relational databases to manage order histories and inventory tracking.
- Banking and Finance:
  - Ensure accuracy and integrity for transactions and account balances.
  - Example: A bank uses SQL databases to record deposits, withdrawals, and loan applications.
- Customer Relationship Management (CRM):
  - Track customer interactions, sales data, and support tickets.
  - Example: Salesforce stores structured client data in relational databases.

Examples of Cloud-Based Relational Databases
- AWS: Amazon RDS (supports MySQL, PostgreSQL, MariaDB, Oracle, and SQL Server).
- Azure: Azure SQL Database.
- Google Cloud: Cloud SQL.

AI Insight:
"Relational databases are ideal for structured, transactional workloads where data integrity and consistency are paramount."

2. NoSQL Databases: Flexible and Scalable

NoSQL databases are designed to handle unstructured or semi-structured data, offering flexibility and scalability. Unlike relational databases, NoSQL databases don't rely on predefined schemas, making them ideal for dynamic and rapidly changing data.

How NoSQL Databases Work
- Data is stored in various formats, such as key-value pairs, documents, columns, or graphs.
- Relationships between data are typically less rigid, allowing for faster changes to the database structure.
- Queries are performed using APIs or custom query languages, depending on the database type.

Types of NoSQL Databases
- Document Databases:
    - Store data as JSON or BSON documents.
    - Example: MongoDB.
- Key-Value Stores:
    - Store data as key-value pairs.
    - Example: Redis.
- Column-Family Databases:
    - Organize data into columns rather than rows.
    - Example: Apache Cassandra.
- Graph Databases:
    - Represent data as nodes and edges for complex relationship mapping.
    - Example: Neo4j.

Key Features of NoSQL Databases
- Flexibility:
    - Dynamic schemas allow for easy adjustments to data structures.
- Horizontal Scalability:
    - Easily scale across multiple servers to handle large datasets.
- High Performance:
    - Optimized for high-speed read and write operations.

Use Cases for NoSQL Databases
- Social Media:
    - Store and analyze user interactions, posts, and connections.
    - Example: Facebook uses graph databases to map relationships between users.
- IoT and Sensor Data:
    - Handle massive volumes of semi-structured data from devices and sensors.
    - Example: A smart home system uses DynamoDB to track sensor activity.

- Real-Time Applications:
  - Power applications that require rapid data retrieval, such as gaming leaderboards or chat systems.
  - Example: Redis is used to manage real-time caching for gaming platforms.

Examples of Cloud-Based NoSQL Databases
- AWS: Amazon DynamoDB.
- Azure: Azure Cosmos DB.
- Google Cloud: Firestore and Bigtable.

AI Insight:
"NoSQL databases are built for speed, scalability, and flexibility, making them a perfect match for modern, dynamic applications."

3. Relational vs. NoSQL Databases: Key Differences
When choosing a database, you'll often have to decide between Relational Databases and NoSQL Databases. Each type serves a different purpose, and understanding their key differences will help you select the best option for your specific needs.

1. Data Structure
- Relational Databases: Store data in tables with rows and columns (like a spreadsheet). Each row represents a record, and each column represents a field (attribute) of that record. This structured format makes it easy to organize, search, and query large datasets using SQL (Structured Query Language).
- NoSQL Databases: Store data in a non-tabular format, such as key-value pairs, documents, graphs, or wide-column stores. Data can be stored as JSON-like documents instead of fixed tables. This flexible structure makes NoSQL ideal for unstructured or semi-structured data.

2. Flexibility and Scalability
- Relational Databases: Use a predefined schema. This means that every row in a table must adhere to the same structure (e.g., all customer records must have the same fields). While this provides consistency, it can be rigid when changes are needed.
- NoSQL Databases: Do not require a fixed schema. New fields can be added to documents at any time, making NoSQL highly flexible. This is useful for handling rapidly changing datasets or big data where the data structure may evolve over time.

3. Query Language
- Relational Databases: Use SQL (Structured Query Language) to query, update, and manage the data. SQL allows for powerful, complex queries using SELECT, JOIN, WHERE, and other operators.
- NoSQL Databases: Do not use SQL. Instead, queries are performed using methods specific to the database. For example, MongoDB uses a query language similar to JSON to retrieve and manipulate documents.

4. Use Cases
- Relational Databases: Best for transactional systems (like banking apps) where data integrity, consistency, and ACID compliance are essential. They are ideal for applications that require complex queries, structured data, and multiple relationships between records.
- Example Use Cases: Banking systems, enterprise resource planning (ERP), and customer relationship management (CRM) platforms.
- NoSQL Databases: Best for scalable, high-speed applications with unstructured or semi-structured data. NoSQL databases handle large, dynamic datasets efficiently and support distributed, horizontal scaling across multiple servers.
- Example Use Cases: Social media platforms, IoT data, content management systems (CMS), and real-time data feeds.

5. Performance and Scalability
- Relational Databases: Use vertical scaling (scaling up by adding more CPU, RAM, or storage to a single server). While relational databases are great for small-to-medium workloads, scaling up can be costly and difficult.
- NoSQL Databases: Use horizontal scaling (scaling out by adding more servers/nodes). This makes NoSQL ideal for handling large, distributed workloads where large amounts of data are stored across multiple servers. This is why NoSQL is often used for big data and real-time applications.

6. ACID vs. BASE
- Relational Databases: Follow the ACID principles (Atomicity, Consistency, Isolation, Durability), ensuring reliable, consistent transactions. This makes relational databases ideal for financial systems, payment gateways, and banking applications.
- NoSQL Databases: Follow the BASE principles (Basically Available, Soft state, Eventually consistent). Instead of guaranteeing immediate consistency, NoSQL focuses on availability and partition tolerance, which is crucial for real-time, high-availability apps like social media feeds.

Summary
- Relational Databases: Use them when you need strong consistency, structured data, and ACID compliance for use cases like financial systems, CRMs, and HR software.
- NoSQL Databases: Use them when you need to handle large, unstructured data with horizontal scalability, real-time data, or high-speed web apps like social networks, e-commerce catalogs, and IoT data.

By understanding the differences in structure, scalability, and performance, you can decide whether relational or NoSQL databases are best for your application.

Choosing the Right Database for Your Needs
When to Use Relational Databases:
- When data integrity is crucial (e.g., banking systems).
- When working with structured data and predefined schemas (e.g., ERP systems).

When to Use NoSQL Databases:
- When handling massive amounts of unstructured or semi-structured data (e.g., IoT data).
- When high-speed, flexible, and scalable data operations are needed (e.g., gaming applications).

AI Insight:
"AI tools can analyze workload characteristics and recommend whether a relational or NoSQL database is more suitable for your application."

Exercises for Readers
- Reflection: Consider a project idea. Would it benefit more from a relational database's structure or a NoSQL database's flexibility?
- Hands-On Activity:
  - Set up a relational database using AWS RDS or Azure SQL. Create a simple table and perform basic SQL queries.
  - Alternatively, deploy a NoSQL database like DynamoDB or MongoDB and test its API queries.
- Comparison Task: Research how a large company (e.g., Netflix, Amazon) uses both relational and NoSQL databases in their architecture.

Relational and NoSQL databases represent two complementary approaches to data management. Relational databases excel in structured, transactional workloads, while NoSQL databases shine in dynamic, high-speed environments. Understanding their differences empowers you to make informed decisions and design efficient, scalable applications.

AI Insight:
"Choosing the right database is about aligning technology with your goals. AI tools simplify this process by evaluating workloads and recommending the best fit."

Key Factors in Choosing Storage and Database Solutions
Selecting the right storage and database solutions is a critical decision in cloud computing. The choices you make will impact performance, scalability, cost, and your ability to meet business objectives. This section explores the key factors to consider when evaluating cloud storage and database options, helping you align solutions with your specific needs.

1. Understanding Your Data Requirements
Data Type
- Structured Data:
  - Organized and follows a predefined schema, such as in relational databases.
  - Example: Customer information, financial transactions.
- Unstructured Data:
  - Data without a predefined format, such as images, videos, or log files.
  - Example: Multimedia content, IoT sensor data.
- Semi-Structured Data:
  - Contains elements of both structured and unstructured data, such as JSON or XML files.
  - Example: API responses, product catalogs.

Key Insight:
- Choose relational databases for structured data and NoSQL databases for unstructured or semi-structured data.
- Opt for object storage for unstructured data and block storage for structured, high-performance workloads.

Access Patterns
- Frequent Access: Choose storage optimized for speed, such as block storage or high-performance databases.
- Infrequent Access: Use cost-effective storage solutions like Amazon S3 Glacier for archival data.

Example: A media company may use object storage for frequent access to video files and archival storage for older content.

2. Scalability and Performance
Scalability Requirements
- Horizontal Scalability:
  - Adding more nodes or instances to distribute data across multiple servers.
  - Common in NoSQL databases and object storage solutions.
- Vertical Scalability:
  - Increasing resources (CPU, memory) in a single instance.
  - Typical for relational databases and block storage.

Performance Considerations
- Low Latency: Block storage and relational databases are best for latency-sensitive applications, such as real-time analytics or transactional systems.
- High Throughput: Object storage and NoSQL databases excel in handling large volumes of data with less emphasis on latency.

Example: An online retailer might use block storage for transaction processing and object storage for storing product images.

3. Cost and Budget Constraints
Cost Models
- Pay-as-You-Go:
  - Flexible pricing based on actual usage, ideal for startups or dynamic workloads.
- Reserved Instances:
  - Discounts for long-term commitments, suitable for predictable workloads.
- Data Transfer Costs:
  - Consider fees for transferring data between regions or services.

Cost Optimization Strategies
- Tiered Storage:
  - Use high-performance storage for active data and archival tiers for rarely accessed data.
- Database Optimization:
  - Use read replicas in relational databases to offload traffic from primary databases.
- Monitor Usage:
  - Leverage tools like AWS Cost Explorer or Azure Cost Management to identify cost-saving opportunities.

AI Insight:
"AI tools can predict usage patterns and recommend cost-effective configurations for storage and databases."

4. Security and Compliance
Data Security Features
- Encryption:
  - Protect data at rest (e.g., S3 encryption) and in transit (e.g., HTTPS, VPN).
- Access Controls:
  - Use IAM policies to grant fine-grained access permissions.
- Monitoring and Alerts:
  - Implement real-time monitoring to detect unauthorized access.

Regulatory Compliance
- GDPR (General Data Protection Regulation):
  - Ensures data privacy and security for European users.
- HIPAA (Health Insurance Portability and Accountability Act):
  - Protects healthcare data.
Example: A healthcare company might choose Azure for its HIPAA-compliant tools and end-to-end encryption.

5. Integration with Existing Systems
Seamless Integration
- Relational Databases: Easily integrate with ERP systems, financial tools, or CRM platforms.
- NoSQL Databases: Integrate with big data pipelines and analytics platforms.
Hybrid Cloud and On-Premises Integration
- Choose solutions like Azure Arc or AWS Outposts for hybrid setups that link on-premises infrastructure with cloud services.
Example: A global enterprise uses hybrid storage solutions to keep sensitive data on-premises while leveraging the cloud for scalability

6. Use Cases and Real-World Scenarios

E-Commerce Platforms
- Storage: Block storage for transactional data and object storage for product images.
- Database: Relational databases (e.g., PostgreSQL) for structured data and NoSQL databases (e.g., DynamoDB) for session data.

Media and Entertainment
- Storage: Object storage for multimedia files and archival storage for older content.
- Database: NoSQL databases (e.g., MongoDB) for metadata indexing.

IoT Applications
- Storage: Scalable object storage for sensor data.
- Database: NoSQL databases (e.g., Cassandra) for real-time processing.

AI and Analytics
- Storage: Object storage for training datasets.
- Database: Relational databases for structured reporting and NoSQL databases for unstructured data analysis.

AI Insight:
"AI-driven use case analysis helps align storage and database choices with specific business needs."

Exercises for Readers
- Reflection: Consider your current project. What are your scalability, performance, and security needs? Which solutions align best?
- Hands-On Activity:
  - Deploy a tiered storage setup on AWS S3 or Azure Blob Storage. Experiment with transitioning data between active and archive tiers.
  - Set up a database and test its scalability by adding data incrementally.
- Comparison Task: Research a company in your industry. How do they use cloud storage and databases to meet their goals?

Choosing the right storage and database solutions is about balancing performance, scalability, cost, and compliance. By understanding your data requirements, evaluating options, and leveraging AI tools for decision-making, you can select solutions that align with your business goals and adapt to future needs.

Conclusion:
Cloud storage and databases are the foundation of any cloud environment, playing a vital role in managing, securing, and scaling data. Chapter 5 provided an in-depth look at the primary storage models, database types, and the critical factors to consider when selecting the right solutions. Each section emphasized the importance of understanding your data requirements, use cases, and the unique strengths of available cloud technologies.

Key Takeaways
1. Types of Cloud Storage: Block, Object, and File Storage
The cloud offers diverse storage models, each suited to specific needs:
- Block Storage: Ideal for high-performance and transactional workloads like databases and VMs.
- Object Storage: Scalable and cost-effective for unstructured data, such as media files and backups.
- File Storage: Familiar and collaborative, perfect for team drives and CMS systems.

Understanding these options enables you to align your storage strategy with workload requirements.

2. Relational and NoSQL Databases
Relational and NoSQL databases represent complementary approaches to data management:
- Relational Databases: Structured, schema-based, and optimized for transactional data integrity.
- NoSQL Databases: Flexible, scalable, and ideal for unstructured or real-time data.

By knowing the strengths and limitations of each, you can make informed choices for projects ranging from e-commerce platforms to AI-driven analytics.

3. Key Factors in Choosing Solutions
Selecting the right storage and database solutions involves evaluating:
- Data Type and Access Patterns: Structured vs. unstructured data and the frequency of access.
- Scalability and Performance Needs: Horizontal vs. vertical scaling and latency vs. throughput.
- Cost Considerations: Optimizing costs through tiered storage, reserved instances, and monitoring.
- Security and Compliance: Ensuring data encryption, access controls, and adherence to regulations.

These factors ensure your choices support current workloads and future growth.

The Bigger Picture
Cloud storage and databases are not one-size-fits-all solutions. They are tools that must be tailored to your specific use cases, whether you're hosting a high-traffic website, analyzing big data, or archiving sensitive information. By understanding the distinct roles of block, object, and file storage, as well as relational and NoSQL databases, you can design a robust and efficient data management strategy.

AI plays a transformative role in optimizing storage and database usage. From analyzing workloads to recommending cost-effective configurations, AI tools enable businesses to make smarter decisions and maximize their cloud investments.

Looking Ahead
With a solid understanding of storage and databases, you're ready to explore the next level of cloud computing. In the upcoming chapter, we'll dive into networking in the cloud, examining virtual private clouds, subnets, load balancers, and how to optimize connectivity for secure, high-performance environments.

AI Insight:
"Storage and databases are the heart of your cloud environment. By leveraging AI to analyze your needs and guide your decisions, you can unlock the full potential of these essential tools."

Chapter 6: Databases in the Cloud

Deep Dive into Relational and NoSQL Databases

Databases are at the core of cloud computing, providing the foundation for data storage, retrieval, and management across applications. In the cloud, databases are more flexible, scalable, and integrated than traditional on-premises systems. This section dives into the specifics of relational databases like MySQL and NoSQL databases like MongoDB, highlighting their unique features, strengths, and use cases.

1. Relational Databases in the Cloud: MySQL

Relational databases are the cornerstone of structured data management. MySQL, one of the most widely used relational database systems, excels in managing structured data through predefined schemas and SQL queries.

Features of MySQL in the Cloud
- Managed Services:
  - Cloud providers like AWS (Amazon RDS), Azure (Azure Database for MySQL), and Google Cloud (Cloud SQL) offer fully managed MySQL services.
  - These services handle backups, patching, and scaling, reducing administrative overhead.
- ACID Compliance:
  - Ensures transactional consistency and reliability, critical for applications requiring high data integrity.
- Integration with Cloud Ecosystems:
  - MySQL integrates seamlessly with other cloud services, such as storage, analytics, and monitoring tools.

Advantages of MySQL in the Cloud
- Scalability:
  - Cloud-based MySQL supports vertical and horizontal scaling to handle growing data and traffic.
- High Availability:
  - Cloud providers offer replication and failover mechanisms, ensuring minimal downtime.
- Ease of Use:
  - Managed MySQL services simplify setup and management, enabling developers to focus on application logic.

Use Cases for MySQL in the Cloud
- E-Commerce Applications:
  - Structured data like customer profiles, product inventories, and order histories.
  - Example: Shopify uses relational databases to manage transaction data efficiently.
- Content Management Systems (CMS):
  - Host blogs, documentation, or websites with well-defined content structures.
  - Example: WordPress, powered by MySQL, is hosted on AWS RDS for scalability and reliability.
- Financial Applications:
  - Record and process sensitive transactions with guaranteed data integrity.
  - Example: A fintech company stores payment records in a MySQL database hosted on Azure.

Challenges of MySQL in the Cloud
- Scaling Complexities:
  - Scaling MySQL horizontally requires sharding, which can be complex to manage.
- Resource Costs:
  - Performance-optimized configurations (e.g., high IOPS storage) can be expensive.

AI Insight:
"Cloud-based relational databases like MySQL leverage AI tools to optimize performance, auto-scale resources, and predict maintenance needs."

2. NoSQL Databases in the Cloud: MongoDB
NoSQL databases break away from rigid schemas, offering flexible and scalable solutions for dynamic and unstructured data. MongoDB, a popular NoSQL database, excels in storing JSON-like documents, making it ideal for modern applications with rapidly evolving data models.

Features of MongoDB in the Cloud
- Document-Oriented Storage:
  - Data is stored as BSON (binary JSON) documents, allowing for flexible schemas.
- Horizontal Scalability:
  - MongoDB supports sharding, distributing data across multiple nodes for large-scale applications.
- Rich Query Capabilities:
  - Developers can perform complex queries using MongoDB's powerful query language.

Advantages of MongoDB in the Cloud
- Flexibility:
  - Adapts easily to changing data structures, making it suitable for agile development environments.
- Global Distribution:
  - Cloud-based MongoDB services, like MongoDB Atlas, enable multi-region deployments for low-latency access.
- Built-In High Availability:
  - Replica sets ensure data redundancy and fault tolerance.

Use Cases for MongoDB in the Cloud
- Real-Time Applications:
  - Power live chat systems, gaming leaderboards, or streaming services.
  - Example: A gaming company uses MongoDB Atlas to store player stats and leaderboard data.
- IoT Data Management:
  - Handle massive streams of semi-structured sensor data.
  - Example: A smart home platform stores device logs and activity data in MongoDB hosted on Google Cloud.
- Evolving Data Models:
  - Adapt quickly to changes in application requirements without complex migrations.
  - Example: A startup uses MongoDB on AWS to iterate rapidly on its app's backend.

Challenges of MongoDB in the Cloud
- Data Consistency:
  - MongoDB prioritizes availability and partition tolerance over strict consistency (CAP theorem).
- Learning Curve:
  - Developers accustomed to SQL may need time to adapt to MongoDB's query language.

AI Insight:
"NoSQL databases like MongoDB thrive in cloud environments, with AI tools optimizing sharding, query performance, and global distribution."

3. Comparing MySQL and MongoDB in the Cloud

When choosing a cloud database, MySQL and MongoDB are two of the most popular options. Each has distinct strengths and use cases, depending on your application's needs for structure, speed, and scalability.

1. Data Structure
- MySQL: MySQL is a relational database that stores data in tables with rows and columns, similar to a traditional spreadsheet. It uses a predefined schema, meaning every record in a table follows the same structure. This makes it ideal for applications where data consistency and relationships are essential, such as financial and enterprise systems.
- MongoDB: MongoDB is a NoSQL database that stores data as documents in a JSON-like format (BSON). Each document can have a different structure, which allows for flexibility when working with unstructured or semi-structured data. This format makes MongoDB suitable for apps that require frequent updates or rapidly changing datasets, like product catalogs or content management systems.

2. Query Language
- MySQL: Uses SQL (Structured Query Language) to perform CRUD (Create, Read, Update, Delete) operations. SQL is known for its powerful query capabilities (like SELECT, JOIN, WHERE, etc.), allowing developers to query multiple tables simultaneously. This makes it a great choice for complex queries and analytics.
- MongoDB: Uses a document-based query language where queries are written in a JSON-like syntax. Instead of SQL statements, developers use methods like find() to search for documents within collections. This approach is often seen as more developer-friendly for web and mobile applications.

3. Use Cases
- MySQL: Ideal for transactional applications that require ACID compliance (Atomicity, Consistency, Isolation, Durability). Examples include banking apps, HR software, CRM tools, and ERP systems where strict data integrity is critical. MySQL is often used in industries like finance, healthcare, and retail.
- MongoDB: Best for applications that need to store large, unstructured, or flexible datasets. Its ability to handle document-based storage makes it a top choice for content management systems (CMS), e-commerce product catalogs, social networks, and IoT data streams. MongoDB is also widely used in real-time applications where speed and scalability are crucial.

4. Schema Flexibility

- MySQL: Requires a fixed schema, meaning each table has a predefined structure that enforces consistency. If you want to add new columns or change the schema, you need to modify the entire table, which can be time-consuming.
- MongoDB: Uses a flexible schema where each document in a collection can have a different structure. This means you can add new fields on the fly without restructuring the entire database. This flexibility makes it ideal for dynamic or fast-changing applications.

5. Scalability

- MySQL: Relies on vertical scaling, meaning you need to increase the server's CPU, RAM, or storage to handle more data. While MySQL supports replication (for read-heavy workloads), it does not scale as easily across multiple servers.
- MongoDB: Supports horizontal scaling through sharding, which splits data across multiple servers. This allows MongoDB to handle massive amounts of data and grow in a distributed system. MongoDB is better suited for apps with large, growing datasets that require real-time availability and scalability.

6. Performance

- MySQL: Performance depends on server resources (CPU, RAM, and disk I/O) since MySQL scales vertically. MySQL can be fast for small to medium-sized datasets but may struggle with high-traffic, large-scale workloads unless replication is used. It's great for read-heavy workloads where data integrity and complex queries are required.
- MongoDB: Performs well for high-velocity, large-volume workloads where data is frequently read, written, or updated. Since MongoDB uses horizontal scaling, it can handle large datasets more effectively than MySQL. For write-heavy applications (like real-time data feeds), MongoDB often outperforms MySQL.

7. ACID Compliance

- MySQL: Fully ACID-compliant, ensuring that every transaction is atomic, consistent, isolated, and durable. This makes MySQL essential for use cases where data integrity is non-negotiable, like financial systems and payment gateways.
- MongoDB: Not traditionally ACID-compliant, but recent versions of MongoDB have introduced support for multi-document ACID transactions. While MongoDB offers strong consistency for single documents, eventual consistency is used in distributed systems.

8. Cloud Deployment
- MySQL: Available as a managed service on AWS RDS, Google Cloud SQL, and Azure Database for MySQL. These managed services handle backups, scaling, and security, allowing companies to focus on application development rather than infrastructure.
- MongoDB: Available through MongoDB Atlas, a fully managed NoSQL service that runs on AWS, Azure, and GCP. MongoDB Atlas provides built-in sharding, backups, and failover support. This makes it easy to deploy MongoDB in a multi-cloud, distributed environment.

9. Cost and Licensing
- MySQL: Available as an open-source database with a commercial version (MySQL Enterprise) for businesses that need advanced features, like security patches and 24/7 support. AWS, Azure, and Google Cloud offer managed MySQL instances that can reduce operational costs.
- MongoDB: MongoDB is also open-source, but it has a commercial version through MongoDB Atlas. While you can self-host MongoDB for free, most businesses use MongoDB Atlas to reduce operational complexity and manage sharding, scaling, and backups automatically.

Summary
- MySQL: Use MySQL if you need a relational database with strong support for ACID transactions, complex queries, and structured data. It's ideal for banking apps, ERP systems, and CRM platforms where data integrity is essential.
- MongoDB: Use MongoDB if you need a NoSQL database for unstructured, flexible, or fast-changing data. It's the top choice for real-time apps, IoT data, social media feeds, and content management systems where horizontal scalability and speed are essential.

By understanding the strengths and limitations of each, you can choose the right database for your specific cloud application needs.

Choosing Between Relational and NoSQL in the Cloud
When to Choose MySQL
- When data is highly structured and relationships are critical.
- When strict consistency is required (e.g., financial transactions).

When to Choose MongoDB
- When working with rapidly evolving or unstructured data.
- When global scalability and low latency are priorities.

AI Insight:
"AI tools can evaluate your workload and recommend whether MySQL or MongoDB is better suited to meet your cloud database needs."

Exercises for Readers
- Reflection: Evaluate a project idea. Would it benefit more from the structured consistency of MySQL or the flexibility of MongoDB?
- Hands-On Activity:
  - Set up a MySQL database using Amazon RDS or Azure Database for MySQL and create a table for a sample application.
  - Deploy a MongoDB instance using MongoDB Atlas and design a flexible schema for storing JSON-like documents.
- Comparison Task: Research how a company like Netflix or Amazon uses both relational and NoSQL databases in their architecture.

Relational and NoSQL databases each offer unique benefits, making them essential tools in the cloud computing landscape. MySQL delivers structured, reliable data management for transactional applications, while MongoDB provides unmatched flexibility and scalability for dynamic, real-time workloads. By understanding their strengths and weaknesses, businesses can design efficient, future-proof cloud architectures.

AI Insight:
"The cloud amplifies the power of databases, combining flexibility with scalability. AI helps optimize database performance, ensuring your applications thrive."

Scalability, Cost-Efficiency, and Performance Considerations
When deploying databases in the cloud, scalability, cost-efficiency, and performance are crucial factors that determine the success of your solution. These considerations directly impact the ability to handle growing workloads, manage expenses, and ensure optimal performance for applications. This section explores how cloud databases address these aspects and provides actionable strategies for maximizing value.

1. Scalability: Adapting to Growing Workloads
Scalability refers to the ability of a database to accommodate increasing data volume and user demand without compromising performance. Cloud databases offer two primary scalability models: vertical scaling and horizontal scaling.

Vertical Scaling (Scaling Up)
Vertical scaling involves increasing the resources of a single database instance, such as CPU, memory, or storage capacity.
- Advantages:
    - Simple to implement and manage.
    - Effective for workloads that require high performance on a single node.
- Challenges:
    - Resource limits eventually cap scalability.
    - Downtime may be required during resource upgrades.
- Use Case:
    - Financial applications with strict transactional requirements often benefit from vertical scaling.

Horizontal Scaling (Scaling Out)
Horizontal scaling adds multiple database nodes to distribute the workload, commonly used in NoSQL databases.
- Advantages:
    - Unlimited scalability for growing workloads.
    - High availability and fault tolerance through data replication.
- Challenges:
    - Complex setup and management, especially in relational databases.
    - Requires sharding or partitioning data effectively.
- Use Case:
    - E-commerce platforms with fluctuating traffic leverage horizontal scaling to handle peak loads.

Cloud Examples of Scalability Solutions:
- Amazon Aurora Auto Scaling: Automatically adjusts capacity based on application demand.
- Azure Cosmos DB: Scales horizontally across regions with guaranteed low-latency access.
- Google Bigtable: Designed for petabyte-scale, real-time workloads.

2. Cost-Efficiency: Managing Resources Wisely
Cost-efficiency ensures you're maximizing the value of your cloud database without overspending. Cloud providers offer various pricing models and tools to help businesses optimize costs.

Key Strategies for Cost-Efficiency
- Choose the Right Pricing Model:
  - Pay-as-You-Go: Flexible, usage-based pricing for unpredictable workloads.
  - Reserved Instances: Discounts for long-term commitments, ideal for steady workloads.
  - Spot Instances: Low-cost, short-term resources for non-critical workloads.
- Leverage Tiered Storage:
  - Use high-performance storage for frequently accessed data and archival tiers for infrequent data.
  - Example: Amazon S3 Glacier for long-term data storage.
- Optimize Resource Allocation:
  - Use read replicas to offload traffic from the primary database, reducing costs.
  - Example: AWS RDS supports read replicas for MySQL and PostgreSQL databases.
- Monitor Usage:
  - Set up alerts to track spending and avoid unexpected charges.
  - Tools like AWS Cost Explorer or Azure Cost Management can identify inefficiencies.

Avoiding Cost Pitfalls
- Over-Provisioning:
  - Allocate only the resources you need to avoid paying for unused capacity.
- Underutilized Resources:
  - Shut down unused instances and optimize storage tiers.
- Data Transfer Costs:
  - Minimize inter-region data transfers, which can incur additional fees.

AI Insight:
"AI-driven cost optimization tools analyze workloads and recommend cost-effective configurations, ensuring businesses spend wisely."

3. Performance Considerations: Optimizing Speed and Reliability

Performance in cloud databases is critical for applications that require fast query execution, low latency, and high reliability. Several factors influence performance, and cloud providers offer tools to monitor and optimize database operations.

Key Performance Factors
- Latency and Throughput:
  - Low Latency: Essential for real-time applications (e.g., gaming, live analytics).
  - High Throughput: Required for processing large volumes of data quickly.
- Replication and Caching:
  - Replication: Improves reliability by creating multiple copies of data across regions.
  - Caching: Reduces query load on databases by storing frequently accessed data in memory.
  - Example: AWS ElastiCache provides in-memory caching for faster data retrieval.
- Query Optimization:
  - Use indexing, partitioning, and query execution plans to improve database performance.
  - Tools like Query Performance Insights (AWS RDS) identify slow queries and suggest optimizations.
- High Availability and Fault Tolerance:
  - Distribute workloads across regions or availability zones to prevent downtime.
  - Use failover mechanisms to ensure seamless recovery in case of node failures.

Cloud Examples of Performance Optimization Tools
- AWS Performance Insights: Identifies bottlenecks and provides recommendations for tuning database performance.
- Azure SQL Intelligent Insights: Uses AI to detect and resolve performance issues automatically.
- Google Cloud SQL Insights: Visualizes query performance for optimized database operations.

AI Insight:
"AI enhances performance by identifying inefficiencies, predicting resource needs, and automating database tuning."

4. Balancing Scalability, Cost, and Performance

Achieving the right balance between scalability, cost-efficiency, and performance is key to designing effective cloud database solutions. Businesses often face trade-offs, but cloud providers and AI tools can help optimize this balance.

Practical Considerations
- Understand Workload Requirements:
  - Prioritize performance for mission-critical applications and cost-efficiency for archival or non-urgent workloads.
- Adopt a Multi-Tiered Strategy:
  - Combine high-performance databases for transactional workloads with scalable NoSQL solutions for analytics.
- Use AI for Predictive Management:
  - AI tools analyze historical data to anticipate traffic spikes, ensuring resources are scaled appropriately without incurring unnecessary costs.

Exercises for Readers
- Reflection: Evaluate your workload. Does it require vertical or horizontal scaling? How can you optimize costs without sacrificing performance?
- Hands-On Activity:
  - Test auto-scaling with a database like AWS Aurora or Azure Cosmos DB. Monitor resource changes during simulated traffic spikes.
- Case Study: Research how a large-scale application, such as Netflix, balances scalability, cost-efficiency, and performance across its global database architecture.

Scalability, cost-efficiency, and performance are the pillars of effective cloud database management. By understanding these factors and leveraging cloud-native tools and AI-powered optimizations, businesses can build robust, scalable, and cost-effective solutions. Whether your workload requires rapid scaling, minimal latency, or budget-conscious configurations, the cloud offers the flexibility to meet your needs.

AI Insight:
"Cloud databases are dynamic tools, but achieving balance requires strategy. AI helps by analyzing workloads, predicting needs, and optimizing configurations for maximum efficiency."

Best Practices for Cloud Database Management
Effective cloud database management is critical for ensuring high availability, security, scalability, and cost efficiency. As cloud databases power mission-critical applications, it's essential to follow best practices that prevent downtime, reduce costs, and secure data. This section will cover the most important principles and techniques to optimize cloud databases for modern business demands.

1. Design for Scalability and Performance
As applications grow, so do the demands on databases. Designing for scalability ensures that the database can handle sudden traffic spikes without crashing or slowing down. Scalability comes in two forms: vertical scaling (scaling up) and horizontal scaling (scaling out). The best approach depends on the type of workload, but for cloud-native applications, horizontal scaling is often preferred.

Key Strategies for Scalability
- Sharding: Split large datasets into smaller, more manageable chunks (shards) that can be distributed across multiple servers.
- Read Replication: Create read-only copies of a database to reduce the load on the primary database. Tools like AWS RDS Read Replicas enable replication across multiple availability zones.
- Partitioning: Split a single database table into multiple partitions for faster query performance. This is often used for time-based data, like logs.

AI Insight:
Tools like AI-driven workload analyzers (like AWS Performance Insights) can suggest changes in database design to improve scalability and reduce query load times.

Actionable Tip:
Use serverless databases like AWS Aurora Serverless to automatically adjust compute capacity based on real-time traffic. This ensures you pay only for the resources you use, while also ensuring high availability.

2. Implement Data Security and Encryption

With growing privacy regulations like GDPR, HIPAA, and CCPA, data security has never been more important. Cloud database best practices prioritize encryption, access control, and user authentication to protect sensitive data.

Best Practices for Database Security
- Encrypt Data at Rest and In Transit:
  - Use AWS KMS (Key Management Service) or Azure Key Vault to manage encryption keys.
  - Enable automatic encryption for RDS, S3, and DynamoDB. For NoSQL databases, encrypt data before storing it.
  - In-transit encryption ensures data is encrypted during transmission via SSL/TLS certificates.
- Use Role-Based Access Control (RBAC) and IAM Policies:
  - Grant the least-privilege access to users and applications.
  - Use IAM Roles instead of static credentials. Grant temporary access keys that expire after a set period.
  - Limit direct access to databases. Use bastion hosts or VPNs to access databases, not public IPs.
- Audit and Monitor Access Logs:
  - Enable AWS CloudTrail to track access to AWS databases.
  - Use Google Cloud's Audit Logs to view access requests and user activities.

AI Insight:
AI-driven security tools like AWS GuardDuty detect anomalous access attempts and alert administrators. Using AI anomaly detection models, threats like data exfiltration or unusual login behavior can be caught in real time.

Actionable Tip:
Automate security compliance by using tools like AWS Config and Azure Policy to enforce encryption and access control policies across all cloud resources.

3. Enable Automated Backups and Disaster Recovery
Data loss can be catastrophic. By enabling automated backups and setting up a disaster recovery plan, businesses ensure that they can recover from database failures quickly and with minimal data loss.

Best Practices for Backups
- Enable Point-in-Time Recovery (PITR):
  - Services like AWS RDS and Azure SQL Database support PITR, allowing you to restore a database to any specific point in time.
  - Backups should be stored in multiple availability zones (AZs) or regions to avoid data loss from regional outages.
- Use Automated Backups:
  - Set up daily snapshots of databases and store them in AWS S3 or Google Cloud Storage.
  - Retain backups for at least 30-90 days to recover from both system failures and human errors (like accidental deletion).
- Test Disaster Recovery Plans:
  - Conduct disaster recovery simulations to ensure that failover systems work. Use AWS Disaster Recovery (DR) tools to test failover processes.
  - Ensure Recovery Point Objectives (RPO) and Recovery Time Objectives (RTO) meet business needs.

AI Insight:
AI tools like AWS Fault Injection Simulator allow companies to run chaos engineering experiments to simulate database failures and test their disaster recovery processes.

Actionable Tip:
Use immutable backups — snapshots that cannot be deleted or altered — to prevent ransomware attacks that attempt to encrypt and delete backups.

4. Monitor and Optimize Database Performance

Performance bottlenecks in cloud databases can impact customer experience and increase operational costs. The best way to maintain optimal performance is to use monitoring tools, track queries, and automate optimizations.

Performance Optimization Best Practices
- Query Optimization:
  - Use query explain plans to identify slow queries.
  - Avoid SELECT * queries; select only the fields you need.
  - Use SQL indexes to speed up queries, especially for large datasets.
- Monitor Database Health:
  - Use tools like AWS CloudWatch, Azure Monitor, and Google Cloud Operations Suite to track metrics such as query latency, CPU usage, and IOPS.
  - Configure alerting rules so that you're notified of issues before they impact users.
- Use AI-Driven Optimization Tools:
  - Tools like AWS Performance Insights and Azure SQL Advisor recommend changes to indexes and queries.
  - AI-based anomaly detection alerts administrators when there are unexpected usage spikes.

Actionable Tip:
Use read replicas for resource-intensive read operations. This offloads read queries from the primary database, improving speed and performance.

5. Reduce Costs with Serverless and On-Demand Databases

Running a cloud database 24/7 can be costly, especially if usage is inconsistent. Using serverless databases allows companies to pay only for what they use. To reduce costs, consider the following:

Cost-Reduction Strategies
- Serverless Databases:
  - Use AWS Aurora Serverless or Google Firestore to avoid paying for "always-on" resources.
  - Serverless options scale automatically, so you only pay for the queries you run.
- Reserved Instances and Savings Plans:
  - Buy Reserved Instances for long-term cost savings on AWS RDS and other managed database services.
  - Use Savings Plans to lock in lower rates on database usage over time.

- AI Cost Optimization Tools:
  - Use tools like AWS Compute Optimizer to identify opportunities to reduce database instance sizes.
  - CloudHealth by VMware tracks and optimizes multi-cloud database costs.

Actionable Tip:
Use usage reports to track the time of day with the lowest query traffic and consider scheduling downtime or hibernation for the database.

6. Ensure Data Consistency and Integrity
Maintaining consistency in a distributed, multi-region environment is one of the biggest challenges for cloud database management. Without proper measures, data can become out of sync.

Data Consistency Best Practices
- Eventual vs. Strong Consistency:
  - Strong consistency ensures immediate updates (used in relational databases like PostgreSQL).
  - Eventual consistency is acceptable for NoSQL databases like DynamoDB.
  - Choose the consistency model that best fits your application needs.
- Replication and Sync Tools:
  - Use AWS Database Migration Service (DMS) to sync on-premises databases with cloud databases.
  - For distributed databases (like AWS DynamoDB Global Tables), data is replicated in multiple regions.
- Maintain ACID Transactions:
  - Use ACID-compliant databases (like MySQL, PostgreSQL) for transactional integrity.
  - Ensure that commits and rollbacks are handled properly in multi-region database setups.

Conclusion:
Databases are the lifeblood of modern cloud environments, powering applications, analytics, and innovation. In Chapter 6, we explored the capabilities and considerations of relational and NoSQL databases, delved into the critical factors of scalability, cost-efficiency, and performance, and established best practices for effective database management in the cloud.

Key Takeaways
1. Relational vs. NoSQL Databases
Relational databases like MySQL provide robust, structured solutions for transactional and highly consistent workloads, while NoSQL databases like MongoDB excel in flexibility, scalability, and unstructured data handling.

What We Learned:
- Relational databases are ideal for structured, schema-driven applications.
- NoSQL databases thrive in dynamic environments with real-time or unstructured data.
- Cloud-native tools enhance both database types, automating scaling and maintenance.

2. Scalability, Cost-Efficiency, and Performance
Cloud databases are built for flexibility and growth, but their effectiveness depends on balancing scalability, cost, and performance.

What We Learned:
- Scalability: Vertical scaling works for single-instance growth, while horizontal scaling supports massive workloads.
- Cost-Efficiency: Tools like auto-scaling, reserved instances, and tiered storage help optimize expenses.
- Performance: Caching, read replicas, and optimized queries ensure low latency and high throughput.

3. Best Practices for Cloud Database Management
Managing databases in the cloud involves a proactive approach to performance, availability, security, and automation.

What We Learned:
- High availability strategies like multi-AZ deployments and automated backups safeguard uptime and data integrity.
- Security measures, including encryption, access controls, and activity monitoring, protect sensitive data.
- Automation through managed services and infrastructure as code reduces manual effort and improves reliability.

The Bigger Picture
Databases in the cloud offer unparalleled opportunities for businesses to innovate and scale efficiently. Whether using relational databases for structured applications or NoSQL solutions for real-time, unstructured data, the cloud enables organizations to adapt to evolving needs. By understanding the fundamentals and following best practices, you can leverage cloud databases to drive growth and streamline operations.

AI plays a pivotal role in optimizing database management, analyzing performance metrics, recommending cost-saving measures, and enhancing security. This partnership between technology and strategy ensures cloud databases remain agile and impactful in a fast-changing digital landscape.

Looking Ahead
With a strong understanding of cloud databases, we now turn to the networking aspects of cloud computing in the next chapter. We'll explore virtual private clouds (VPCs), subnets, load balancers, and how to design secure, high-performance networks that connect your cloud resources seamlessly.

AI Insight:
"Cloud databases are not just tools—they're enablers of innovation. With AI guiding your strategy, you can build database systems that are resilient, efficient, and aligned with your goals."

Chapter 7: Networking in the Cloud

Understanding VPCs, Subnets, and Network Configurations

Networking is a core component of cloud computing, enabling secure communication between resources, applications, and users. Virtual Private Clouds (VPCs), subnets, and network configurations form the backbone of cloud networking. This section explains their roles, how they work together, and why they are critical for designing efficient and secure cloud environments.

1. Virtual Private Clouds (VPCs)

A Virtual Private Cloud (VPC) is an isolated virtual network within a public cloud. It provides full control over network settings, including IP address ranges, subnets, and routing configurations.

Key Features of VPCs
- Isolation:
  - Each VPC operates independently, ensuring privacy for your resources.
- Customizability:
  - Define your network's structure, including subnets, routing tables, and internet gateways.
- Scalability:
  - Easily expand your VPC to accommodate new resources without disrupting existing configurations.

Use Cases for VPCs
- Secure Environments:
  - Host sensitive workloads in a controlled network space.
  - Example: A healthcare application storing patient data can use a VPC with strict access controls.
- Hybrid Architectures:
  - Extend on-premises networks to the cloud for hybrid setups using VPNs or direct connections.
  - Example: A corporate database connected securely to cloud applications.

Cloud Provider Examples:
- AWS: Amazon VPC.
- Azure: Virtual Network (VNet).
- Google Cloud: VPC.

2. Subnets: Dividing Your Network
Subnets are subdivisions of a VPC that segregate network resources into smaller, manageable segments. Each subnet resides in a specific availability zone (AZ), enabling resource placement for performance and redundancy.

Key Features of Subnets
- Segmentation:
  - Separate resources based on functionality, such as application servers, databases, or public-facing services.
- Public vs. Private Subnets:
  - Public Subnets: Accessible from the internet; often used for web servers or load balancers.
  - Private Subnets: Isolated from the internet; used for sensitive resources like databases.
- Traffic Control:
  - Use network access control lists (NACLs) and security groups to manage traffic flow between subnets.

Use Cases for Subnets
- Multi-Tier Architectures:
  - Deploy web servers in a public subnet and databases in a private subnet for security and performance.
- Load Balancing:
  - Spread workloads across subnets in different AZs for fault tolerance.

Example: A web application deployed on AWS might use:
- A public subnet for hosting the frontend.
- A private subnet for backend services.

3. Network Configurations: Building a Connected Cloud
Network configurations define how resources within and outside the VPC communicate. Proper configurations are essential for seamless connectivity, security, and performance.

Essential Network Configuration Components
- Routing Tables:
  - Direct traffic within the VPC and between external networks.
  - Example: A route to an internet gateway enables public internet access, while a route to a VPN connects to on-premises resources.
- Internet Gateways and NAT Gateways:
  - Internet Gateway: Allows public internet access for resources in public subnets.
  - NAT Gateway: Enables resources in private subnets to access the internet without being exposed.

- DNS Services:
  - Configure custom domain names and internal DNS for seamless resource identification.
  - Example: AWS Route 53 or Azure DNS.
- Firewalls and Security Groups:
  - Define inbound and outbound traffic rules for individual instances or subnets.
  - Example: Allow HTTP traffic to a web server but block SSH from unauthorized IPs.

Why VPCs, Subnets, and Configurations Matter
Security and Isolation
- VPCs and subnets provide boundaries that separate workloads, protecting sensitive data and reducing the risk of unauthorized access.
Scalability and Flexibility
- Subnets and routing tables allow networks to scale seamlessly as your cloud environment grows.
Optimized Performance
- By placing resources in specific AZs or subnets, you can optimize latency and throughput while ensuring redundancy.

AI Insight:
"AI tools simplify network configurations by suggesting optimal setups based on workload requirements, security policies, and performance needs."

Exercises for Readers
- Reflection: Identify a potential cloud deployment scenario in your business. How would you structure VPCs and subnets for security and performance?
- Hands-On Activity:
  - Create a VPC in AWS with public and private subnets. Deploy an EC2 instance in each subnet and configure communication between them.
- Case Study: Research how a major enterprise leverages VPCs and subnets for their cloud infrastructure.

Understanding VPCs, subnets, and network configurations is crucial for building secure, scalable, and efficient cloud environments. These components form the foundation of cloud networking, enabling businesses to control traffic, isolate resources, and optimize performance. With AI-powered tools and cloud-native services, configuring networks has become more accessible and intuitive, allowing organizations to focus on innovation rather than complexity.

Role of Load Balancers and Content Delivery Networks (CDNs)

In cloud computing, ensuring that applications are highly available, scalable, and responsive is critical. Load balancers and Content Delivery Networks (CDNs) play essential roles in achieving these goals by distributing traffic efficiently and optimizing content delivery. This section explores their functions, benefits, and how they complement each other to enhance performance and reliability.

1. Load Balancers: Distributing Traffic Efficiently

A load balancer is a service that distributes incoming traffic across multiple servers to ensure no single server is overwhelmed. This improves availability, scalability, and fault tolerance for applications.

Types of Load Balancers
- Application Load Balancers (ALB):
  - Operates at the application layer (Layer 7 of the OSI model).
  - Routes traffic based on HTTP/HTTPS requests, such as URL paths or headers.
  - Example Use Case: Directing traffic to different microservices in a containerized environment.
- Network Load Balancers (NLB):
  - Operates at the transport layer (Layer 4).
  - Distributes traffic based on IP protocols (TCP/UDP), ideal for low-latency scenarios.
  - Example Use Case: Handling real-time gaming traffic or VoIP calls.
- Classic Load Balancers (CLB):
  - Supports both Layer 4 and Layer 7 operations but lacks advanced features found in ALB or NLB.

Key Benefits of Load Balancers
- Scalability:
  - Automatically distributes traffic to new instances as they are added, supporting horizontal scaling.
- High Availability:
  - Ensures continuous uptime by rerouting traffic away from failed servers or instances.
- Performance Optimization:
  - Reduces server load by evenly distributing traffic and prioritizing healthy instances.

97

Cloud Examples of Load Balancers
- AWS Elastic Load Balancer (ELB): Supports ALB, NLB, and CLB for diverse workloads.
- Azure Load Balancer: Provides Layer 4 balancing for virtual networks.
- Google Cloud Load Balancing: Offers global, software-defined load balancing with built-in redundancy.

2. Content Delivery Networks (CDNs): Accelerating Content Delivery

A Content Delivery Network (CDN) is a geographically distributed network of servers that delivers web content to users based on their location. CDNs cache content at edge servers, reducing latency and improving load times.

How CDNs Work
- Caching:
  - Static content (e.g., images, videos, stylesheets) is stored on edge servers closest to the user.
- Content Routing:
  - Requests are directed to the nearest edge server, minimizing latency and improving response times.
- Dynamic Content Delivery:
  - While CDNs excel at caching static content, many now support dynamic content delivery by optimizing origin fetches.

Key Benefits of CDNs
- Improved Performance:
  - Reduces latency and speeds up website loading times, especially for global audiences.
- Scalability:
  - Handles surges in traffic without overloading origin servers.
- Enhanced Security:
  - Mitigates Distributed Denial of Service (DDoS) attacks by absorbing malicious traffic at edge servers.

Cloud Examples of CDNs
- AWS CloudFront: Fully integrated with AWS services for caching and secure content delivery.
- Azure Content Delivery Network: Delivers high-bandwidth content globally with low latency.
- Google Cloud CDN: Integrates with Google Cloud Load Balancing for efficient content delivery.

3. Complementary Roles of Load Balancers and CDNs
Load balancers and CDNs work together to create robust, scalable, and high-performing applications. While load balancers focus on distributing traffic among servers, CDNs optimize content delivery to end-users.

How They Work Together
- Global Traffic Distribution:
  - CDNs route user requests to the nearest edge server, while load balancers manage traffic within the cloud infrastructure.
- Fault Tolerance and High Availability:
  - Load balancers reroute traffic to healthy servers, while CDNs ensure cached content remains available even during server outages.
- Enhanced User Experience:
  - CDNs improve page load times for users, while load balancers ensure backend servers operate efficiently.

Example Use Case:
A video streaming platform uses:
- CDNs to cache and deliver videos to users worldwide.
- Load balancers to distribute requests for user authentication and video recommendations across multiple servers.

Why Load Balancers and CDNs Are Critical
Business Benefits
- Resilience:
  - Together, load balancers and CDNs reduce downtime and ensure uninterrupted service.
- Cost Efficiency:
  - CDNs offload static content delivery, reducing bandwidth costs.
- Global Reach:
  - Enable businesses to deliver consistent performance across regions.

AI Insight:
"AI integrates with load balancers and CDNs to predict traffic spikes, optimize routing, and enhance end-user experiences."

Exercises for Readers
- Reflection: Consider a high-traffic application. How could load balancers and CDNs be implemented to improve performance and reliability?
- Hands-On Activity:
  - Configure an AWS Elastic Load Balancer with CloudFront. Simulate a traffic spike to observe how requests are handled.
- Case Study: Research how platforms like Netflix or YouTube use CDNs and load balancers to deliver content efficiently to millions of users.

Load balancers and CDNs are indispensable for building scalable and high-performing cloud applications. By distributing traffic intelligently and delivering content rapidly, these technologies ensure a seamless user experience even under heavy demand. Combined with AI-driven optimizations, they empower businesses to scale globally while maintaining reliability and cost efficiency.

AI Insight:
"Load balancers and CDNs act as the gatekeepers and accelerators of the cloud. With AI-powered enhancements, they provide the backbone for resilient and responsive applications."

AI-Powered Solutions for Optimizing Network Performance
Artificial Intelligence (AI) is transforming cloud networking by enabling smarter, faster, and more efficient management of complex infrastructures. AI-powered solutions optimize network performance through predictive analytics, real-time monitoring, automated configurations, and advanced troubleshooting. This section explores how AI integrates into cloud networking to enhance connectivity, reduce latency, and improve reliability.

1. AI in Network Traffic Management
AI tools analyze and manage network traffic patterns to ensure optimal performance. These tools help balance loads, predict traffic surges, and identify bottlenecks before they impact users.

How AI Improves Traffic Management
- Predictive Traffic Analysis:
  - AI analyzes historical traffic data to forecast demand and allocate resources dynamically.
  - Example: Anticipating increased traffic during an e-commerce sale and pre-scaling network capacity.

- Dynamic Load Balancing:
  - AI-powered load balancers distribute traffic intelligently across resources, optimizing performance and minimizing latency.
  - Example: AWS Elastic Load Balancing uses AI to monitor and adjust traffic routing in real-time.
- Bottleneck Detection:
  - AI tools identify congestion points in the network and recommend adjustments, such as rerouting traffic or increasing bandwidth.

2. Real-Time Monitoring and Anomaly Detection
AI enhances network monitoring by continuously analyzing performance metrics and identifying anomalies that may indicate potential issues.

Key Features of AI-Powered Monitoring
- Proactive Alerting:
  - Detects unusual patterns in network traffic or resource usage, such as unexpected spikes or drops.
  - Example: Azure Network Watcher uses AI to alert administrators about packet loss or high latency.
- Root Cause Analysis:
  - AI tools diagnose the cause of performance issues faster than manual processes.
  - Example: Google Cloud Operations Suite uses AI to analyze logs and pinpoint the source of network delays.
- Performance Benchmarking:
  - Compares current network performance against historical data to highlight areas for improvement.

3. Automated Network Optimization
AI reduces manual intervention by automating complex network configurations and adjustments, ensuring networks remain efficient and resilient.

Applications of Automation in Networking
- Dynamic Routing:
  - AI adjusts routing tables automatically to direct traffic along the most efficient paths.
  - Example: AI-powered routing in SD-WAN (Software-Defined Wide Area Network) solutions dynamically adapts to changes in traffic or network conditions.
- QoS (Quality of Service) Adjustments:
  - AI prioritizes critical traffic, such as VoIP or video streaming, over less time-sensitive data.

- Policy Enforcement:
  - Ensures compliance with security and performance policies by automatically adjusting access controls and configurations.

AI Insight:
"Automation not only improves performance but also reduces the risk of human error in complex network environments."

4. AI-Driven Security Enhancements
AI strengthens network security by detecting and mitigating threats faster and more effectively than traditional methods.

Security Benefits of AI-Powered Networking
- DDoS Attack Mitigation:
  - AI detects and blocks Distributed Denial of Service (DDoS) attacks in real-time by analyzing traffic patterns.
  - Example: AWS Shield Advanced uses AI to protect against large-scale DDoS attacks.
- Intrusion Detection Systems (IDS):
  - AI identifies unusual behavior that may indicate a breach, such as unauthorized access attempts or data exfiltration.
- Encryption Optimization:
  - AI monitors and adjusts encryption protocols to ensure secure data transmission without compromising performance.

5. Enhancing CDN Performance with AI
AI integrates seamlessly with Content Delivery Networks (CDNs) to optimize content delivery and improve end-user experiences.

AI-Powered CDN Capabilities
- Intelligent Caching:
  - AI predicts frequently accessed content and preloads it on edge servers for faster delivery.
  - Example: Google Cloud CDN uses AI to cache high-demand content closer to users.
- Load Forecasting:
  - Anticipates regional traffic patterns to scale edge server resources accordingly.
- Latency Reduction:
  - AI analyzes network routes and selects the fastest paths for content delivery.

Why AI-Powered Solutions Matter
Business Benefits
- Improved Efficiency:
  - AI automates resource allocation, ensuring networks perform at their best with minimal manual oversight.
- Cost Savings:
  - Optimized traffic routing and resource scaling reduce unnecessary expenses.
- Enhanced User Experience:
  - Faster, more reliable networks lead to better application performance and user satisfaction.

AI Insight:
"AI isn't just an enhancement—it's a necessity for managing the complexity of modern cloud networks."

Exercises for Readers
- Reflection: Consider how AI-powered tools could optimize your current network setup. What specific challenges could AI address?
- Hands-On Activity:
  - Use AWS CloudWatch or Azure Network Watcher to monitor network traffic and identify potential bottlenecks.
  - Experiment with an AI-driven SD-WAN solution to optimize routing in a multi-region deployment.
- Case Study: Research how a leading company like Netflix or Amazon uses AI to enhance their network performance and content delivery.

AI-powered solutions are revolutionizing cloud networking by offering predictive analytics, real-time monitoring, and automated optimization. These tools enhance performance, reliability, and security, ensuring networks can handle growing complexity and demand. By integrating AI into your network strategy, you can create a resilient, cost-effective, and high-performing cloud environment.

AI Insight:
"AI transforms cloud networking into a proactive and self-optimizing ecosystem, enabling businesses to focus on innovation rather than infrastructure."

Conclusion:
Networking is the backbone of cloud computing, enabling seamless communication, secure data transfers, and efficient application delivery. Chapter 7 explored the foundational components of cloud networking, including Virtual Private Clouds (VPCs), subnets, load balancers, Content Delivery Networks (CDNs), and the transformative role of AI-powered solutions. Together, these technologies ensure that cloud infrastructures remain scalable, secure, and high-performing.

Key Takeaways
1. Understanding VPCs, Subnets, and Network Configurations
VPCs and subnets form the fundamental structure of cloud networks, offering isolation, security, and scalability. By configuring routing tables, gateways, and firewalls, businesses can create robust network environments tailored to their specific needs.

What We Learned:
- VPCs provide isolated, customizable virtual networks.
- Subnets enable segmentation of resources for improved security and performance.
- Proper network configurations ensure efficient traffic flow and connectivity.

2. Role of Load Balancers and CDNs
Load balancers distribute traffic across resources to maintain uptime and optimize performance, while CDNs accelerate content delivery by caching data at edge locations. Together, they enhance scalability, reliability, and user experiences.

What We Learned:
- Load balancers prevent resource overload and improve fault tolerance.
- CDNs minimize latency by delivering cached content closer to users.
- These technologies complement each other, ensuring global scalability and high availability.

3. AI-Powered Solutions for Optimizing Network Performance

AI enhances cloud networking by providing predictive analytics, automating configurations, and identifying performance bottlenecks in real-time. From dynamic traffic management to advanced security measures, AI transforms networks into intelligent ecosystems.

What We Learned:
- AI-powered tools automate load balancing, routing, and anomaly detection.
- Real-time monitoring and predictive insights ensure optimal performance and security.
- AI-driven CDNs and SD-WAN solutions improve scalability and cost-efficiency.

The Bigger Picture

Cloud networking is essential for modern applications, enabling businesses to scale globally, maintain reliability, and deliver superior user experiences. By integrating load balancers, CDNs, and AI-powered tools, organizations can create networks that are efficient, resilient, and adaptive to future demands.

AI's role in cloud networking goes beyond automation—it empowers businesses with data-driven insights and proactive optimizations. This partnership between human expertise and AI ensures that cloud networks are not only high-performing but also cost-effective and secure.

Looking Ahead

With a solid understanding of cloud networking, we now turn to security in the cloud in the next chapter. We'll explore best practices for protecting your cloud infrastructure, securing data, and leveraging AI tools to stay ahead of evolving threats.

AI Insight:

"Networking in the cloud is the bridge that connects resources, users, and data. AI ensures this bridge is robust, efficient, and scalable, enabling businesses to focus on innovation."

Chapter 8: Security in the Cloud

Core Principles: Identity and Access Management (IAM), Encryption, and Compliance
Security in the cloud is a top priority for businesses looking to protect sensitive data and maintain trust with their customers. This section explores the core principles of cloud security—Identity and Access Management (IAM), encryption, and compliance. These principles form the foundation of a secure cloud environment, safeguarding against threats while meeting regulatory requirements.

1. Identity and Access Management (IAM)
IAM is a framework for managing user identities and their access to cloud resources. By implementing IAM, businesses can ensure that only authorized individuals have access to specific data and services.

Key Features of IAM
- Granular Access Controls:
  - Define permissions at various levels, such as users, groups, and roles.
  - Example: An admin has full access to cloud resources, while a developer has access only to the development environment.
- Multi-Factor Authentication (MFA):
  - Adds an extra layer of security by requiring multiple verification methods (e.g., password and one-time code).
- Temporary Credentials:
  - Use time-limited credentials to minimize exposure to sensitive data.
  - Example: AWS IAM roles provide temporary access for applications or services.

Best Practices for IAM
- Least Privilege Principle:
  - Grant the minimum level of access necessary for users to perform their tasks.
- Regular Audits:
  - Periodically review and update IAM policies to remove outdated or unnecessary permissions.
- Use Identity Federation:
  - Integrate IAM with existing identity providers (e.g., Active Directory) for streamlined user management.

AI Insight:
"AI-powered IAM solutions detect unusual access patterns, flagging potential breaches before they escalate."

2. Encryption: Protecting Data at Rest and in Transit
Encryption ensures that data is unreadable without the proper decryption key, providing a critical layer of security for sensitive information.

Types of Encryption
- Data at Rest:
  - Encrypt stored data using algorithms like AES-256.
  - Example: AWS S3 supports server-side encryption with automatic key management.
- Data in Transit:
  - Protect data as it moves between systems using protocols like HTTPS or TLS.
  - Example: Enforcing TLS for API communications secures data transfer between applications.
- Key Management:
  - Securely manage encryption keys using services like AWS KMS or Azure Key Vault.

Best Practices for Encryption
- Automate Encryption:
  - Enable default encryption for storage buckets, databases, and other resources.
- Rotate Keys Regularly:
  - Update encryption keys periodically to minimize the impact of a compromised key.
- Use End-to-End Encryption:
  - Ensure data remains encrypted throughout its lifecycle, from sender to recipient.

AI Insight:
"AI-driven key management systems automate key rotation and detect weak encryption configurations."

3. Compliance: Meeting Regulatory Standards
Compliance ensures that cloud environments adhere to industry standards and legal regulations, protecting businesses from penalties and reputational damage.

Key Compliance Standards
- General Data Protection Regulation (GDPR):
  - Protects the personal data of European Union (EU) citizens.
- Health Insurance Portability and Accountability Act (HIPAA):
  - Sets standards for safeguarding healthcare data in the U.S.
- Payment Card Industry Data Security Standard (PCI DSS):
  - Regulates the storage and transmission of credit card information.

Best Practices for Compliance
- Understand Regional Regulations:
  - Identify the regulations applicable to your industry and geography.
- Use Compliance Tools:
  - Leverage tools like AWS Artifact or Azure Compliance Manager to monitor adherence.
- Maintain Detailed Logs:
  - Store audit logs to demonstrate compliance during inspections or audits.

Cloud Provider Support for Compliance
- AWS: Offers pre-configured compliance reports and services for GDPR, HIPAA, and PCI DSS.
- Azure: Provides regulatory compliance blueprints for faster implementation.
- Google Cloud: Offers compliance certifications and tools for data protection.

AI Insight:
"AI streamlines compliance by continuously monitoring configurations and flagging potential violations."

Why These Principles Matter
Security and Trust
IAM ensures that resources are accessed only by authorized users, encryption protects sensitive data, and compliance builds trust with customers and regulators. Together, they form a robust defense against breaches and legal risks.

AI's Role in Core Security
AI strengthens these principles by automating tasks like anomaly detection in IAM, optimizing encryption protocols, and monitoring compliance in real time.

Exercises for Readers
- Reflection: Assess your current security setup. Are IAM, encryption, and compliance integrated effectively?
- Hands-On Activity:
  - Configure an IAM policy in AWS to enforce least privilege access.
  - Enable server-side encryption for a storage bucket and test data transfer with TLS.
- Case Study: Research how a leading organization manages cloud security to comply with GDPR or HIPAA.

The core principles of cloud security—IAM, encryption, and compliance—are essential for protecting data, ensuring privacy, and meeting regulatory standards. By implementing these practices effectively and leveraging AI-powered tools, businesses can create secure cloud environments that inspire confidence and resilience.

AI Insight:
"Core security principles are the foundation of a strong cloud strategy. With AI-driven enhancements, these principles become smarter, faster, and more reliable."

Understanding Shared Responsibility Between Providers and Customers

One of the defining aspects of cloud security is the shared responsibility model, where security responsibilities are divided between the cloud provider and the customer. This collaboration ensures the cloud environment is secure, resilient, and compliant. Understanding these roles is critical to prevent gaps in security that can lead to vulnerabilities.

1. What is the Shared Responsibility Model?

The shared responsibility model defines which security tasks are handled by the cloud provider and which are managed by the customer. The division depends on the type of cloud service—Infrastructure as a Service (IaaS), Platform as a Service (PaaS), or Software as a Service (SaaS).

Provider's Responsibilities
- Infrastructure Security:
  - Physical security of data centers, network infrastructure, and hardware.
  - Example: AWS, Azure, and Google Cloud ensure their facilities are protected against unauthorized access and natural disasters.
- Core Cloud Services:
  - Secure delivery and operation of compute, storage, and networking resources.
  - Example: Providers regularly patch and update the underlying hardware and hypervisors.
- Compliance Certifications:
  - Providers obtain certifications like ISO 27001, SOC 2, and PCI DSS for their infrastructure.

Customer's Responsibilities
- Application Security:
  - ○ Secure configuration of cloud resources and applications.
  - ○ Example: Setting up security groups in AWS or implementing proper firewall rules.
- Identity Management:
  - ○ Managing access controls and ensuring users follow the least privilege principle.
  - ○ Example: Configuring IAM policies to restrict sensitive operations to administrators.
- Data Security:
  - ○ Encrypting sensitive data and managing encryption keys.
  - ○ Example: Enabling encryption for S3 buckets and ensuring secure data transmission.

2. Responsibility Breakdown by Service Model
Infrastructure as a Service (IaaS)
- Provider: Manages physical infrastructure, virtualization, and network security.
- Customer: Configures virtual machines, storage, and network security.

Example: A customer using AWS EC2 must secure their operating system, configure IAM roles, and implement security patches for their applications.

Platform as a Service (PaaS)
- Provider: Handles infrastructure and platform-level services, including runtime environments.
- Customer: Focuses on securing applications and managing user access.

Example: In Azure App Service, the provider handles OS and runtime updates, while the customer manages application-level security.

Software as a Service (SaaS)
- Provider: Manages the application, infrastructure, and underlying services.
- Customer: Ensures proper user access controls and data security.

Example: A company using Google Workspace must enforce strong password policies and enable MFA for users.

3. Key Challenges in Shared Responsibility

- Misconfigurations:
  - Many security incidents result from customer-side misconfigurations, such as open storage buckets or overly permissive IAM policies.
  - Solution: Regularly audit and monitor configurations using tools like AWS Config or Azure Security Center.
- Data Ownership and Protection:
  - While providers ensure infrastructure security, customers must secure sensitive data.
  - Solution: Use encryption for data at rest and in transit, and adopt robust key management practices.
- Understanding Boundaries:
  - Customers may assume providers are responsible for tasks that fall under their scope.
  - Solution: Familiarize yourself with the shared responsibility model and clearly define roles during onboarding.

4. Benefits of the Shared Responsibility Model

Increased Security Resilience:
- Providers handle physical and foundational security, freeing customers to focus on application and data security.

Scalability and Flexibility:
- Customers can scale their workloads without worrying about infrastructure security.

Collaboration and Innovation:
- The shared model fosters a collaborative approach, allowing businesses to leverage provider expertise while retaining control over sensitive aspects.

Best Practices for Managing Shared Responsibility
- Understand Provider Policies:
  - Review security documentation and service agreements to clarify roles and responsibilities.
- Automate Compliance Checks:
  - Use tools like Azure Policy or AWS Security Hub to ensure continuous compliance with best practices.
- Leverage Provider Security Services:
  - Use built-in tools like Google Cloud Armor or AWS Shield for enhanced protection against threats.
- Regular Training and Awareness:
  - Educate teams about their responsibilities in the shared model to prevent missteps.

Exercises for Readers
- Reflection: Assess your current cloud setup. Are you aware of your responsibilities within the shared model?
- Hands-On Activity:
  - Review a service you use (e.g., AWS S3, Azure VM). Identify which security tasks are your responsibility and which are the provider's.
- Case Study: Research a security breach caused by a shared responsibility misunderstanding. How could it have been prevented?

The shared responsibility model is central to cloud security, ensuring a collaborative approach to safeguarding resources. By understanding the division of roles, customers can effectively secure their applications and data while relying on providers for infrastructure and compliance. AI-powered tools further simplify this process by identifying risks, automating compliance, and strengthening the partnership between providers and customers.

AI Insight:
"The shared responsibility model empowers businesses to focus on innovation while maintaining robust security, with AI serving as a vigilant partner in identifying and addressing potential vulnerabilities."

Key Tools for Ensuring Cloud Security
Cloud providers offer a suite of tools to help businesses secure their environments, protect data, and maintain compliance. These tools address various aspects of security, including identity management, threat detection, encryption, and monitoring. This section explores the most important tools for ensuring cloud security and how they work together to create a robust defense.

1. Identity and Access Management (IAM) Tools
IAM tools control access to cloud resources by defining who can access what and under what conditions. They enforce the principle of least privilege and prevent unauthorized access.

Popular IAM Tools
- AWS Identity and Access Management (IAM):
  - Manage users, roles, and policies to control access to AWS resources.
  - Supports multi-factor authentication (MFA) and fine-grained permissions.

- Azure Active Directory (AAD):
  - A centralized identity solution for managing access across Azure resources and third-party apps.
  - Integrates with on-premises directories for seamless user management.
- Google Cloud Identity:
  - Offers identity federation, role-based access control, and device management.

Key Features of IAM Tools
- Fine-Grained Permissions: Define resource-specific access policies.
- Conditional Access: Restrict access based on factors like location or device type.
- Automated Monitoring: Detect suspicious login attempts and revoke compromised credentials.

AI Insight:
"AI-driven IAM tools identify unusual access patterns and recommend stronger access controls."

2. Threat Detection and Intrusion Prevention Tools
These tools proactively monitor cloud environments to identify and mitigate security threats, such as unauthorized access or malicious attacks.

Top Threat Detection Tools
- AWS GuardDuty:
  - Uses machine learning to detect threats across AWS environments by analyzing logs, DNS queries, and VPC flow data.
- Azure Security Center:
  - Provides advanced threat detection and recommendations to improve security configurations.
- Google Cloud Security Command Center (SCC):
  - Offers real-time visibility into potential threats and misconfigurations across GCP resources.

Key Features of Threat Detection Tools
- Anomaly Detection: Identify unusual activity patterns that may indicate security breaches.
- Automated Alerts: Notify administrators immediately when a threat is detected.
- Actionable Recommendations: Provide steps to mitigate risks and harden configurations.

3. Encryption and Key Management Tools

Encryption tools protect data by making it unreadable without the proper decryption keys, while key management solutions ensure encryption keys are stored and rotated securely.

Top Encryption Tools
- AWS Key Management Service (KMS):
  - Manage and control encryption keys for AWS services and customer applications.
- Azure Key Vault:
  - Store and manage encryption keys, passwords, and certificates securely.
- Google Cloud Key Management Service:
  - Protect encryption keys and integrate them with GCP services for seamless security.

Best Practices for Using Encryption Tools
- Enable default encryption for all storage services.
- Use customer-managed keys (CMK) for greater control over encryption.
- Regularly rotate keys to minimize risks associated with compromised keys.

AI Insight:
"AI-powered key management systems automate key rotation and monitor for weak encryption configurations."

4. Security Monitoring and Compliance Tools

Monitoring and compliance tools help businesses maintain visibility into their cloud environments and ensure adherence to regulatory requirements.

Popular Monitoring Tools
- AWS CloudTrail:
  - Tracks and logs user activity, providing an audit trail for AWS accounts.
- Azure Monitor:
  - Monitors resource performance and sends alerts for potential security issues.
- Google Cloud Operations Suite:
  - Provides real-time insights into system performance and user activity logs.

Top Compliance Tools
- AWS Artifact:
  - Offers access to compliance reports and agreements for AWS services.

- Azure Compliance Manager:
  - Helps organizations assess compliance against standards like GDPR and HIPAA.
- Google Cloud Assured Workloads:
  - Ensures workloads meet compliance requirements with preconfigured environments.

AI Insight:
"AI integrates with monitoring tools to detect compliance violations and recommend corrective actions."

5. Network Security Tools

Network security tools secure traffic within and outside the cloud environment, preventing unauthorized access and mitigating attacks.

Popular Network Security Tools
- AWS Shield:
  - Protects against Distributed Denial of Service (DDoS) attacks.
- Azure Firewall:
  - Offers a stateful firewall service to protect Azure resources.
- Google Cloud Armor:
  - Defends against large-scale attacks with IP-based restrictions and rate limiting.

Key Features of Network Security Tools
- Traffic Filtering: Block unauthorized traffic and allow only trusted sources.
- Real-Time Threat Mitigation: Respond to attacks as they occur.
- Integration with Monitoring Tools: Combine with threat detection solutions for a holistic security strategy.

AI Insight:
"AI-powered firewalls analyze traffic patterns and automatically adapt to emerging threats."

6. Backup and Disaster Recovery Tools

Backup tools ensure data recovery in the event of data loss, while disaster recovery tools help restore cloud environments quickly during outages.

Top Tools for Backup and Recovery
- AWS Backup:
  - Centralized backup management for AWS resources.
- Azure Site Recovery:
  - Replicates applications and data across regions for seamless recovery.
- Google Cloud Backup and DR:
  - Offers integrated backup and disaster recovery solutions.

Best Practices for Backup and Recovery
- Schedule regular backups to minimize data loss.
- Test recovery processes to ensure reliability during actual events.
- Use multi-region backups for greater resilience.

Why These Tools Matter
Comprehensive Security
By leveraging these tools, businesses can address all aspects of cloud security, from access control and threat detection to encryption and compliance.

AI's Role in Cloud Security Tools
AI integrates across these tools to enhance capabilities, automating responses, predicting threats, and reducing human error.

Exercises for Readers
- Reflection: Which security tools does your current cloud environment lack? How can they enhance your security posture?
- Hands-On Activity:
  - Enable AWS GuardDuty or Azure Security Center for your environment and review their findings.
  - Configure an encryption key in AWS KMS or Azure Key Vault and test data encryption.
- Case Study: Research how a leading organization uses cloud security tools to protect its infrastructure and maintain compliance.

The right combination of cloud security tools provides a robust defense against modern threats while ensuring compliance and maintaining operational efficiency. AI-powered enhancements elevate these tools, enabling faster detection, smarter prevention, and seamless automation. By integrating these solutions into your cloud strategy, you can build a secure and resilient cloud environment.

AI Insight:
"Cloud security tools, combined with AI's intelligence, transform security into a proactive and adaptive shield, ensuring businesses remain secure in a rapidly evolving digital landscape."

Conclusion:
Security is the cornerstone of cloud computing, protecting sensitive data, applications, and infrastructure from ever-evolving threats. Chapter 8 delved into the foundational principles of cloud security, the shared responsibility model, and the essential tools and strategies for maintaining a secure cloud environment. Together, these elements ensure businesses can confidently innovate while safeguarding their assets.

Key Takeaways
1. Core Principles of Cloud Security
Identity and Access Management (IAM), encryption, and compliance form the backbone of cloud security.
- IAM ensures that only authorized users can access specific resources.
- Encryption protects data at rest and in transit, rendering it unreadable without the proper keys.
- Compliance frameworks like GDPR and HIPAA ensure adherence to legal and industry standards.

What We Learned: By adopting these principles, businesses can establish a secure foundation for their cloud operations.

2. The Shared Responsibility Model
The shared responsibility model emphasizes collaboration between cloud providers and customers.
- Providers handle infrastructure security, compliance certifications, and service availability.
- Customers manage application security, identity controls, and data protection.

What We Learned: Understanding and adhering to this model prevents security gaps and ensures seamless operations.

3. Key Tools for Ensuring Cloud Security

Cloud providers offer a range of tools to address specific security needs, from IAM and threat detection to encryption and disaster recovery.

- IAM tools control access and enforce least privilege policies.
- Threat detection solutions monitor and respond to suspicious activity in real-time.
- Encryption and key management tools protect data, while monitoring tools ensure compliance and visibility.

What We Learned: Leveraging these tools creates a comprehensive security framework that is proactive, resilient, and scalable.

The Bigger Picture

Security in the cloud is an ongoing effort that requires vigilance, regular updates, and the integration of best practices. By understanding core principles, embracing shared responsibility, and utilizing advanced security tools, businesses can build environments that are not only secure but also adaptable to future challenges.

AI plays a transformative role in modern cloud security, automating complex tasks, detecting threats faster, and optimizing resource allocation. This partnership between human expertise and AI-powered tools strengthens security frameworks and ensures businesses remain resilient in a constantly evolving threat landscape.

Looking Ahead

With security as a strong foundation, we now move to the next chapter: Cloud-Native Applications. This chapter will explore containers, Kubernetes, serverless computing, and how to design applications optimized for the cloud.

AI Insight:

"Cloud security isn't static—it's a dynamic process that evolves with new challenges and innovations. With AI as a partner, businesses can stay ahead of the curve, ensuring their cloud environments remain secure and robust."

Chapter 9: AI-Enhanced Security in the Cloud

How AI Detects and Mitigates Threats Proactively
Artificial Intelligence (AI) is revolutionizing cloud security by providing advanced capabilities to detect, prevent, and respond to threats in real-time. Traditional security systems rely on predefined rules and human oversight, which can be slow and reactive. AI-powered systems, on the other hand, analyze vast amounts of data, identify patterns, and adapt to evolving threats, offering a proactive and robust defense against cyberattacks.

1. Real-Time Threat Detection
AI enhances threat detection by continuously monitoring network traffic, user behavior, and system activity to identify anomalies that may indicate malicious activity.

Key Techniques in AI Threat Detection
- Anomaly Detection:
  - AI algorithms identify unusual patterns or deviations from baseline behavior.
  - Example: Detecting an abnormal number of login attempts from an unrecognized location.
- Behavioral Analysis:
  - Machine learning models analyze user and system behavior to identify threats.
  - Example: Spotting unusual data transfer activities that may indicate data exfiltration.
- Log Analysis:
  - AI examines security logs to detect hidden threats, such as suspicious API calls or unauthorized access attempts.
  - Example: Google Cloud Operations Suite uses AI to flag anomalies in log data.

AI Insight:
"AI's ability to analyze large datasets in real-time ensures that even subtle or emerging threats are detected before they escalate."

2. Threat Prediction and Prevention
AI not only detects current threats but also predicts future attacks based on historical data and global trends.

How AI Predicts Threats
- Pattern Recognition:
  - AI identifies recurring attack patterns and flags similar attempts in progress.
  - Example: Recognizing phishing email patterns across multiple organizations and warning users before they act.

- Threat Intelligence Integration:
  - AI integrates with threat intelligence databases to stay updated on global attack vectors and vulnerabilities.
  - Example: AWS GuardDuty leverages global threat intelligence to enhance its detection capabilities.
- Predictive Analytics:
  - AI models assess risk levels based on current activity and suggest preventive measures.
  - Example: Predicting DDoS attacks during high-traffic periods and pre-scaling resources to mitigate impact.

3. Automated Response and Mitigation

AI automates threat responses, reducing the time between detection and action. This minimizes the damage caused by security incidents and alleviates the burden on human teams.

Examples of AI-Driven Responses
- Quarantine and Isolation:
  - AI isolates compromised systems or accounts to prevent further spread.
  - Example: Automatically disabling access for a user showing signs of credential compromise.
- Dynamic Firewall Adjustments:
  - AI modifies firewall rules in real-time to block malicious IPs or restrict access to vulnerable services.
  - Example: Azure Firewall dynamically blocking traffic from known attack sources.
- Data Encryption on Threat Detection:
  - Automatically encrypts sensitive data when a threat is detected.
  - Example: Triggering end-to-end encryption on suspicious database activity.

AI Insight:
"By automating responses, AI reduces reaction time from minutes to seconds, often neutralizing threats before they cause harm."

4. AI's Role in Ransomware and DDoS Defense

Ransomware Detection and Prevention
- AI monitors file systems for signs of ransomware encryption, such as rapid file renaming or unauthorized access.
- Example: AI halts ransomware attacks by stopping malicious processes and restoring files from backups.

DDoS Mitigation
- AI analyzes traffic patterns to distinguish between legitimate users and attack traffic.

- AI-driven systems scale resources preemptively or divert malicious traffic using tools like AWS Shield Advanced.

Challenges in AI Threat Detection
- False Positives:
  - Overly sensitive models may flag normal behavior as threats, leading to unnecessary disruptions.
  - Solution: Continuously train models with updated data to refine accuracy.
- Data Privacy Concerns:
  - AI systems must balance threat detection with user privacy.
  - Solution: Implement privacy-preserving techniques, such as anonymized data analysis.
- Adaptability of Attackers:
  - Cybercriminals may use AI to develop more sophisticated attacks.
  - Solution: Continuously update and improve AI algorithms to stay ahead of attackers.

Why AI-Driven Threat Detection Matters
Proactive Defense
- AI shifts the security paradigm from reactive to proactive, enabling organizations to stay ahead of attackers.
Scalability and Efficiency
- AI scales effortlessly to monitor vast, dynamic cloud environments, offering consistent protection without manual oversight.
Enhanced Accuracy
- Machine learning models improve over time, reducing false positives and improving threat detection accuracy.

AI Insight:
"AI turns the cloud into a self-defending environment, capable of predicting and mitigating threats with minimal human intervention."

Exercises for Readers
- Reflection: What areas of your cloud environment could benefit most from AI-powered threat detection and mitigation?
- Hands-On Activity:
  - Enable an AI-driven threat detection tool like AWS GuardDuty or Azure Security Center. Review its findings and suggested actions.
- Case Study: Research how an organization like Netflix or Dropbox uses AI to enhance their cloud security.

AI's ability to detect and mitigate threats proactively is transforming cloud security. By analyzing patterns, predicting attacks, and automating responses, AI creates a robust and adaptive defense system. As threats grow more sophisticated, AI will continue to play a critical role in securing cloud environments, allowing businesses to innovate with confidence.

AI Insight:
"AI-powered security systems are the silent guardians of the cloud, tirelessly protecting against known and unknown threats."

Automating Security Monitoring and Incident Response
Automation is a game-changer in cloud security, enabling organizations to detect, respond to, and neutralize threats with unprecedented speed and efficiency. By leveraging AI-powered tools and automated workflows, businesses can reduce the burden on human teams, ensure consistent monitoring, and minimize the impact of security incidents. This section explores how automation transforms security monitoring and incident response in cloud environments.

1. Automated Security Monitoring
Traditional monitoring relies on manual analysis and predefined rules, which can be slow and prone to errors. Automated security monitoring, powered by AI and machine learning, offers real-time insights and proactive defense mechanisms.

How Automated Monitoring Works
- Continuous Data Collection:
  - Automated tools gather data from logs, network traffic, and application activity.
  - Example: AWS CloudTrail and Azure Monitor collect and analyze activity logs across cloud environments.
- Real-Time Analysis:
  - AI algorithms process vast amounts of data to identify anomalies, suspicious behavior, or potential threats.
  - Example: Google Cloud Security Command Center uses AI to flag unusual access patterns or misconfigurations.
- Risk Scoring:
  - Incidents are prioritized based on severity, allowing teams to focus on high-risk issues first.
  - Example: Tools like Splunk or AWS Security Hub assign risk scores to detected threats.

Benefits of Automated Monitoring
- Faster Threat Detection: Real-time analysis reduces the time to detect security breaches.
- Scalability: Automated tools can monitor complex, multi-region environments without manual intervention.
- Consistency: Eliminates human error, ensuring comprehensive and accurate monitoring.

AI Insight:
"AI enhances monitoring by identifying subtle patterns that might be missed by traditional systems."

2. Automated Incident Response
Incident response involves identifying, containing, and resolving security incidents to minimize their impact. Automation accelerates this process, enabling swift and coordinated actions.

How Automated Incident Response Works
- Incident Detection and Classification:
  - AI systems categorize incidents based on predefined policies and severity.
  - Example: An unauthorized login attempt triggers a "medium severity" alert, while a detected data exfiltration is classified as "high severity."
- Orchestrated Response Actions:
  - Automated workflows execute predefined actions based on the incident type.
  - Example: Upon detecting malware, a system isolates the infected instance, runs antivirus scans, and restores from backup if necessary.
- Dynamic Remediation:
  - AI-driven tools adapt responses based on evolving threat scenarios.
  - Example: If an attacker attempts multiple login methods, the system progressively tightens access controls.

Examples of Automated Responses
- Quarantine and Isolation: Automatically isolating compromised resources to prevent lateral movement.
- Firewall Rule Updates: Blocking malicious IP addresses in real-time.
- Credential Revocation: Disabling access for users or devices involved in suspicious activities.
- Data Restoration: Automatically restoring affected systems from backups after malware removal.

3. Integrating Automation with Security Operations
Automated security tools work best when integrated with existing security operations and workflows, creating a seamless and efficient ecosystem.

Key Integration Points
- SIEM (Security Information and Event Management) Tools:
  - Combine automated monitoring with centralized log analysis and reporting.
  - Example: Splunk or IBM QRadar integrates AI insights for actionable recommendations.
- SOAR (Security Orchestration, Automation, and Response) Platforms:
  - Coordinate automated incident response across multiple tools and systems.
  - Example: Palo Alto Cortex XSOAR integrates workflows for threat containment, investigation, and remediation.
- AI-Driven Analytics Dashboards:
  - Provide visual insights into detected threats, ongoing incidents, and response effectiveness.
  - Example: AWS Security Hub consolidates alerts and provides compliance status in a single interface.

4. Overcoming Challenges in Security Automation
While automation offers significant advantages, its implementation comes with challenges that must be addressed.

Common Challenges
- False Positives:
  - Overly sensitive systems may trigger unnecessary alerts, overwhelming teams.
  - Solution: Refine algorithms and train AI models with accurate data to improve precision.
- Over-Automation Risks:
  - Blindly relying on automation may lead to unintended consequences, such as blocking legitimate users.
  - Solution: Implement human oversight for critical decisions and high-impact actions.
- Complex Integration:
  - Integrating automation tools with legacy systems can be time-consuming and complex.
  - Solution: Use cloud-native solutions that offer seamless integration with modern cloud environments.

5. Why Automation Matters

Faster Incident Response
- Automation drastically reduces response times, ensuring that threats are neutralized before they cause significant harm.

Improved Efficiency
- Automated workflows allow security teams to focus on strategic initiatives rather than routine tasks.

Cost Savings
- By reducing manual effort and downtime, automation lowers operational costs and enhances resource utilization.

AI Insight:
"Automation isn't just about speed; it's about precision and scalability, enabling businesses to secure their environments without compromise."

Exercises for Readers
- Reflection: Identify security processes in your cloud environment that could benefit from automation. What tasks take the most time or are prone to human error?
- Hands-On Activity:
  - Use a SOAR platform like Cortex XSOAR or AWS Security Hub to automate a basic incident response workflow.
- Case Study: Research how an enterprise like Microsoft or Netflix uses automation to enhance their security operations.

Automating security monitoring and incident response is no longer optional—it's essential for businesses operating in complex and fast-paced cloud environments. AI-driven tools enhance efficiency, improve accuracy, and ensure faster threat resolution, empowering organizations to stay ahead of evolving security challenges. By integrating automation into your security strategy, you create a resilient and adaptive defense framework that scales with your needs.

AI Insight:
"With AI and automation at the helm, cloud security becomes proactive, precise, and always vigilant, ensuring businesses are prepared for the challenges of tomorrow."

Examples of AI-Driven Tools Like AWS GuardDuty and Azure Sentinel

AI-driven tools are transforming cloud security by providing advanced capabilities for threat detection, monitoring, and incident response. Tools like AWS GuardDuty and Azure Sentinel leverage machine learning and automation to identify vulnerabilities, flag malicious activities, and enable swift mitigation. This section highlights these tools, their key features, and how they can enhance your cloud security strategy.

1. AWS GuardDuty: Intelligent Threat Detection

AWS GuardDuty is a managed threat detection service that continuously monitors AWS environments for malicious activity and unauthorized behavior. It uses machine learning, threat intelligence, and behavioral analysis to protect resources.

Key Features of AWS GuardDuty
- Behavioral Threat Detection:
  o Identifies unusual patterns in network traffic, API calls, and login attempts.
  o Example: Flagging an EC2 instance exhibiting anomalous traffic that may indicate a compromised server.
- Integrated Threat Intelligence:
  o Combines AWS's internal threat intelligence with third-party data to detect known attack vectors.
  o Example: Recognizing IP addresses associated with botnets or phishing campaigns.
- Automated Remediation:
  o Works with AWS Lambda to trigger automated workflows for incident response.
  o Example: Isolating an instance that has been flagged for suspicious activity.

Use Cases for AWS GuardDuty
- Monitoring for Data Exfiltration: Detects unusual S3 bucket access patterns that may indicate data theft.
- Protecting Web Applications: Identifies and mitigates SQL injection and cross-site scripting attempts.

AI Insight:
"GuardDuty's AI-driven analysis helps businesses detect even subtle anomalies, providing a proactive defense against emerging threats."

2. Azure Sentinel: Cloud-Native SIEM and SOAR

Azure Sentinel is Microsoft's cloud-native Security Information and Event Management (SIEM) and Security Orchestration, Automation, and Response (SOAR) solution. It aggregates and analyzes security data from multiple sources to provide comprehensive threat detection and response capabilities.

Key Features of Azure Sentinel
- Unified Threat Detection:
  - Collects and correlates security data across on-premises, cloud, and hybrid environments.
  - Example: Monitoring login attempts across Azure Active Directory and on-premises systems for suspicious activity.
- AI-Powered Threat Hunting:
  - Uses built-in AI models to detect threats and recommend mitigation actions.
  - Example: Identifying a ransomware attack in progress by analyzing unusual file encryption patterns.
- Customizable Playbooks:
  - Enables automated responses through predefined workflows.
  - Example: Blocking an IP address and notifying administrators after detecting brute-force login attempts.

Use Cases for Azure Sentinel
- Hybrid Cloud Monitoring: Provides visibility into security across multi-cloud and on-premises environments.
- Advanced Threat Hunting: Leverages AI and machine learning to identify hidden threats in large datasets.

AI Insight:
"Azure Sentinel's AI capabilities empower security teams to hunt for sophisticated threats with precision and speed."

3. Comparing AWS GuardDuty and Azure Sentinel

When it comes to cloud security and threat detection, AWS GuardDuty and Azure Sentinel are two of the most prominent tools used by businesses to detect, analyze, and respond to security threats. Each tool offers unique features and is best suited for specific cloud environments.

1. Purpose and Function
- AWS GuardDuty: Threat detection service that continuously monitors AWS accounts, workloads, and data. It uses machine learning and anomaly detection to identify suspicious behavior, such as unauthorized access attempts, API misuse, or compromised EC2 instances. GuardDuty focuses on internal AWS security.
- Azure Sentinel: Cloud-native SIEM (Security Information and Event Management) and SOAR (Security Orchestration, Automation, and Response) platform. It aggregates security data from multiple sources (not just Azure) to provide full security event visibility and incident response automation. Azure Sentinel is more comprehensive as it integrates with multi-cloud and on-premise systems.

2. Cloud Integration
- AWS GuardDuty: Primarily built to work with AWS environments. It analyzes logs from services like CloudTrail, VPC Flow Logs, and DNS logs. It works seamlessly within AWS but has limited support for third-party, non-AWS services.
- Azure Sentinel: Works with Azure, AWS, Google Cloud, and on-premises environments. Sentinel can collect security data from third-party tools like Firewalls, VPNs, and endpoint security platforms. This makes Sentinel ideal for multi-cloud and hybrid environments.

3. Detection and Alerts
- AWS GuardDuty: Uses machine learning, anomaly detection, and threat intelligence feeds to detect unauthorized access, unusual API calls, and account compromises. Alerts are ranked as low, medium, or high to prioritize response efforts.
- Azure Sentinel: Uses AI-driven anomaly detection to identify unusual behavior, similar to GuardDuty. However, Sentinel also includes behavioral analytics and machine learning models to detect sophisticated threats. It correlates events across multiple systems (Azure, AWS, and on-premise), making it more effective for cross-platform threat detection.

4. Automation and Incident Response
- AWS GuardDuty: GuardDuty does not directly automate incident response, but it integrates with AWS Security Hub, AWS Lambda, and AWS CloudWatch to trigger incident responses. For example, you can automate blocking malicious IP addresses or isolating compromised instances.
- Azure Sentinel: Offers full SOAR capabilities (Security Orchestration, Automation, and Response). Sentinel can automatically trigger incident response actions through Logic Apps and Playbooks. It allows users to create automated workflows to contain, investigate, and respond to threats without manual intervention.

5. Use Cases
- AWS GuardDuty: Best for AWS-native environments that want a lightweight, automated threat detection system. It's ideal for businesses looking to monitor VPC network activity, API usage, and EC2 instance anomalies. Since GuardDuty only works within AWS, it's best for companies that use AWS as their primary cloud provider.
- Example Use Cases:
  - Detect compromised EC2 instances.
  - Monitor unusual API calls (like unauthorized IAM activity).
  - Alert admins of port scanning attempts on VPC networks.
- Azure Sentinel: Best for multi-cloud, hybrid cloud, and on-premises environments. It offers a single pane of glass for managing security events across Azure, AWS, Google Cloud, and on-premise systems. Sentinel excels in centralized log collection, SIEM analytics, and automated incident response workflows.
- Example Use Cases:
  - Monitor cross-cloud security threats from AWS, Azure, and Google Cloud.
  - Aggregate log data from VPNs, firewalls, and third-party security tools.
  - Automate threat response using Playbooks and Logic Apps to block malicious IPs.

6. Pricing and Cost

- AWS GuardDuty: Charges are based on the amount of data analyzed from CloudTrail logs, VPC flow logs, and DNS logs. Costs depend on the volume of log data analyzed and the frequency of anomalies. GuardDuty is considered more cost-effective for AWS-native environments.
- Azure Sentinel: Uses a pay-as-you-go pricing model based on the ingestion of log data (measured in GB) from Azure and other systems. Sentinel costs can be higher if a company integrates data from multiple sources (e.g., third-party firewalls or VPN logs). Multi-cloud monitoring costs more since more data must be ingested.

7. Customization and Extensibility

- AWS GuardDuty: Offers limited customization. It detects threats using pre-built machine learning models and threat intelligence from AWS, but users cannot modify these models. GuardDuty works best when paired with AWS Security Hub to correlate findings from multiple AWS security services.
- Azure Sentinel: Offers extensive customization with the ability to create custom rules, custom Playbooks, and custom Logic Apps for automation. Sentinel also integrates with Microsoft 365 Defender, Azure Security Center, and third-party SIEMs.

8. Threat Intelligence Sources

- AWS GuardDuty: Relies on threat intelligence feeds from AWS's threat intelligence database as well as third-party security intelligence feeds. The insights are used to recognize known malicious IPs, domains, and URLs.
- Azure Sentinel: Uses threat intelligence from Microsoft's security intelligence network, which is one of the largest threat intelligence databases in the world. Sentinel also allows businesses to ingest custom threat intelligence feeds from third-party sources like VirusTotal and Recorded Future.

9. Reporting and Dashboards

- AWS GuardDuty: Alerts are displayed in the AWS Management Console under GuardDuty's interface. Reports can be viewed via AWS Security Hub for a centralized threat view. For deeper reporting, companies must export data to AWS CloudWatch or AWS CloudTrail for custom dashboards.
- Azure Sentinel: Provides advanced custom dashboards and visualizations. Users can create dashboards with data from Azure, AWS, and third-party sources. Sentinel has pre-built templates for dashboards, allowing security analysts to track incident timelines, user activity, and security trends.

Summary
- AWS GuardDuty: Best for AWS-native threat detection. It is lightweight, affordable, and easy to set up. It integrates well with other AWS services but has limited visibility outside AWS. It is best for companies that are 100% AWS-based.
- Azure Sentinel: Best for companies with multi-cloud, hybrid, or on-premises environments. Sentinel provides centralized log collection, cross-cloud security analytics, and full SIEM + SOAR capabilities. It is ideal for large enterprises that require multi-cloud visibility, centralized dashboards, and automated threat response.

By understanding the strengths of AWS GuardDuty and Azure Sentinel, companies can choose the right security platform to protect their cloud environment. If your company relies on AWS-only infrastructure, GuardDuty is a simple, cost-effective option. If you need multi-cloud and cross-platform threat detection, Azure Sentinel provides more advanced SIEM and SOAR capabilities.

4. Other AI-Driven Tools in Cloud Security
Google Cloud Security Command Center (SCC)
- Provides a centralized dashboard for monitoring vulnerabilities and threats across Google Cloud resources.
- AI Features: Analyzes IAM policies, identifies misconfigurations, and flags potential risks.

Splunk Security Cloud
- A powerful SIEM platform that uses AI to correlate security data and detect complex threats.
- AI Features: Predicts potential security incidents based on historical trends and real-time activity.

IBM QRadar
- A comprehensive SIEM tool for threat detection and compliance reporting.
- AI Features: Uses AI to prioritize threats and recommend responses based on context.

5. Benefits of Using AI-Driven Tools
- Proactive Threat Detection:
  - AI identifies threats before they cause harm, reducing downtime and potential damage.
- Reduced Manual Effort:
  - Automates routine tasks like log analysis, allowing security teams to focus on strategic issues.

- Scalability:
  - AI-powered tools handle growing workloads effortlessly, ensuring security in dynamic cloud environments.

AI Insight:
"AI-driven tools like GuardDuty and Sentinel enable businesses to move beyond reactive defenses, creating proactive and resilient security systems."

Exercises for Readers
- Reflection: Evaluate your cloud environment. Which AI-driven tools could address your current security challenges?
- Hands-On Activity:
  - Set up AWS GuardDuty or Azure Sentinel in a test environment. Explore their dashboards and test basic threat detection scenarios.
- Case Study: Research how a major enterprise uses AI-driven security tools to protect its cloud infrastructure. Identify the benefits they achieved.

AI-driven tools like AWS GuardDuty and Azure Sentinel exemplify the future of cloud security, combining advanced analytics, automation, and machine learning to address modern threats. By adopting these tools, businesses can create adaptive and proactive security strategies that evolve with the threat landscape.

AI Insight:
"AI-powered security tools are your most vigilant allies in the cloud, offering 24/7 protection and empowering teams to focus on innovation instead of firefighting."

Conclusion:
AI is revolutionizing cloud security, enabling organizations to detect threats, respond to incidents, and protect resources with unprecedented precision and speed. Chapter 9 explored how AI enhances every aspect of cloud security, from proactive threat detection to automated responses and advanced tools like AWS GuardDuty and Azure Sentinel. Together, these innovations form a dynamic and adaptive defense strategy tailored to the complex demands of cloud environments.

Key Takeaways
1. Proactive Threat Detection
AI-powered systems continuously monitor cloud environments, analyzing behavior patterns, network traffic, and system logs to identify anomalies.

- What We Learned: AI's ability to predict and detect threats in real time shifts security from a reactive process to a proactive one, reducing the time to detect and mitigate incidents.

2. Automating Security Monitoring and Incident Response
Automation powered by AI accelerates threat resolution, enabling businesses to neutralize risks before they escalate.
- What We Learned: Tools that automate workflows, such as isolating compromised systems or blocking malicious IPs, enhance both efficiency and accuracy in managing incidents.

3. AI-Driven Tools Like AWS GuardDuty and Azure Sentinel
Specialized tools integrate AI with cloud services to provide comprehensive security solutions.
- What We Learned: AWS GuardDuty and Azure Sentinel exemplify how AI can enhance threat detection, automate responses, and simplify security management for businesses of all sizes.

The Bigger Picture
AI has transformed cloud security into a proactive, adaptive, and efficient process. By automating repetitive tasks, predicting threats, and enabling faster responses, AI allows security teams to focus on strategic initiatives rather than operational challenges. Tools like GuardDuty, Sentinel, and other AI-driven solutions empower businesses to scale confidently in the cloud while maintaining robust protection.

AI also mitigates common security challenges such as false positives, resource mismanagement, and human error. By continuously learning from data, AI enhances its effectiveness over time, staying ahead of evolving threats and enabling organizations to innovate securely.

Looking Ahead
With a strong understanding of AI's role in cloud security, we now turn to Chapter 10: Cloud-Native Applications. In the next chapter, we'll explore the design and deployment of cloud-native solutions, including containers, serverless computing, and microservices, to harness the full potential of the cloud.

Chapter 10: Cloud-Native Applications

Introduction to Containers, Kubernetes, and Serverless Architectures

Cloud-native applications are designed to take full advantage of cloud computing capabilities, offering flexibility, scalability, and efficiency. At the heart of this approach are containers, Kubernetes, and serverless architectures. These technologies redefine how applications are developed, deployed, and managed, enabling businesses to innovate faster and scale seamlessly.

1. Containers: Lightweight Application Environments

A container is a lightweight, portable unit of software that includes an application and all its dependencies, enabling it to run consistently across different environments. Containers are built on operating system virtualization, isolating applications without the overhead of virtual machines (VMs).

Key Features of Containers
- Portability:
  - Run the same container image across development, testing, and production environments.
  - Example: Deploy a containerized web application from a developer's laptop to a cloud platform without modifications.
- Efficiency:
  - Share the host OS kernel, reducing resource consumption compared to VMs.
  - Example: Run multiple containerized microservices on a single server without significant overhead.
- Rapid Deployment:
  - Start and stop containers in seconds, enabling faster updates and rollbacks.

Popular Container Tools
- Docker: The most widely used container platform for building and running containerized applications.
- Podman: A daemonless alternative to Docker, designed for secure container management.

2. Kubernetes: Orchestrating Containers at Scale

While containers are ideal for individual applications, managing them at scale can become complex. Kubernetes solves this challenge by providing an orchestration platform to deploy, manage, and scale containerized applications.

Key Features of Kubernetes
- Automated Scaling:
  - Adjusts the number of running containers based on traffic and resource needs.
  - Example: Scale a web application during peak hours and reduce resources during off-peak times.
- Self-Healing:
  - Detects and replaces failed containers automatically.
  - Example: Restarting a crashed container without manual intervention.
- Load Balancing:
  - Distributes traffic across containers to ensure high availability and performance.

Kubernetes Architecture Components
- Pods: The smallest deployable unit, consisting of one or more containers.
- Nodes: Machines (virtual or physical) that run pods.
- Cluster: A collection of nodes managed by Kubernetes.

Popular Kubernetes Platforms
- Google Kubernetes Engine (GKE): Fully managed Kubernetes service on Google Cloud.
- Amazon Elastic Kubernetes Service (EKS): Kubernetes on AWS.
- Azure Kubernetes Service (AKS): Kubernetes on Azure.

AI Insight:
"AI enhances Kubernetes management by predicting resource needs and automating cluster optimization."

3. Serverless Architectures: Abstracting Infrastructure Management

Serverless computing eliminates the need to manage infrastructure, allowing developers to focus solely on writing code. In a serverless model, the cloud provider handles provisioning, scaling, and maintenance of servers.

Key Features of Serverless Architectures
- Event-Driven Execution:
  - Functions are triggered by events such as API requests, database updates, or file uploads.
  - Example: A function runs to process an image when it's uploaded to a storage bucket.
- Automatic Scaling:
  - Resources scale automatically based on demand, from zero to thousands of requests.
  - Example: Handling occasional traffic spikes without pre-allocating resources.

- Pay-As-You-Go Pricing:
  - Customers pay only for the compute time used, reducing costs for intermittent workloads.

Popular Serverless Platforms
- AWS Lambda: Runs code in response to events.
- Azure Functions: A serverless computing service on Azure.
- Google Cloud Functions: Supports event-driven applications on Google Cloud.

Why These Technologies Matter
Efficiency and Agility
- Containers, Kubernetes, and serverless architectures streamline development and deployment, enabling faster iteration and innovation.

Scalability and Resilience
- These technologies ensure applications can scale dynamically and recover quickly from failures, meeting the demands of modern cloud-native workloads.

Cost-Effectiveness
- Serverless computing reduces costs by charging only for actual resource usage, while containers and Kubernetes optimize resource allocation at scale.

AI Insight:
"AI accelerates the adoption of cloud-native technologies by automating deployment, monitoring, and scaling processes."

Exercises for Readers
- Reflection: How could your applications benefit from adopting containers, Kubernetes, or serverless architectures?
- Hands-On Activity:
  - Create a Docker container for a simple web application and deploy it on a Kubernetes cluster.
  - Experiment with an event-driven serverless function using AWS Lambda or Google Cloud Functions.
- Case Study: Research how companies like Netflix or Spotify leverage cloud-native technologies to deliver scalable and resilient services.

Containers, Kubernetes, and serverless architectures are the building blocks of cloud-native applications, empowering organizations to innovate faster, reduce costs, and scale effortlessly. By adopting these technologies, businesses can create applications that are agile, resilient, and optimized for the cloud.

AI Insight:
"Cloud-native technologies enable organizations to harness the full potential of the cloud, with AI providing the intelligence to optimize and scale them seamlessly."

Building Scalable and Resilient Microservices
Microservices architecture is a cloud-native approach to designing applications as a collection of small, independent services. Each service focuses on a specific function, enabling teams to develop, deploy, and scale them independently. Building scalable and resilient microservices requires careful planning, robust design principles, and leveraging cloud-native tools.

1. What Are Microservices?
Microservices are an architectural style where applications are broken down into small, modular services. These services communicate with each other using lightweight protocols, such as REST APIs, gRPC, or message queues.

Key Characteristics of Microservices
- Independence:
  - Each microservice operates as a standalone component with its own codebase and database.
- Modularity:
  - Services are designed to perform specific functions, making them easier to develop and maintain.
- Technology Agnosticism:
  - Teams can use different programming languages or frameworks for each service.

Example:
An e-commerce application might have separate microservices for user authentication, product catalog, shopping cart, and payment processing.

2. Designing for Scalability

Scalability ensures that microservices can handle increased workloads efficiently without degrading performance.

Key Strategies for Scalable Microservices
- Decouple Services:
  - Design services to be loosely coupled so they can scale independently.
  - Example: A payment processing service should not depend on the product catalog to function.
- Horizontal Scaling:
  - Use container orchestration platforms like Kubernetes to add or remove instances of services based on demand.
  - Example: Scale up the order service during Black Friday sales and scale down afterward.
- Asynchronous Communication:
  - Use message queues like RabbitMQ or Kafka to decouple services and handle high volumes of requests.
  - Example: A notification service processes messages from a queue rather than waiting for synchronous API calls.

Cloud-Native Tools for Scalability
- AWS Elastic Kubernetes Service (EKS): Automatically scales containerized microservices.
- Azure Service Bus: Enables scalable message queuing and event-driven architectures.
- Google Cloud Pub/Sub: Provides global message queueing for asynchronous communication.

AI Insight:
"AI-driven monitoring tools predict traffic patterns and automatically scale microservices to handle peak loads."

3. Ensuring Resilience

Resilience ensures that microservices remain operational and recover quickly from failures. This is critical for maintaining user trust and minimizing downtime.

Key Strategies for Resilient Microservices
- Implement Circuit Breakers:
  - Use circuit breaker patterns to prevent cascading failures when a service is overloaded or down.
  - Example: If the payment gateway service is unavailable, return a fallback message instead of crashing the entire application.
- Replication and Redundancy:
  - Deploy multiple instances of critical services across different availability zones.
  - Example: Run three replicas of the authentication service to ensure continuous availability.
- Service Mesh:
  - Use service mesh technologies like Istio or Linkerd to handle communication between microservices and add resilience features like retries and failover.
  - Example: Automatically rerouting traffic to a healthy instance if one replica fails.
- Health Checks and Monitoring:
  - Continuously monitor the health of services using Kubernetes probes or tools like Prometheus.
  - Example: Remove unhealthy instances from the load balancer pool to maintain high availability.

4. Challenges and Solutions

Challenges in Building Microservices
- Complexity:
  - Managing multiple services increases complexity compared to monolithic architectures.
- Data Consistency:
  - Ensuring data consistency across services can be difficult in distributed systems.
- Latency:
  - Communication between services can introduce latency.

Solutions
- Adopt DevOps Practices:
  - Automate testing, deployment, and monitoring using CI/CD pipelines.
- Use Distributed Tracing:
  - Tools like Jaeger or Zipkin help trace requests across services, identifying bottlenecks.
- Implement Event Sourcing:
  - Record all changes as events to maintain consistency and auditability.

AI Insight:
"AI-powered observability tools provide real-time insights into the health and performance of microservices, simplifying troubleshooting and optimization."

5. Why Build Microservices?
Scalability and Agility
- Microservices allow teams to scale specific parts of an application independently and make rapid changes without affecting the entire system.

Resilience
- By isolating failures, microservices ensure that issues in one service do not bring down the entire application.

Innovation
- Microservices enable teams to adopt new technologies or experiment with features without disrupting other components.

Exercises for Readers
- Reflection: Identify an application in your organization that could benefit from being broken into microservices. What challenges might you face?

Hands-On Activity:
- Create a microservice using Docker & deploy it on Kubernetes.
- Use a message queue like RabbitMQ to enable communication between two microservices.
- Case Study: Research how companies like Netflix or Amazon use microservices to build scalable, resilient systems.

Microservices architecture empowers organizations to build applications that are scalable, resilient, and optimized for cloud environments. By leveraging containers, orchestration platforms like Kubernetes, and tools for asynchronous communication, businesses can create agile systems that adapt to changing demands. With AI enhancing monitoring, scaling, and troubleshooting, microservices become an even more powerful foundation for modern cloud-native applications.

Examples of Cloud-Native Application Workflows

Cloud-native application workflows exemplify how modern applications are designed and deployed to maximize scalability, resilience, and efficiency. These workflows integrate containers, microservices, serverless architectures, and orchestration tools to streamline processes. This section provides real-world examples of cloud-native workflows to illustrate their benefits and implementation strategies.

1. E-Commerce Application Workflow

An e-commerce application often handles fluctuating traffic, requires high availability, and integrates multiple services like inventory, payment processing, and user management.

Workflow Overview
- User Interaction Layer:
  - Frontend: A React or Angular web application served via a Content Delivery Network (CDN) for low latency.
  - Backend: A REST or GraphQL API hosted in containers or as serverless functions.
- Service Layer:
  - Authentication Microservice: Manages user login and session tokens.
  - Product Catalog Microservice: Handles product listings and inventory updates.
  - Order Processing Microservice: Processes payments and creates orders.
- Asynchronous Processing:
  - Message queues (e.g., RabbitMQ or AWS SQS) handle events like order confirmations and inventory updates.
- Data Storage:
  - Relational Database: Stores user profiles and orders.
  - NoSQL Database: Caches product catalog data for faster access.
- Monitoring and Scaling:
  - Kubernetes scales microservices based on traffic patterns.
  - Prometheus and Grafana monitor performance and alert on anomalies.

Example Implementation:
- AWS Stack: Frontend on CloudFront, backend on AWS Lambda, and database on Amazon DynamoDB.
- Azure Stack: Frontend on Azure CDN, backend on Azure Functions, and database on Cosmos DB.

2. Video Streaming Platform Workflow

A video streaming platform must deliver content quickly to users worldwide while ensuring scalability and minimal buffering.

Workflow Overview
- Content Delivery:
  - Videos are stored in cloud object storage (e.g., AWS S3 or Google Cloud Storage) and distributed via a CDN (e.g., AWS CloudFront or Azure CDN).
- User Interaction:
  - Users authenticate via an IAM-integrated service.
  - A microservice handles user subscriptions and content recommendations.
- Video Processing Pipeline:
  - Step 1: Upload videos to cloud storage.
  - Step 2: Serverless functions (e.g., AWS Lambda or Azure Functions) trigger video encoding into multiple resolutions and formats.
  - Step 3: Store processed videos in storage buckets for distribution.
- Real-Time Analytics:
  - AI-driven analytics monitor playback performance and recommend content based on user behavior.
- Scalability and Resilience:
  - Kubernetes or serverless services automatically scale during peak streaming hours.

Example Implementation:
- AWS Stack: Video encoding with AWS Elemental MediaConvert, delivery via CloudFront, and recommendations powered by Amazon Personalize.
- Google Cloud Stack: Encoding with Cloud Video Intelligence, delivery via Google Cloud CDN, and analytics using BigQuery.

3. Serverless Event-Driven Workflow

Event-driven workflows are ideal for applications that require minimal resource usage until triggered by specific events, such as file uploads or database updates.

Workflow Overview
- Trigger Event:
  - A file upload to a cloud storage bucket (e.g., AWS S3 or Google Cloud Storage) initiates the workflow.
- Processing Layer:
  - A serverless function processes the file, such as resizing images or extracting metadata.

- Data Storage and Notification:
  - Processed data is stored in a database.
  - Notifications are sent to users via an event stream or messaging service (e.g., AWS SNS or Azure Event Grid).
- AI Integration:
  - Use AI models for advanced processing, such as image recognition or sentiment analysis.

Example Implementation:
- AWS Stack: S3 triggers a Lambda function to process files, with results stored in DynamoDB and notifications sent via SNS.
- Azure Stack: Azure Blob Storage triggers an Azure Function, with output stored in Cosmos DB and notifications sent via Azure Notification Hubs.

4. IoT Device Workflow
IoT applications process data from distributed devices, requiring efficient handling of data streams and real-time analysis.

Workflow Overview
- Device Connectivity:
  - Devices connect to a cloud-based IoT hub (e.g., AWS IoT Core, Azure IoT Hub) to send telemetry data.
- Data Ingestion and Processing:
  - Stream processing tools (e.g., Apache Kafka or AWS Kinesis) analyze incoming data in real-time.
- AI Analytics:
  - AI models detect anomalies, such as equipment failures or unusual environmental conditions.
- Actionable Insights and Storage:
  - Insights are stored in databases for reporting and triggering automated responses, such as sending alerts or activating backup systems.
- Dashboard Monitoring:
  - A web dashboard visualizes IoT device performance and analytics.

Example Implementation:
- AWS Stack: IoT Core for connectivity, Kinesis for stream processing, and SageMaker for AI analytics.
- Azure Stack: IoT Hub, Stream Analytics, and Azure Machine Learning for predictions.

Benefits of Cloud-Native Workflows
- Scalability:
  - Handle growing workloads effortlessly by leveraging containers, serverless functions, and orchestration platforms.
- Cost-Effectiveness:
  - Pay-as-you-go pricing models reduce costs by scaling resources dynamically.
- Flexibility:
  - Modular architectures make it easy to add or modify components without disrupting the entire system.
- Resilience:
  - Built-in redundancy and failover mechanisms ensure high availability.

AI Insight:
"AI optimizes cloud-native workflows by automating scaling, predicting resource needs, and analyzing operational performance."

Exercises for Readers
- Reflection: Identify a workflow in your organization that could benefit from a cloud-native approach. How could modular components improve scalability or resilience?
- Hands-On Activity:
  - Create a basic serverless workflow using AWS Lambda or Azure Functions triggered by an event.
  - Build a microservices-based workflow with Kubernetes for a simple e-commerce application.
- Case Study: Research a real-world cloud-native application workflow, such as Spotify's microservices architecture or Uber's event-driven systems.

Cloud-native application workflows enable businesses to build scalable, resilient, and efficient systems tailored to dynamic user demands. Whether it's powering e-commerce platforms, processing IoT data, or delivering video streams, these workflows exemplify the versatility and power of cloud-native technologies. By leveraging AI and automation, businesses can optimize these workflows further, ensuring they remain competitive in a fast-evolving digital landscape.

AI Insight:
"Cloud-native workflows unlock the full potential of the cloud, with AI ensuring these workflows are always optimized, adaptive, and efficient."

Conclusion:
Cloud-native applications embody the transformative potential of the cloud, enabling businesses to build systems that are scalable, resilient, and cost-efficient. Chapter 10 explored the foundational technologies of containers, Kubernetes, and serverless architectures, delved into the design principles of microservices, and illustrated real-world workflows to showcase how these components work together. These concepts form the backbone of modern cloud-native development, empowering organizations to innovate and adapt with agility.

Key Takeaways
1. The Role of Cloud-Native Technologies
Containers, Kubernetes, and serverless architectures enable developers to focus on building robust applications without the complexity of managing infrastructure.

- What We Learned: These technologies optimize resource utilization, simplify deployments, and offer unparalleled scalability.

2. Building Scalable and Resilient Systems
Microservices architecture enhances modularity and independence, making applications easier to scale and maintain. With tools like Kubernetes and service meshes, developers can ensure resilience and fault tolerance.

- What We Learned: Designing for scalability and resilience is critical for cloud-native success, especially in dynamic and high-demand environments.

3. Real-World Workflows
Cloud-native workflows, such as those used in e-commerce, video streaming, and IoT applications, demonstrate the versatility and power of this approach.

- What We Learned: Modular workflows allow organizations to build applications that scale dynamically, recover quickly, and deliver seamless user experiences.

The Bigger Picture
Cloud-native applications are not just about leveraging the latest technologies—they represent a paradigm shift in how applications are designed, deployed, and managed. By embracing this approach, organizations can respond faster to market demands, reduce operational costs, and achieve greater innovation.

AI enhances the potential of cloud-native applications by automating scaling, optimizing workflows, and predicting resource needs. This integration between cloud-native principles and AI ensures that applications remain efficient, resilient, and aligned with business goals.

Looking Ahead
With a solid understanding of cloud-native application development, the next chapter focuses on AI and Machine Learning in the Cloud. We will explore how cloud platforms enable businesses to harness AI's power for predictive analytics, automation, and decision-making, driving the next wave of innovation.

AI Insight:
"Cloud-native applications redefine what's possible in the digital age, and with AI as a partner, these systems become smarter, faster, and more responsive to change."

Chapter 11: AI and Machine Learning in the Cloud

Tools for Building AI/ML Models in the Cloud

The cloud has revolutionized artificial intelligence (AI) and machine learning (ML) development by offering powerful tools and platforms that simplify the process of building, training, and deploying models. Platforms like AWS SageMaker, Azure Machine Learning, and Google Cloud AI Platform provide robust, scalable, and cost-effective solutions for data scientists and developers. This section explores the key tools available in the cloud for AI/ML workflows, their features, and how they can be leveraged to accelerate innovation.

1. AWS SageMaker: End-to-End ML Development

AWS SageMaker is a fully managed service that simplifies the machine learning workflow, from data preparation to model deployment.

Key Features of AWS SageMaker
- Integrated Development Environment:
    - Includes SageMaker Studio, a web-based IDE for developing and debugging ML models.
    - Example: Use pre-built Jupyter notebooks to experiment with algorithms.
- Automated Machine Learning (AutoML):
    - SageMaker Autopilot automatically selects algorithms and tunes models based on your data.
    - Example: Automatically train and deploy a classification model with minimal manual intervention.
- Distributed Training:
    - Allows large-scale model training using multiple GPUs or TPUs.
- Deployment and Monitoring:
    - One-click deployment for hosting models on managed infrastructure.
    - Built-in tools for monitoring model performance and detecting drift.

Use Cases for SageMaker
- Building recommendation systems for e-commerce platforms.
- Training predictive models for financial risk assessment.

AI Insight:
"SageMaker's integration with other AWS services like S3, Lambda, and Athena creates a seamless workflow for building AI-powered applications."

2. Azure Machine Learning: Enterprise-Grade AI Development

Azure Machine Learning (Azure ML) offers a comprehensive platform for developing, training, and deploying machine learning models at scale.

Key Features of Azure ML
- Drag-and-Drop Interface:
  - The Designer tool allows users to create ML pipelines visually without coding.
  - Example: Drag and drop modules to preprocess data, train models, and deploy endpoints.
- MLOps Integration:
  - Supports CI/CD for machine learning through automated pipelines and reproducible workflows.
- Built-in Algorithms and Frameworks:
  - Access pre-trained models or build your own using popular frameworks like TensorFlow and PyTorch.
- Responsible AI Features:
  - Includes interpretability tools and fairness assessments to ensure ethical model development.
  - Example: Evaluate model bias with built-in explainability metrics.

Use Cases for Azure ML
- Deploying real-time fraud detection systems in banking.
- Automating predictive maintenance in manufacturing.

AI Insight:
"Azure ML's enterprise-grade features make it ideal for businesses seeking scalable and reliable AI solutions with integrated governance."

3. Google Cloud AI Platform: Data-Driven Innovation

Google Cloud AI Platform is designed to accelerate machine learning workflows by leveraging Google's expertise in AI and data analytics.

Key Features of Google Cloud AI Platform
- Vertex AI:
  - Combines data engineering, model training, and MLOps in a unified interface.
  - Example: Use AutoML for image classification without writing code.
- Pre-Trained Models and APIs:
  - Access models for natural language processing (NLP), speech recognition, and image analysis.

- BigQuery ML Integration:
  - Build and deploy ML models directly from Google BigQuery without moving data.
- Custom Training:
  - Train custom models using TensorFlow, PyTorch, or scikit-learn on Google's infrastructure.

Use Cases for Google Cloud AI Platform
- Building real-time analytics dashboards for e-commerce.
- Automating sentiment analysis for customer feedback.

AI Insight:
"Google Cloud AI Platform excels at integrating advanced analytics with AI development, making it a powerful tool for data-driven applications."

4. Other Cloud AI/ML Tools
IBM Watson Studio:
- Focused on enterprise AI with strong NLP capabilities and explainability tools.

Alibaba Cloud Machine Learning Platform for AI:
- Provides easy-to-use tools for businesses in Asia-Pacific markets.

Hugging Face on Cloud Platforms:
- Offers pre-trained transformer models for NLP tasks across AWS, Azure, and Google Cloud.

How Cloud Tools Simplify AI/ML Workflows
- Accessibility:
  - Cloud platforms democratize AI/ML by reducing the need for specialized infrastructure.
  - Example: Small startups can leverage the same computing power as large enterprises.
- Scalability:
  - Dynamic resource allocation ensures models can train efficiently, even with large datasets.
- Integration:
  - Seamless integration with data storage, analytics, and deployment tools speeds up development.
- Cost Efficiency:
  - Pay-as-you-go pricing eliminates the need for upfront hardware investments.

Exercises for Readers
- Reflection: Which cloud platform aligns best with your AI/ML needs? Consider factors like budget, scalability, and ease of use.
- Hands-On Activity:
  - Set up a simple model training workflow using SageMaker, Azure ML, or Google Cloud AI Platform.
  - Experiment with AutoML features to build a quick prototype.
- Case Study: Research how a leading company (e.g., Spotify, Airbnb) uses cloud tools to accelerate AI/ML innovation.

Cloud platforms like SageMaker, Azure ML, and Google Cloud AI Platform are reshaping AI/ML development by offering accessible, scalable, and feature-rich environments. These tools empower businesses to harness the potential of AI without the complexity of managing infrastructure. By leveraging these platforms, organizations can innovate faster, build better models, and stay competitive in an AI-driven world.

Key Use Cases: Predictive Analytics, NLP, and Computer Vision
AI and machine learning (ML) in the cloud unlock transformative potential for businesses by enabling advanced use cases like predictive analytics, natural language processing (NLP), and computer vision. These applications address real-world challenges, offering insights, automation, and innovative solutions across industries. This section explores these use cases, their impact, and how cloud-based AI tools make them accessible.

1. Predictive Analytics: Forecasting and Decision-Making
Predictive analytics uses historical data and machine learning algorithms to predict future outcomes, enabling proactive decision-making and risk management.

How Predictive Analytics Works
- Data Collection:
  - Historical and real-time data are gathered from various sources, such as sensors, transactions, or logs.
- Feature Engineering:
  - Significant data attributes are extracted to improve model accuracy.
- Model Training:
  - ML models are trained to detect patterns and correlations in the data.

- Predictions and Recommendations:
  - The trained model generates predictions, such as demand forecasts or risk scores.

Use Cases
- Demand Forecasting:
  - Retailers predict product demand to optimize inventory and reduce stockouts.
  - Example: Amazon uses predictive analytics to forecast customer preferences and streamline its supply chain.
- Fraud Detection:
  - Financial institutions identify fraudulent transactions in real time.
  - Example: Credit card companies use predictive models to flag suspicious activities.
- Customer Churn Prediction:
  - Businesses predict which customers are likely to leave and design retention strategies.
  - Example: Subscription services use predictive models to offer personalized incentives.

AI Insight:
"Predictive analytics transforms raw data into actionable foresight, allowing businesses to stay ahead of challenges and opportunities."

2. Natural Language Processing (NLP): Interpreting and Generating Human Language

NLP enables machines to understand, interpret, and generate human language, powering applications that enhance communication and automate workflows.

How NLP Works
- Text Processing:
  - Input text is tokenized, cleaned, and structured for analysis.
- Feature Extraction:
  - Semantic and syntactic features, such as word embeddings, are derived from the text.
- Model Application:
  - Pre-trained or custom models are used to analyze or generate language.

Use Cases
- Sentiment Analysis:
  - Analyzes customer feedback to gauge satisfaction and identify trends.
  - Example: E-commerce platforms monitor product reviews for quality improvement.

- Chatbots and Virtual Assistants:
  - Automates customer support and enhances user interaction.
  - Example: Google Dialogflow powers conversational AI chatbots for businesses.
- Language Translation:
  - Translates content across languages, making information accessible globally.
  - Example: Google Translate uses NLP to provide real-time language translation.

Cloud NLP Tools
- AWS Comprehend: Performs sentiment analysis, entity recognition, and topic modeling.
- Azure Text Analytics: Provides key phrase extraction, language detection, and sentiment analysis.
- Google Cloud Natural Language API: Analyzes syntax and sentiment in text data.

AI Insight:
"NLP bridges the gap between humans and machines, enabling intuitive and intelligent interactions."

3. Computer Vision: Understanding Visual Data
Computer vision empowers machines to interpret and analyze visual inputs like images and videos, enabling advanced automation and insight extraction.

How Computer Vision Works
- Image Processing:
  - Images are preprocessed (e.g., resizing, normalization) to enhance quality.
- Feature Detection:
  - Algorithms extract features like edges, shapes, or patterns from images.
- Model Application:
  - ML models classify, segment, or detect objects in the visual data.

Use Cases
- Object Detection:
  - Identifies objects in images or videos for security, automation, or retail.
  - Example: Autonomous vehicles detect pedestrians and traffic signs.

- Facial Recognition:
  - Verifies identity for authentication or surveillance.
  - Example: Smartphones use facial recognition to unlock devices securely.
- Quality Control:
  - Inspects manufacturing products for defects.
  - Example: Factories use computer vision to automate quality assurance.

Cloud Computer Vision Tools
- AWS Rekognition: Detects objects, faces, and activities in images and videos.
- Azure Computer Vision: Performs OCR, object detection, and image analysis.
- Google Cloud Vision API: Recognizes text, objects, and logos in images.

AI Insight:
"Computer vision enables machines to see and analyze the world, driving automation and innovation across industries."

How Cloud Platforms Support These Use Cases
Accessibility and Scalability
- Cloud platforms democratize AI use cases, allowing businesses of all sizes to access powerful ML models and tools.

Integration with Existing Systems
- Seamless integration with data storage, APIs, and deployment pipelines ensures efficient implementation.

AI-Enhanced Features
- Built-in AI features, such as pre-trained models and automated workflows, reduce development time and complexity.

Exercises for Readers
- Reflection: Identify which AI/ML use case (predictive analytics, NLP, or computer vision) could solve a problem in your organization.
- Hands-On Activity:
  - Use AWS SageMaker or Google AI Platform to build a predictive analytics model.
  - Experiment with AWS Rekognition or Azure Computer Vision to analyze image datasets.
- Case Study: Research how a company like Netflix, Tesla, or Amazon uses one of these use cases to gain a competitive advantage.

Predictive analytics, NLP, and computer vision represent the forefront of AI applications, addressing challenges and creating opportunities across industries. Cloud platforms make these use cases accessible, scalable, and efficient, empowering businesses to innovate without the constraints of traditional infrastructure. By leveraging these technologies, organizations can unlock insights, improve processes, and transform user experiences.

AI Insight:
"AI use cases like predictive analytics, NLP, and computer vision are no longer futuristic—they are practical solutions driving business success today."

Scaling Machine Learning Workloads with Cloud Infrastructure

Machine learning (ML) workloads often demand significant computational resources, especially for training large models or processing massive datasets. Cloud infrastructure is uniquely suited to meet these demands by providing scalable, on-demand resources and tools that optimize performance and efficiency. This section explores how cloud infrastructure enables businesses to scale ML workloads, the key strategies involved, and the tools available to streamline the process.

1. Why Scale ML Workloads in the Cloud?

Scaling ML workloads in the cloud offers numerous advantages over traditional on-premises setups:

Key Benefits
- Elastic Resource Allocation:
  - Cloud platforms dynamically allocate compute, storage, and networking resources based on workload requirements.
  - Example: Scale GPU instances during training and reduce them after completion to save costs.
- Global Accessibility:
  - Teams can access and collaborate on ML projects from anywhere, using centralized cloud resources.
- Cost Efficiency:
  - Pay-as-you-go pricing eliminates the need for expensive hardware investments and maintenance.
- Seamless Integration with AI/ML Tools:
  - Cloud platforms integrate with AI/ML tools, simplifying workflows from data preprocessing to model deployment.

AI Insight:
"Cloud scalability empowers businesses to experiment with ML models of varying complexity without worrying about resource limitations."

2. Strategies for Scaling ML Workloads
Scaling ML workloads involves optimizing resources and processes to handle increasing data volumes and computational demands effectively.

Distributed Training
- What It Is: Training ML models across multiple machines or GPUs simultaneously to reduce training time.
- How It Works: Splits data into smaller batches processed in parallel across distributed nodes.
- Example: Training a deep learning model on AWS EC2 instances with multiple GPUs using PyTorch's distributed data parallelism.

Auto-scaling
- What It Is: Automatically adjusts compute resources based on workload requirements.
- How It Works: Cloud services monitor resource utilization and scale up or down dynamically.
- Example: Azure Machine Learning adjusts VM sizes and counts during peak training periods.

Spot Instances for Cost Efficiency
- What It Is: Using cloud providers' surplus compute capacity at discounted rates.
- How It Works: Spot instances offer temporary resources for non-urgent tasks, reducing costs significantly.
- Example: Using AWS Spot Instances for model experimentation and non-critical workloads.

Leveraging AI-Optimized Hardware
- What It Is: Using specialized hardware like GPUs, TPUs, or FPGAs designed for ML tasks.
- How It Works: Cloud platforms offer access to hardware optimized for parallel processing and matrix computations.
- Example: Training transformer models with Google Cloud TPUs to accelerate matrix-heavy computations.

Data Sharding and Caching
- What It Is: Dividing large datasets into manageable chunks and caching frequently accessed data.
- How It Works: Improves data processing speed by reducing latency and avoiding redundant computations.
- Example: Using Amazon S3 and SageMaker's Pipe Mode to stream data directly to ML algorithms during training.

3. Tools for Scaling ML Workloads
Cloud platforms provide specialized tools and services to simplify and optimize scaling.

AWS Tools
- AWS SageMaker:
  - Supports distributed training, automatic model tuning, and elastic inference for efficient resource usage.
- Amazon Elastic Kubernetes Service (EKS):
  - Orchestrates containerized ML workloads for scalability and fault tolerance.
- AWS Batch:
  - Automates batch processing for large-scale data preprocessing and ML training tasks.

Azure Tools
- Azure Machine Learning:
  - Provides autoscaling compute clusters, MLOps integration, and hyperparameter tuning.
- Azure Batch AI:
  - Manages distributed training jobs and optimizes resource allocation.
- Azure Kubernetes Service (AKS):
  - Orchestrates scalable containerized applications and ML workflows.

Google Cloud Tools
- Vertex AI:
  - Combines distributed training, hyperparameter tuning, and model optimization in one platform.
- Google Kubernetes Engine (GKE):
  - Scales containerized ML workloads using Kubernetes.
- Preemptible VMs:
  - Provides low-cost instances for temporary or experimental ML workloads.

4. Best Practices for Scaling ML Workloads
- Optimize Data Pipelines:
  - Ensure data preprocessing and ingestion are efficient to avoid bottlenecks.
  - Example: Use Apache Spark on Google Dataproc for distributed data processing.
- Use Managed Services:
  - Leverage managed ML services to reduce operational complexity.
  - Example: Use SageMaker to handle infrastructure management automatically.

- Monitor Resource Utilization:
  - Continuously monitor and adjust resources to balance performance and cost.
  - Example: Use AWS CloudWatch or Azure Monitor to track GPU and CPU usage during training.
- Experiment with AutoML:
  - Automate model selection and tuning for faster experimentation.
  - Example: Google AutoML for quick prototyping of image classification models.

5. Scaling Beyond Training: Deployment and Inference

Scaling ML workloads isn't limited to training; deployment and inference also require scalable infrastructure:
- Model Deployment:
  - Use container orchestration tools like Kubernetes to deploy models as microservices.
  - Example: Host a recommendation engine as a REST API on GKE.
- Batch and Real-Time Inference:
  - Optimize for different inference needs—batch jobs for large datasets or real-time APIs for immediate predictions.
  - Example: Azure ML supports batch scoring for offline predictions and endpoint APIs for real-time scoring.
- Serverless Inference:
  - Use serverless platforms to scale inference workloads dynamically.
  - Example: Deploy models on AWS Lambda for event-driven predictions.

Exercises for Readers
- Reflection: What aspects of your ML workflows could benefit most from cloud scaling?
- Hands-On Activity:
  - Set up distributed training for a deep learning model using SageMaker or Vertex AI.
  - Deploy a containerized ML model on Kubernetes and test its scalability.
- Case Study: Research how OpenAI scales its models using distributed training and specialized hardware in the cloud.

Scaling machine learning workloads is a critical challenge that cloud infrastructure addresses with unparalleled flexibility and power. By leveraging distributed training, autoscaling, and specialized hardware, businesses can train complex models faster and more efficiently. The cloud's managed tools and services further simplify this process, making advanced AI/ML workflows accessible to organizations of all sizes.

AI Insight:
"Scaling ML workloads in the cloud is not just about adding resources—it's about optimizing processes, reducing costs, and enabling innovation at scale."

Conclusion:
AI and machine learning have become essential tools for businesses seeking to innovate, automate, and gain actionable insights. Chapter 11 explored how cloud platforms make these technologies accessible, scalable, and practical for real-world applications. From powerful development tools to transformative use cases and scalable infrastructure, the cloud empowers organizations to unlock AI's full potential.

Key Takeaways
1. Tools for AI/ML Development
Cloud platforms like AWS SageMaker, Azure Machine Learning, and Google Cloud AI Platform provide comprehensive tools for building, training, and deploying AI/ML models.
- What We Learned: These platforms simplify workflows, enable rapid experimentation, and integrate seamlessly with other cloud services.

2. Real-World Use Cases
Applications such as predictive analytics, natural language processing (NLP), and computer vision demonstrate how AI/ML solves complex challenges across industries.
- What We Learned: These use cases drive innovation, from automating customer interactions to uncovering insights in massive datasets.

3. Scaling AI/ML Workloads
Cloud infrastructure enables organizations to scale AI/ML workloads dynamically, reducing training times and optimizing costs.
- What We Learned: Distributed training, auto-scaling, and AI-optimized hardware ensure efficient resource utilization for even the most demanding workloads.

The Bigger Picture
AI and ML in the cloud represent a paradigm shift in how businesses approach problem-solving and innovation. By leveraging cloud platforms, organizations of all sizes can develop sophisticated models, deploy scalable solutions, and derive actionable insights without the need for extensive in-house infrastructure.

The scalability, accessibility, and efficiency of cloud-based AI/ML workflows are further amplified by the integration of advanced tools and automation. Whether it's training a complex deep learning model or deploying a real-time recommendation engine, the cloud ensures these processes are seamless and cost-effective.

Looking Ahead
With a strong foundation in AI and machine learning in the cloud, the next chapter focuses on Automation, DevOps, and AIOps. We'll explore how cloud platforms enable infrastructure as code (IaC), continuous integration/continuous deployment (CI/CD) pipelines, and AI-powered operational tools to streamline development and operations.

AI Insight:
"AI and ML in the cloud are not just about building models—they are about creating smarter, more efficient systems that adapt, learn, and drive progress in a dynamic world."

Chapter 12: Automation, DevOps, and AIOps

Infrastructure as Code (IaC) for Automated Deployments

Infrastructure as Code (IaC) is a foundational practice in modern cloud computing, enabling teams to define and manage infrastructure using code. IaC automates the deployment, scaling, and management of cloud resources, replacing manual configurations with repeatable, efficient, and error-free processes. This section explores the principles, benefits, and tools of IaC, with a focus on its role in automated deployments.

1. What is Infrastructure as Code (IaC)?

IaC is the practice of defining cloud infrastructure—such as servers, networks, and storage—using declarative or imperative programming languages. Instead of manually provisioning resources through a cloud provider's interface, IaC allows developers to write code that automates these tasks.

Declarative vs. Imperative IaC
- Declarative IaC: Specifies the desired state of infrastructure. The system determines the steps to achieve that state.
  - Example: AWS CloudFormation templates describe the final configuration of resources.
- Imperative IaC: Details the exact steps required to provision infrastructure.
  - Example: Writing scripts in Ansible or Python to configure resources step-by-step.

AI Insight:
"Declarative IaC simplifies automation by focusing on outcomes, while imperative IaC offers flexibility for custom processes."

2. Benefits of IaC

IaC transforms infrastructure management by introducing consistency, efficiency, and scalability.

Key Benefits
- Automation:
  - Automates repetitive tasks like resource provisioning, reducing manual errors.
  - Example: Automatically deploy a multi-tier application with network configurations using Terraform.
- Consistency:
  - Ensures environments remain identical across development, testing, and production stages.
  - Example: Deploy the same infrastructure for a staging environment to mimic production settings.

- Version Control:
  - IaC files can be stored in version control systems like Git, enabling change tracking and rollback.
  - Example: Restore infrastructure to a previous state after an unsuccessful deployment.
- Scalability:
  - Facilitates horizontal scaling by automating resource provisioning based on demand.
  - Example: Use auto-scaling groups in AWS defined through an IaC template.
- Speed:
  - Rapidly deploy or update infrastructure with minimal manual intervention.
  - Example: Spin up a Kubernetes cluster in minutes using a pre-written script.

3. Popular IaC Tools
Several IaC tools simplify infrastructure automation, each catering to specific use cases and cloud platforms.

AWS CloudFormation
- A declarative IaC tool that automates the provisioning of AWS resources.
- Key Features:
  - Supports JSON or YAML templates.
  - Integrates with AWS SAM for serverless application management.
- Use Case: Deploy a web application stack with EC2 instances, load balancers, and databases.

Terraform (by HashiCorp)
- A widely used multi-cloud IaC tool.
- Key Features:
  - Platform-agnostic, supports AWS, Azure, Google Cloud, and more.
  - Enables modular code for reusable configurations.
- Use Case: Provision a hybrid cloud infrastructure spanning multiple providers.

Azure Resource Manager (ARM) Templates
- The native IaC tool for Azure environments.
- Key Features:
  - Allows JSON-based templates to define Azure resources.
  - Integrates seamlessly with Azure DevOps.
- Use Case: Set up a scalable virtual network with VMs and storage accounts in Azure.

Google Cloud Deployment Manager
- A declarative IaC tool for Google Cloud resources.
- Key Features:
  - YAML or Python templates to define infrastructure.
  - Supports advanced features like input validation.
- Use Case: Automate the deployment of a BigQuery data pipeline.

Ansible
- An imperative tool focused on configuration management and IaC.
- Key Features:
  - Uses simple YAML syntax in playbooks.
  - Works well for provisioning and post-deployment configuration.
- Use Case: Configure server environments after deployment.

AI Insight:
"Tools like Terraform and Ansible are critical for multi-cloud strategies, ensuring seamless automation across diverse environments."

4. Best Practices for IaC
Modularize Code
- Break down IaC scripts into reusable modules for scalability and simplicity.
- Example: Create separate Terraform modules for networking, storage, and compute resources.

Use CI/CD Pipelines
- Integrate IaC workflows into continuous integration/continuous deployment (CI/CD) pipelines for automated testing and deployment.
- Example: Validate IaC templates using AWS CodePipeline before deploying infrastructure.

Implement Drift Detection
- Monitor and correct deviations between the declared and actual state of infrastructure.
- Example: Use Terraform's state management to identify and resolve drift.

Secure IaC Files
- Protect sensitive information, such as API keys, by using tools like AWS Secrets Manager or HashiCorp Vault.

Test Configurations
- Use sandbox environments to test IaC scripts before deploying to production.
- Example: Test CloudFormation templates in a development account to avoid disrupting production.

5. AI's Role in Enhancing IaC
AI for Drift Detection
- AI systems monitor infrastructure configurations and alert teams to discrepancies.
- Example: AI-powered insights recommend corrections for misconfigured cloud resources.

AI-Driven Optimization
- Machine learning models analyze IaC scripts to suggest performance optimizations or cost-saving measures.
- Example: AI identifies underutilized resources and recommends rightsizing or termination.

Exercises for Readers
- Reflection: What aspects of your infrastructure management could benefit from adopting IaC?
- Hands-On Activity:
  - Write a Terraform script to deploy a simple web application with a backend database.
  - Create a CloudFormation template to provision an auto-scaling EC2 instance in AWS.
- Case Study: Research how Netflix or Spotify uses IaC to manage large-scale, multi-cloud infrastructure.

Infrastructure as Code is a cornerstone of modern cloud operations, enabling organizations to automate deployments, ensure consistency, and scale resources efficiently. By integrating IaC with cloud platforms and DevOps practices, businesses can achieve faster deployments, reduced errors, and enhanced collaboration. As AI continues to evolve, it will further refine IaC workflows, making them smarter, faster, and more adaptive.

AI Insight:
"IaC transforms cloud infrastructure management from a manual process into a seamless, automated system, with AI driving further optimization and scalability."

Role of AI in DevOps Pipelines and AIOps Platforms
AI is reshaping the landscape of DevOps and IT operations by introducing automation, intelligence, and predictive capabilities into pipelines and platforms. By leveraging machine learning, AI optimizes resource utilization, accelerates deployment cycles, and enables proactive issue detection and resolution. This section dives deeper into how AI integrates into DevOps pipelines and AIOps platforms, providing detailed insights and actionable strategies for modern cloud environments.

1. Understanding AI in DevOps Pipelines

AI enhances DevOps pipelines by improving the efficiency and reliability of software development and delivery processes.

How AI Fits into DevOps Pipelines
- Continuous Integration (CI):
  - AI-driven tools analyze code commits in real time to detect errors or inefficiencies before they reach production.
  - Example: Tools like SonarQube use machine learning to identify code vulnerabilities and enforce quality standards.
- Continuous Delivery (CD):
  - AI predicts deployment risks and automates rollbacks when anomalies are detected.
  - Example: AI models assess whether a deployment might degrade performance based on historical data.
- Testing Automation:
  - AI optimizes test cases, prioritizing the most critical ones to reduce pipeline execution time.
  - Example: An AI-powered testing tool identifies redundant tests and focuses on scenarios with high defect probability.
- Performance Monitoring:
  - AI monitors build and deployment pipelines for bottlenecks and inefficiencies.
  - Example: Real-time alerts notify developers about resource contention or long-running build processes.

2. AIOps Platforms: Intelligent IT Operations

AIOps (Artificial Intelligence for IT Operations) platforms revolutionize how IT environments are managed, ensuring scalability, performance, and reliability.

Key Functions of AIOps Platforms
- Anomaly Detection:
  - AI models analyze logs, metrics, and events to identify unusual patterns.
  - Example: Detecting an unexpected spike in latency during off-peak hours.
- Predictive Insights:
  - Machine learning predicts system failures before they occur, enabling proactive remediation.
  - Example: Anticipating server crashes due to increasing memory usage trends.
- Automated Root Cause Analysis:
  - AI correlates data from multiple sources to pinpoint the cause of incidents quickly.
  - Example: Identifying that a high CPU usage issue is caused by a specific application version.

- Incident Response Automation:
  - AIOps automates routine incident responses, reducing downtime and operational overhead.
  - Example: Automatically restarting a failed service or scaling up resources during traffic spikes.
- Resource Optimization:
  - AI identifies underutilized or overburdened resources and recommends adjustments.
  - Example: Recommending rightsizing an over-provisioned virtual machine to reduce costs.

3. Practical Applications of AI in DevOps and AIOps
DevOps Pipelines
- Code Quality Enforcement:
  - AI enforces coding standards and detects potential bugs early in the development cycle.
  - Example: A CI pipeline integrates AI tools like GitHub Copilot to provide code suggestions and detect vulnerabilities.
- Dynamic Deployment Strategies:
  - AI supports canary or blue-green deployments by analyzing real-time metrics to decide whether to proceed or roll back.
  - Example: Allowing only 5% of traffic to access a new feature and gradually increasing based on AI analysis of user feedback.
- Optimized Testing:
  - AI dynamically selects the most relevant test cases for a build, saving time and resources.
  - Example: Tools like Testim leverage machine learning to prioritize tests based on historical defect data.

AIOps Platforms
- Real-Time Monitoring and Alerting:
  - AI integrates with observability tools like Prometheus or Datadog to provide advanced monitoring.
  - Example: Detecting and alerting about unusual spikes in database query times.
- Incident Management:
  - AI reduces mean time to resolution (MTTR) by automating ticket assignment and response.
  - Example: Integrating AI with ITSM tools like ServiceNow to route tickets based on priority and context.
- Proactive Maintenance:
  - AI predicts hardware failures and schedules maintenance before disruptions occur.
  - Example: Using AI-driven insights to replace aging hard drives in data centers.

4. Tools and Platforms for AI in DevOps and AIOps

For DevOps Pipelines
- Jenkins with AI Plugins: Automates build and deployment processes with AI-powered optimizations.
- GitHub Copilot: Uses AI to suggest code, detect vulnerabilities, and enforce quality.
- Test.ai: Applies machine learning to optimize and automate testing workflows.

For AIOps Platforms
- Splunk ITSI: Monitors IT infrastructure with AI-driven insights for root cause analysis and performance optimization.
- Moogsoft: Uses machine learning for event correlation and incident management.
- Datadog: Provides advanced observability and AI-driven alerting to monitor application health.

5. Best Practices for Leveraging AI in DevOps and AIOps
- Start with Small Use Cases:
  - Implement AI in specific areas, such as anomaly detection or test optimization, before scaling.
- Integrate AI with Existing Tools:
  - Ensure AI integrates seamlessly with current DevOps and ITSM workflows.
- Leverage Feedback Loops:
  - Use feedback from AI recommendations to improve models and refine processes continuously.
- Ensure Explainability:
  - Choose AI tools that provide insights into their decisions, ensuring transparency and trust.
- Monitor AI Performance:
  - Regularly evaluate AI models to ensure they remain accurate and effective.

Exercises for Readers
- Reflection: Identify areas in your DevOps pipeline or IT operations where AI could provide the most value.
- Hands-On Activity:
  - Set up an AI-powered tool like Moogsoft for incident management or GitHub Copilot for code quality enforcement.
  - Integrate AIOps insights into a real-time monitoring system like Datadog.
- Case Study: Research how companies like Netflix or Spotify use AI to enhance DevOps efficiency and operational reliability.

The integration of AI into DevOps and IT operations through pipelines and AIOps platforms enables businesses to automate, optimize, and innovate. By leveraging AI-driven insights, organizations can enhance code quality, reduce downtime, and deliver faster, more reliable applications. As cloud environments grow in complexity, AI serves as a critical partner in ensuring scalability and resilience.

AI Insight:
"The power of AI in DevOps and AIOps lies in its ability to transform reactive processes into proactive and predictive systems, ensuring efficiency and reliability."

Continuous Integration/Continuous Delivery (CI/CD) Best Practices

Continuous Integration (CI) and Continuous Delivery (CD) are core DevOps practices that automate the process of integrating, testing, and deploying code changes. These practices improve development efficiency, reduce errors, and enable rapid delivery of high-quality software. This section provides an in-depth exploration of best practices for CI/CD pipelines, ensuring that they are efficient, scalable, and aligned with modern cloud-driven workflows.

1. Core Principles of CI/CD

Before diving into best practices, it's essential to understand the foundational principles of CI/CD.

Continuous Integration (CI):
- Developers frequently integrate their code into a shared repository.
- Automated builds and tests run with every integration to detect issues early.
- Goal: Identify and resolve integration errors quickly to maintain a stable codebase.

Continuous Delivery (CD):
- Code changes that pass automated tests are automatically prepared for release to production.
- Deployment is a consistent, repeatable process with minimal manual intervention.
- Goal: Ensure software is always ready for deployment.

2. CI/CD Best Practices

Automate Everything
- Automation is the cornerstone of CI/CD. From code integration to testing and deployment, every step should be automated to reduce manual errors and speed up the pipeline.
- Use Cases:
  - Automate builds using Jenkins, CircleCI, or GitHub Actions.
  - Automate testing with frameworks like Selenium for UI testing or JUnit for unit testing.
- Benefits:
  - Consistent workflows reduce variability.
  - Faster feedback loops ensure developers can address issues quickly.

Keep Pipelines Fast
Optimize pipeline speed to avoid bottlenecks and keep developers productive.
- Techniques:
  - Parallelize tasks like testing and building.
  - Cache dependencies to avoid redundant downloads.
  - Use containerized environments for faster, consistent builds.
- Example:
  - Use Docker to ensure consistent environments for CI jobs across teams.

Test Early and Often
Testing should occur at every stage of the pipeline to catch issues as early as possible.
- Best Practices:
  - Write unit tests for individual components.
  - Implement integration tests to ensure components work together.
  - Run end-to-end tests to validate overall functionality.
- AI Integration:
  - Use AI-driven tools to prioritize tests based on historical defect patterns.
  - Example: Tools like Test.ai optimize test coverage by identifying high-risk code areas.

Adopt Trunk-Based Development
Use trunk-based development to simplify integrations and reduce merge conflicts.
- What It Involves:
  - Developers commit code changes to a shared main branch frequently.
  - Feature branches are short-lived and integrated as soon as changes are stable.
- Benefits:
  - Reduces code divergence, making integration easier.
  - Encourages collaboration and rapid feedback.

Use Blue-Green or Canary Deployments
Minimize user impact during deployments by gradually rolling out changes.
- Blue-Green Deployment:
  - Maintain two production environments: one live (blue) and one idle (green).
  - Route traffic to the green environment after verifying the new version.
  - Roll back instantly by switching traffic back to blue if issues arise.
- Canary Deployment:
  - Deploy changes to a small subset of users before rolling them out to everyone.
  - Use AI to analyze user feedback and system performance during the canary phase.

Monitor and Observe Pipelines
Real-time monitoring and observability are crucial for identifying and resolving pipeline issues quickly.
- Best Practices:
  - Integrate observability tools like Prometheus and Grafana to monitor CI/CD pipelines.
  - Set up alerts for critical metrics such as build failures, deployment times, and resource utilization.
- AI Tools:
  - AI platforms like Datadog and Splunk analyze logs to detect anomalies and suggest resolutions.

Secure the CI/CD Pipeline
CI/CD pipelines are an attractive target for attackers, so security must be a priority.
- Best Practices:
  - Use secure credentials management tools like AWS Secrets Manager or HashiCorp Vault.
  - Scan code repositories for vulnerabilities with tools like SonarQube or Snyk.
  - Apply role-based access control (RBAC) to limit pipeline access.

Implement Rollbacks and Recovery
Even with rigorous testing, deployments can fail. Robust rollback mechanisms are essential.
- Strategies:
  - Use versioned deployments to roll back to the previous stable release.
  - Maintain backups of configuration and database changes.

- Example:
  - Kubernetes Helm makes it easy to roll back failed deployments.

3. Tools for CI/CD Implementation
Jenkins
- Open-source automation server for building, deploying, and testing applications.
- Supports integration with plugins for Kubernetes, Docker, and Git.

GitHub Actions
- CI/CD service integrated into GitHub repositories.
- Ideal for lightweight, scalable workflows with YAML-based configuration.

CircleCI
- Offers containerized environments for fast, consistent builds.
- Includes tools for testing, deployment, and monitoring.

Azure DevOps
- Comprehensive CI/CD suite with native support for Azure services.
- Integrates with Azure Kubernetes Service (AKS) for automated deployments.

4. Challenges in CI/CD and How to Overcome Them
Challenge 1: Long Build Times
- Solution: Use parallel processing and caching to optimize pipelines.

Challenge 2: Flaky Tests
- Solution: Regularly review and refine test cases to eliminate unreliable ones.

Challenge 3: Tool Overload
- Solution: Standardize on a minimal set of tools to reduce complexity.

Challenge 4: Scaling Pipelines
- Solution: Use auto-scaling infrastructure to handle large workloads dynamically.

Exercises for Readers
- Reflection: Assess your organization's current CI/CD pipeline. Are there inefficiencies or gaps in automation?
- Hands-On Activity:
  - Create a CI/CD pipeline with Jenkins or GitHub Actions to build and test a simple application.
  - Implement a blue-green deployment strategy for a web application hosted on AWS.
- Case Study: Research how companies like Google or Netflix optimize their CI/CD pipelines to support frequent, reliable releases.

CI/CD is the backbone of modern software delivery, enabling teams to release updates faster and with greater confidence. By following best practices like automating workflows, testing thoroughly, and monitoring pipelines, organizations can achieve a streamlined, reliable development lifecycle. When paired with AI-driven insights, CI/CD pipelines become even more efficient, resilient, and adaptable to the demands of modern cloud environments.

AI Insight:
"CI/CD pipelines with AI-enhanced automation allow businesses to innovate at speed without compromising quality or reliability."

Conclusion:
Automation, DevOps, and AIOps are the driving forces behind efficient and scalable cloud operations. Chapter 12 explored the critical components and best practices that empower teams to streamline workflows, enhance collaboration, and ensure system reliability. By combining automation with AI-driven insights, organizations can not only keep pace with rapid development cycles but also proactively address challenges in complex environments.

Key Takeaways
- Infrastructure as Code (IaC):
  - IaC automates infrastructure provisioning, ensuring consistency, speed, and scalability.
  - Tools like Terraform, CloudFormation, and Ansible simplify deployments while reducing errors.
- AI in DevOps and AIOps:
  - AI enhances DevOps pipelines by predicting issues, optimizing resources, and automating testing.
  - AIOps platforms enable proactive monitoring, anomaly detection, and automated incident resolution.
- CI/CD Best Practices:
  - Automation, testing, and robust deployment strategies ensure faster and more reliable software releases.
  - Techniques like blue-green and canary deployments, combined with AI-driven optimizations, minimize risks.

The Bigger Picture
Automation and AI are not just tools; they are catalysts for innovation in the cloud. By adopting the practices and tools outlined in this chapter, organizations can achieve a higher level of agility, reliability, and efficiency. Whether it's automating deployments with IaC, optimizing DevOps workflows with AI, or implementing resilient CI/CD pipelines, these strategies position businesses for success in the competitive cloud era.

Looking Ahead
The next chapter, Cloud Storage and Databases, delves into managing and optimizing data in the cloud, covering topics like storage types, database solutions, and best practices for data architecture.

AI Insight:
"Automation and AI are transforming cloud operations, enabling businesses to work smarter, adapt faster, and innovate confidently."

Chapter 13: AI-Driven Cost Optimization

Using AI Tools to Monitor and Forecast Cloud Costs

Managing cloud costs is one of the most critical challenges for organizations adopting cloud computing. While cloud platforms offer flexibility and scalability, uncontrolled resource usage can lead to unexpected and escalating expenses. AI-driven tools provide advanced capabilities to monitor, analyze, and forecast cloud costs, enabling businesses to maintain financial control while optimizing resource utilization.

1. Why AI for Cost Management?

Traditional cost-monitoring tools provide basic insights into resource usage, but they often fall short in identifying inefficiencies or predicting future expenses. AI-powered solutions go beyond static reports by offering real-time analysis, predictive forecasting, and actionable recommendations.

Key Benefits of AI in Cost Management
1. Proactive Monitoring:
   o AI continuously tracks resource usage and alerts users about anomalies or trends.
   o Example: Detecting an unused virtual machine that's consuming storage and compute resources.
2. Predictive Forecasting:
   o Machine learning models analyze historical data to predict future costs based on usage patterns.
   o Example: Forecasting next month's cloud bill for a rapidly scaling application.
3. Optimized Resource Allocation:
   o AI identifies over-provisioned resources and suggests right-sizing or alternative configurations.
   o Example: Recommending a reserved instance instead of an on-demand instance for consistent workloads.

AI Insight:
"AI not only tells you what you're spending but also why and how to spend more effectively."

2. AI Tools for Monitoring Cloud Costs

Each major cloud provider offers AI-driven cost management tools, along with third-party solutions that integrate across platforms.

AWS Cost Explorer
- Capabilities:
  - Uses machine learning to analyze cost and usage data.
  - Provides forecasts based on historical spending patterns.
- AI Features:
  - Detects anomalies in spending, such as unexpected spikes in resource usage.
  - Suggests optimizations like switching to reserved instances.
- Example Use Case:
  - Identifying underutilized EC2 instances and recommending cost-saving alternatives.

Azure Cost Management and Billing
- Capabilities:
  - Offers AI-powered insights to monitor spending and optimize resource allocation.
  - Tracks spending across subscriptions and resource groups.
- AI Features:
  - Predicts future spending trends and provides budget alerts.
  - Recommends resource consolidation to minimize waste.
- Example Use Case:
  - Forecasting monthly costs for a Kubernetes cluster based on workload scaling patterns.

Google Cloud Billing Reports
- Capabilities:
  - Tracks and visualizes costs across projects, services, and regions.
  - Integrates with BigQuery for advanced cost analysis.
- AI Features:
  - Provides recommendations for idle resource cleanup and cost-efficiency improvements.
  - Predicts spending trends based on project activity.
- Example Use Case:
  - Analyzing storage usage trends to optimize costs for BigQuery datasets.

Third-Party Tools
- CloudHealth by VMware:
  - Provides multi-cloud cost insights with AI-driven recommendations.
  - Ideal for businesses using hybrid or multi-cloud setup

- Spot.io:
    - Specializes in optimizing cloud costs by dynamically allocating resources.
- FinOps Platforms:
    - Tools like Harness FinOps help teams manage cloud costs collaboratively, integrating AI to forecast budgets and track efficiency.

3. Forecasting Cloud Costs with AI
Forecasting is a critical aspect of cost optimization, enabling organizations to plan budgets effectively and avoid surprises.

How AI Forecasting Works
- Historical Data Analysis:
    - AI models analyze past usage patterns and cost data to identify trends.
- Usage Correlations:
    - AI correlates resource usage with application activity, scaling events, or seasonal factors.
    - Example: Predicting increased compute costs during a holiday sale for an e-commerce site.
- Scenario Simulation:
    - Models simulate different usage scenarios to project costs under various conditions.
    - Example: Estimating costs for a new product launch with expected traffic spikes.

Benefits of AI Forecasting
- Accurate Budget Planning:
    - Aligns financial planning with technical operations by predicting costs reliably.
- Preemptive Cost Control:
    - Identifies potential cost overruns early, enabling corrective action.
- Scalability Awareness:
    - Helps teams understand the financial impact of scaling decisions.

AI Insight:
"AI turns cloud cost forecasting from guesswork into a data-driven science."

4. Challenges and Solutions in AI-Driven Cost Management
Challenge 1: Data Quality
- Poorly tagged resources or incomplete usage data can affect AI accuracy.
- Solution: Implement rigorous tagging policies and ensure data completeness.

Challenge 2: Complexity of Multi-Cloud Environments
- Managing costs across multiple providers is more complex.
- Solution: Use third-party tools like CloudHealth that aggregate and analyze multi-cloud data.

Challenge 3: Resistance to Recommendations
- Teams may be hesitant to trust AI-driven cost-saving suggestions.
- Solution: Start with non-critical resources to validate AI recommendations and build confidence.

Exercises for Readers
- Reflection: Which cloud resources in your organization are likely candidates for AI-driven cost optimization?
- Hands-On Activity:
  - Use AWS Cost Explorer, Azure Cost Management, or Google Cloud Billing to analyze your current cloud spending.
  - Test AI-powered recommendations for resource optimization and evaluate their impact.
- Case Study: Research how a leading company (e.g., Airbnb or Lyft) uses AI tools to control cloud costs effectively.

AI tools are transforming cloud cost management by providing real-time insights, accurate forecasting, and actionable recommendations. By integrating these tools into their workflows, organizations can achieve significant cost savings, optimize resource usage, and align cloud spending with business objectives. With AI as a partner, businesses can ensure that they're not just using the cloud effectively but doing so cost-efficiently.

AI Insight:
"Effective cost management isn't just about spending less—it's about spending smarter, with AI guiding the way."

Identifying and Addressing Inefficiencies in Resource Usage
Inefficient resource usage in cloud environments can lead to
spiraling costs, degraded performance, and wasted capacity.
Identifying and addressing these inefficiencies is a key component
of cost optimization. Leveraging AI-powered tools and practices
allows organizations to pinpoint underutilized resources, optimize
workloads, and ensure cloud investments deliver maximum value.

1. Common Causes of Inefficiencies in Cloud Resource Usage
Understanding the typical sources of inefficiency is the first step in
addressing them.

Over-Provisioning
- Description: Allocating more resources than needed to handle
  workloads, often as a precaution against peak demand.
- Example: Running an EC2 instance with 32 CPUs when the
  workload requires only 8 CPUs.
- Impact: Leads to unnecessarily high costs with minimal
  performance benefits.

Underutilized Resources
- Description: Resources that remain idle or are used below
  capacity for extended periods.
- Example: Persistent storage volumes attached to instances that
  are no longer active.
- Impact: Idle resources contribute to costs without providing
  value.

Inefficient Workload Placement
- Description: Deploying workloads in regions or zones that
  increase costs or latency.
- Example: Running applications in high-cost regions like the US
  East Coast when cheaper options exist in other regions.
- Impact: Increases expenses and may degrade user experience.

Redundant Resources
- Description: Duplicate or unnecessary resources resulting from
  improper scaling or failed decommissioning.
- Example: Retaining old snapshots or outdated load balancers
  no longer in use.
- Impact: Adds to storage costs and creates clutter in the
  environment.

AI Insight:
"Many inefficiencies stem from a lack of visibility into cloud
environments—a challenge AI tools are uniquely positioned to
solve."

2. Using AI to Detect Inefficiencies

AI-powered tools analyze resource usage data to identify patterns of inefficiency and provide actionable insights.

Capabilities of AI Tools

- Resource Utilization Analysis:
  - Monitors CPU, memory, and disk usage across instances to identify underutilized or over-provisioned resources.
  - Example: AI detects that a database server operates at only 15% CPU usage and recommends downsizing.
- Idle Resource Detection:
  - Identifies resources that are consuming costs without contributing to workloads.
  - Example: Flags unattached storage volumes or inactive virtual machines for review.
- Anomaly Detection:
  - Uses machine learning to detect unusual spikes or drops in resource usage.
  - Example: Identifies a misconfigured process consuming excessive compute power.
- Workload Optimization Recommendations:
  - Suggests optimal resource configurations based on historical and real-time data.
  - Example: Recommends converting on-demand instances to reserved instances for steady-state workloads.

3. Steps to Address Inefficiencies

Step 1: Conduct a Resource Audit

- Use cloud-native tools like AWS Trusted Advisor, Azure Advisor, or Google Cloud Recommender to generate a detailed report of resource usage.
- Action: Identify unused or low-utilization resources, such as detached storage or idle instances.

Step 2: Optimize Compute Resources

- Right-size virtual machines or containers based on workload requirements.
- Implement auto-scaling to adjust resources dynamically in response to demand.
- Action: Transition predictable workloads to reserved instances or savings plans for cost efficiency.

Step 3: Streamline Storage

- Delete obsolete snapshots, unused volumes, outdated backups.
- Transition data to lower-cost storage tiers (e.g., Amazon S3 Glacier for archival data).
- Action: Use AI tools to analyze data access patterns and optimize storage placement.

Step 4: Consolidate Workloads
- Combine workloads with similar patterns to maximize resource usage and reduce duplication.
- Example: Deploy multiple lightweight services on a single Kubernetes node rather than separate VMs.

Step 5: Optimize Networking
- Evaluate data transfer costs and configure traffic routing to minimize expenses.
- Use content delivery networks (CDNs) to reduce egress costs for frequently accessed content.
- Action: Implement AI-driven recommendations for optimizing network traffic flow.

Step 6: Automate Resource Management
- Use automation tools to clean up unused resources regularly and enforce governance policies.
- Example: Configure a script or Lambda function to delete unattached storage volumes automatically.

4. Tools for Identifying and Addressing Inefficiencies
AWS Trusted Advisor
- Provides cost-saving recommendations by identifying underutilized resources, over-provisioned instances, and unused elastic IPs.
- AI Features: Uses machine learning to prioritize actionable recommendations.

Azure Advisor
- Offers tailored recommendations to optimize cost, performance, and reliability.
- Example: Recommends resizing underutilized VMs or consolidating storage accounts.

Google Cloud Recommender
- Provides insights into idle resources, optimal machine types, and data transfer configurations.
- Example: Flags VM instances with less than 10% CPU utilization for downsizing.

Spot.io
- Specializes in optimizing compute costs by dynamically allocating resources and terminating idle instances.
- AI Features: Predicts resource needs and allocates resources accordingly.

Kubecost
- Focused on Kubernetes environments, Kubecost monitors resource usage and highlights inefficiencies in cluster management.
- Example: Identifies over-provisioned pods and suggests adjustments.

5. Best Practices for Preventing Inefficiencies
- Implement Governance Policies:
  - Enforce policies for tagging resources and decommissioning unused assets.
- Automate Regular Cleanups:
  - Schedule automated cleanup jobs for orphaned resources, such as unattached disks or expired snapshots.
- Monitor Usage Regularly:
  - Use dashboards and alerts to track resource usage and identify inefficiencies in real time.
- Optimize Continuously:
  - Periodically review and refine resource configurations based on workload changes and AI recommendations.

AI Insight:
"Continuous monitoring and optimization are essential to ensure resources remain efficient as workloads evolve."

Exercises for Readers
- Reflection: Identify areas in your organization's cloud environment where resource inefficiencies might exist.
- Hands-On Activity:
  - Use AWS Trusted Advisor or Azure Advisor to generate a report on underutilized resources in your cloud account.
  - Implement a right-sizing recommendation and measure the cost savings achieved.
- Case Study: Research how a major company, such as Lyft or Spotify, optimized cloud resource usage to reduce costs and improve performance.

Identifying and addressing inefficiencies in resource usage is a continuous process that combines monitoring, analysis, and action. AI-powered tools provide unparalleled visibility into resource utilization, enabling organizations to optimize workloads and reduce costs proactively. By implementing the strategies outlined in this section, readers can ensure their cloud environments are both cost-efficient and high-performing.

Practical Tips for Budget Management

Effective budget management is essential for controlling cloud costs, maximizing resource utilization, and aligning expenses with business goals. With the flexibility of cloud computing comes the challenge of keeping spending in check, especially in dynamic environments where costs can quickly spiral out of control. This section provides actionable tips and strategies for managing cloud budgets effectively, leveraging best practices and AI-driven tools.

1. Define a Clear Budget Strategy

Before diving into tools and optimization tactics, organizations must establish a well-defined budget strategy.

Key Steps to Create a Budget
- Set Budget Limits:
  - Define spending limits for individual projects, teams, or departments.
  - Example: Allocate $10,000 per month for the development environment.
- Identify Critical Resources:
  - Prioritize resources that drive business goals and focus budget allocations accordingly.
  - Example: Invest more in production databases than in testing environments.
- Plan for Growth:
  - Account for scaling needs or seasonal fluctuations in resource usage.
  - Example: Include higher budget allowances for Black Friday traffic spikes.

AI Insight:
"Budget strategies work best when they're dynamic, adapting to real-time changes in resource usage and business priorities."

2. Leverage AI-Powered Budget Tools

AI tools are invaluable for monitoring, forecasting, and optimizing cloud budgets in real-time.

Recommended Tools
- AWS Budgets:
  - Tracks and alerts users about spending against predefined limits.
  - AI Features: Suggests optimizations for underutilized or redundant resources.
- Azure Cost Management and Billing:
  - Provides detailed cost analysis and forecasting for Azure environments.

- AI Features: Predicts spending trends and recommends cost-saving measures.
- Google Cloud Budgets and Alerts:
  - Tracks spending and sends real-time alerts when thresholds are exceeded.
  - AI Features: Offers recommendations for optimizing resource configurations.
- Third-Party Tools:
  - Tools like CloudHealth, Harness FinOps, and Spot.io provide multi-cloud cost management capabilities with AI-driven insights.

Practical Tip: Enable real-time alerts for budget thresholds to avoid unexpected overages.

3. Implement Budget Tracking Policies
Tracking policies ensure that cloud spending is monitored and managed consistently across teams and projects.

Steps for Effective Budget Tracking
- Tagging Resources:
  - Use consistent tags (e.g., team, project, environment) to track costs by category.
  - Example: Tag resources as "Dev," "QA," or "Production" to allocate budgets accurately.
- Monitor Key Metrics:
  - Focus on metrics like cost per user, cost per transaction, or resource utilization rate.
  - Example: Track compute costs as a percentage of total workload expenses.
- Regular Budget Reviews:
  - Schedule monthly or quarterly budget reviews to assess spending trends and make adjustments.
  - Example: Identify and decommission unused resources during each review.

4. Optimize Spending with Reserved Resources
Cloud providers offer discounts for reserving resources in advance, making them an effective way to manage predictable workloads.

Key Strategies
- Use Reserved Instances:
  - Commit to a specific amount of compute capacity for one or three years to receive significant discounts.
  - Example: Save up to 75% on AWS EC2 instances with reserved pricing.

- Adopt Savings Plans:
    - Flexible plans that reduce costs for steady-state workloads while allowing resource adjustments.
    - Example: Azure Reserved VM Instances or Google Committed Use Discounts.
- Combine Spot and Reserved Resources:
    - Use spot instances for non-critical workloads and reserved resources for production.
    - Example: Deploy a CI/CD pipeline on spot instances while running databases on reserved instances.

AI Insight:
"AI tools can analyze workload patterns to recommend the optimal mix of reserved and on-demand resources."

5. Encourage Cost-Conscious Development
Empower teams to make informed decisions that align with budget goals.

Key Practices
- Educate Teams on Cloud Costs:
    - Provide training on the cost implications of resource choices.
    - Example: Teach developers to evaluate the cost impact of deploying large-scale Kubernetes clusters.
- Integrate Cost Insights into DevOps Pipelines:
    - Use CI/CD tools to display cost estimates during deployment stages.
    - Example: Jenkins integrates with cloud billing APIs to show expected costs before deployment.
- Enforce Budget Policies:
    - Set automated limits or restrictions for non-production environments.
    - Example: Automatically shut down unused development instances after 8 PM.

6. Automate Budget Management
Automation reduces manual oversight and ensures consistent enforcement of budget policies.

Automation Strategies
- Auto-Scaling:
    - Automatically adjust resource allocation based on demand to avoid over-provisioning.
    - Example: Use AWS Auto Scaling for EC2 instances to match workload requirements.

- Scheduled Shutdowns:
  - Automate the shutdown of non-essential resources during off-hours.
  - Example: Use Azure Automation to stop development VMs overnight.
- Automated Alerts and Actions:
  - Set up alerts for budget thresholds and trigger automated responses, like scaling down workloads or notifying teams.
  - Example: Configure Google Cloud Functions to terminate idle instances once costs exceed a predefined limit.

7. Continuously Optimize Costs

Budget management is an ongoing process, requiring continuous evaluation and optimization.

Best Practices
- Review Budget Allocations Regularly:
  - Adjust budgets based on changing priorities or business goals.
- Leverage AI for Cost Forecasting:
  - Use predictive analytics to anticipate budget requirements and prevent overages.
- Experiment with Cost-Saving Strategies:
  - Test strategies like moving workloads to cheaper regions or adopting multi-cloud solutions.

Exercises for Readers
- Reflection: Identify the top three cloud services consuming your budget. Are they aligned with your business priorities?
- Hands-On Activity:
  - Set up a budget in AWS Budgets or Azure Cost Management. Enable alerts for 80% and 100% of the budget threshold.
  - Analyze your spending trends using an AI-powered tool and implement one recommendation.
- Case Study: Research how a major company, like Spotify or Lyft, uses cloud budget management to achieve financial efficiency.

Practical budget management is essential for maximizing the value of cloud investments. By leveraging AI-driven tools, adopting reserved resource strategies, and enforcing cost-conscious practices, organizations can maintain control over their cloud spending while supporting innovation and scalability. With proactive monitoring and continuous optimization, businesses can strike the perfect balance between cost efficiency and performance.

Conclusion:
Effective cost management is critical for maximizing the value of cloud computing while avoiding unnecessary expenses. In this chapter, we explored how AI-driven tools and strategies empower organizations to monitor, forecast, and optimize cloud spending. By addressing inefficiencies in resource usage and implementing practical budget management techniques, businesses can ensure financial control and scalability.

Key Takeaways
- AI as a Cost Management Ally:
  - AI tools like AWS Cost Explorer, Azure Cost Management, and third-party solutions provide actionable insights into resource usage and spending trends.
  - Predictive analytics and anomaly detection help organizations stay ahead of cost overruns.
- Identifying Inefficiencies:
  - Common inefficiencies such as over-provisioning, idle resources, and redundant workloads can be identified and resolved with AI-powered monitoring tools.
  - Regular audits, automated cleanup, and workload optimization reduce unnecessary expenses.
- Budget Management Practices:
  - Clear budget strategies, reserved resource commitments, and cost-conscious development practices ensure sustainable cloud operations.
  - Automation, tagging, and proactive alerts enforce accountability and financial discipline.

The Bigger Picture
AI-driven cost optimization is more than just a way to save money —it's a strategic approach to aligning cloud spending with business goals. By integrating AI tools into budget management workflows, organizations can create a culture of financial efficiency, enabling them to innovate without the fear of runaway costs. This balance between performance and affordability is crucial in today's cloud-first world.

Looking Ahead
The next chapter, Hybrid and Multi-Cloud Strategies, explores how organizations can leverage multiple cloud environments to improve flexibility, avoid vendor lock-in, and achieve optimal workload placement.

AI Insight:
"AI transforms cloud cost management from a reactive process into a proactive strategy, empowering businesses to innovate with confidence."

Chapter 14: Monitoring, Scaling, and Performance Optimization

Effective monitoring, scaling, and performance optimization are essential to ensuring that cloud environments remain efficient, reliable, and responsive to dynamic workloads. With the integration of AI-driven tools and proactive strategies, organizations can achieve high availability, resource efficiency, and seamless scalability. This chapter explores techniques for observability, scaling, and performance tuning, providing actionable insights and best practices.

Techniques for Observability and Proactive Scaling

Observability is the ability to understand and monitor the internal state of a system based on the data it generates. Proactive scaling ensures resources are dynamically adjusted to meet workload demands, preventing performance bottlenecks or over-provisioning.

1. Observability: Gaining Insights into Cloud Environments

Observability focuses on three pillars: metrics, logs, and traces.
- Metrics:
  - Quantitative data that reflects system performance, such as CPU usage, memory consumption, or response times.
  - Example Tool: Prometheus collects and visualizes metrics, offering insights into resource utilization.
- Logs:
  - Detailed records of system events, helping diagnose issues or track anomalies.
  - Example Tool: AWS CloudWatch Logs aggregates and analyzes log data from multiple sources.
- Traces:
  - Provides end-to-end visibility into request flows, highlighting latency or bottlenecks.
  - Example Tool: Jaeger or Zipkin trace distributed applications.

Proactive Observability Techniques:
- Dashboards: Use tools like Grafana to visualize key metrics and logs in real-time.
- Alerts: Set up alerts for threshold breaches, such as high CPU usage or latency spikes.
- Automation: Leverage AI tools to analyze observability data and predict potential failures.

2. Proactive Scaling: Matching Resources to Demand
Scaling ensures that cloud resources dynamically adapt to workload requirements.
- Horizontal Scaling:
  - Adds or removes instances to handle fluctuations in traffic.
  - Example: A web application increases its EC2 instances during a flash sale and reduces them afterward.
- Vertical Scaling:
  - Adjusts the capacity of existing resources, such as increasing memory or CPU for a VM.
  - Example: Scaling up a database instance to accommodate a surge in queries.
- Predictive Scaling with AI:
  - AI models analyze historical and real-time data to anticipate demand and scale resources accordingly.
  - Example: Google Cloud AutoML forecasts traffic spikes and adjusts Kubernetes pods.

AI Tools for Performance Tuning and Resource Allocation
AI-driven tools are transforming how cloud resources are optimized by offering intelligent insights and automated recommendations.

1. AI in Performance Tuning
AI identifies inefficiencies in workloads and recommends adjustments for optimal performance.
- Load Balancer Optimization:
  - AI analyzes traffic patterns and configures load balancers to distribute traffic efficiently.
  - Example: AWS Elastic Load Balancer with AI integration ensures even distribution across EC2 instances.
- Query Optimization:
  - Machine learning models improve database performance by analyzing and optimizing query execution plans.
  - Example: AI-powered tools in Azure SQL Database recommend index creation or query rewrites.
- Application Profiling:
  - AI profiles application performance to detect code inefficiencies or resource contention.
  - Example: New Relic AI highlights slow API endpoints and suggests refactoring.

2. Resource Allocation with AI
- Dynamic Allocation:
  - AI tools allocate resources based on workload priorities and usage trends.
  - Example: Kubernetes with AI-powered HPA (Horizontal Pod Autoscaler) adjusts pods in real-time.
- Spot Instance Management:
  - AI predicts availability and pricing for spot instances, ensuring cost-effective scaling.
  - Example: Spot.io automates the use of AWS Spot Instances to balance cost and performance.
- Rightsizing Recommendations:
  - AI analyzes historical data to recommend the ideal size for virtual machines or containers.
  - Example: Azure Advisor suggests resizing underutilized VMs for cost savings.

Best Practices for Maintaining High Availability
High availability ensures that applications remain accessible and operational despite failures or fluctuations in demand.

1. Building Resilient Architectures
- Fault Tolerance:
  - Design systems that continue functioning even when individual components fail.
  - Example: Use auto-healing groups in AWS Auto Scaling to replace failed instances.
- Redundancy:
  - Deploy resources across multiple availability zones or regions to avoid single points of failure.
  - Example: Host a database in a primary region with a replica in a secondary region.
- Load Balancing:
  - Distribute traffic across multiple instances to ensure even load distribution.
  - Example: AWS Elastic Load Balancer handles traffic spikes without degrading performance.

2. Monitoring for Availability
- Health Checks:
  - Regularly monitor resource health using tools like AWS CloudWatch or Azure Monitor.
  - Example: Detecting unhealthy EC2 instances and triggering automatic replacement.
- Disaster Recovery Testing:
  - Simulate failures to validate recovery strategies.
  - Example: Use Chaos Engineering tools like Gremlin to test system resilience.

- Real-Time Analytics:
  - Monitor latency, response times, and error rates using tools like Datadog or Splunk.

3. Proactive Maintenance
- Patch Management:
  - Automate software updates to prevent vulnerabilities or performance degradation.
  - Example: AWS Systems Manager automates patching across instances.
- Scalability Testing:
  - Perform load testing to ensure systems can handle peak traffic scenarios.
  - Example: Use Apache JMeter to simulate high-traffic loads.
- Scheduled Resource Cleanup:
  - Remove unused resources to maintain an efficient environment.
  - Example: Automate snapshot deletion using AWS Lambda functions.

Exercises for Readers
- Reflection: Identify gaps in your current observability and scaling strategies. Which AI tools could fill these gaps?
- Hands-On Activity:
  - Configure a real-time observability dashboard using Grafana.
  - Set up predictive scaling with Google Kubernetes Engine or AWS Auto Scaling.
- Case Study: Research how a leading company (e.g., Netflix or Shopify) maintains high availability and optimizes performance in its cloud environment.

Monitoring, scaling, and performance optimization are essential practices for ensuring that cloud environments deliver consistent, reliable, and cost-effective results. By leveraging AI-driven tools and adhering to best practices, organizations can achieve a balance between efficiency and resilience, keeping their systems prepared for any challenge. Whether it's proactive scaling, intelligent resource allocation, or building highly available architectures, these strategies form the backbone of successful cloud operations.

AI Insight:
"AI-powered observability, scaling, and optimization redefine how cloud systems adapt, ensuring peak performance under any circumstances."

Conclusion:
Effective monitoring, scaling, and performance optimization are critical for maintaining a reliable, efficient, and cost-effective cloud environment. This chapter explored how AI-driven tools and best practices enable organizations to gain deeper insights into system behavior, proactively scale resources, and fine-tune performance.

Key Takeaways
1. Observability and Proactive Scaling:
   o Observability pillars (metrics, logs, traces) provide actionable insights into system performance.
   o Proactive scaling, powered by AI, ensures resources align dynamically with workload demands.
2. AI-Driven Performance Optimization:
   o Tools like AWS Elastic Load Balancer, Kubernetes HPA, and New Relic AI automate and optimize resource allocation and application performance.
   o AI recommendations for workload placement, rightsizing, and query optimization reduce inefficiencies.
3. High Availability Best Practices:
   o Fault-tolerant, redundant architectures, combined with real-time monitoring and disaster recovery testing, ensure systems remain operational during failures or demand surges.
   o Automation tools enhance availability by handling updates, resource cleanup, and scaling efficiently.

The Bigger Picture
As organizations increasingly rely on the cloud to support mission-critical applications, monitoring, scaling, and optimization become non-negotiable pillars of success. AI amplifies these practices, transforming reactive processes into proactive strategies that maximize efficiency, reliability, and scalability. By adopting these techniques, readers can ensure their cloud environments remain robust and responsive to evolving demands.

Looking Ahead
The next chapter, Cost Management and FinOps, dives deeper into strategies for aligning cloud spending with organizational objectives, ensuring financial efficiency without compromising performance.

AI Insight:
"By leveraging AI and best practices, monitoring and scaling evolve from manual tasks into intelligent, automated processes that drive cloud success."

Chapter 15: Cost Management and FinOps

Cost management is a critical component of effective cloud computing, ensuring businesses can leverage the scalability and flexibility of the cloud without incurring unnecessary expenses. Financial Operations (FinOps) introduces a strategic framework to align cloud spending with business objectives, enabling teams to track, optimize, and forecast expenses. This chapter explores FinOps strategies, essential tools, and actionable methods to forecast costs for future projects.

1. Introduction to FinOps and Its Importance
What is FinOps?
Financial Operations, or FinOps, is a collaborative financial management approach tailored to the dynamic nature of cloud computing. It combines best practices from finance, operations, and technology to provide visibility, accountability, and efficiency in cloud spending.

Why FinOps is Essential
- Dynamic Pricing Models:
  - Cloud providers operate on a pay-as-you-go model, which requires continuous monitoring to avoid overspending.
- Cross-Team Collaboration:
  - FinOps bridges the gap between engineering, finance, and leadership, ensuring unified decision-making.
- Scalability Challenges:
  - As cloud usage scales, so do costs. FinOps ensures scaling is efficient and cost-effective.
- AI Integration:
  - Modern FinOps integrates AI tools for real-time monitoring, predictive analytics, and automated recommendations.

AI Insight:
"FinOps transforms cloud cost management into a proactive, collaborative process, enabling teams to align spending with business goals."

2. Core Principles of FinOps
FinOps operates on several foundational principles that guide effective cloud budgeting and cost management.
Visibility
- Provide stakeholders with clear insights into cloud spending.
- Best Practices:
  - Use dashboards to monitor real-time costs.
  - Implement resource tagging for granular cost tracking.

Accountability
- Assign ownership of cloud spending to individual teams or departments.
- Best Practices:
  - Align budgets with specific projects or workloads.
  - Conduct regular reviews to ensure teams stay within budget.

Optimization
- Continuously evaluate and optimize cloud spending for efficiency.
- Best Practices:
  - Right-size resources and eliminate redundancies.
  - Adopt reserved instances or savings plans for predictable workloads.

3. Tools for Tracking and Optimizing Expenses

Cloud Provider Tools
- AWS Cost Management
  - Real-time cost monitoring and forecasting.
  - Budget alerts for overages.
  - Example Use Case: Identifying and eliminating unused EC2 instances.
- Azure Cost Management and Billing
  - Detailed cost analysis for Azure services.
  - AI-powered recommendations for optimization.
  - Example Use Case: Transitioning underutilized resources to a cheaper pricing tier.
- Google Cloud Billing
  - Spending insights and budgeting tools.
  - Cost forecasts based on historical trends.
  - Example Use Case: Monitoring multi-project costs with BigQuery integration.

Third-Party Tools
- CloudHealth by VMware
  - Tracks multi-cloud spending and provides optimization insights.
  - Ideal for enterprises with hybrid or multi-cloud setups.
- Spot.io
  - Focuses on automating resource allocation to reduce costs.
  - Excels in managing spot instances for non-critical workloads.
- Harness FinOps
  - Integrates with DevOps pipelines to provide real-time cost estimates during deployments.

4. FinOps Strategies for Cloud Budgeting

Establishing Budgets and Cost Centers
- Set Budget Thresholds:
  - Define spending limits for projects, teams, or services.
  - Example: Allocate $5,000 per month for a development environment.
- Tagging Resources:
  - Use tags to track costs by project, department, or environment.
  - Example: Tag resources with labels like "Production" or "QA" for easier attribution.
- Track Key Metrics:
  - Monitor metrics like cost per transaction or cost per user.
  - Example: Track how much a single API call costs for a SaaS product.

Automating Cost Management
- Real-Time Alerts:
  - Configure alerts for budget breaches or unusual spending patterns.
  - Example: AWS Budgets sends notifications when costs exceed 80% of the allocated budget.
- Scheduled Cleanups:
  - Automate the decommissioning of unused resources.
  - Example: Use AWS Lambda to remove unattached EBS volumes weekly.
- Auto-Scaling:
  - Implement dynamic resource scaling to avoid over-provisioning.
  - Example: Azure Autoscale adjusts VM instances based on real-time demand.

5. Forecasting Costs for Future Projects

Accurate cost forecasting helps organizations plan budgets effectively and avoid unexpected overages.

1. How AI Enhances Cost Forecasting
- Historical Data Analysis:
  - AI models analyze past spending patterns to predict future costs.
  - Example: Predicting next month's Kubernetes cluster costs based on current usage trends.
- Scenario Modeling:
  - Simulate different scenarios, such as traffic spikes or workload scaling.
  - Example: Estimate costs for a product launch with a projected 200% traffic increase.

- Usage Correlation:
  - Correlate resource usage with business metrics like customer growth or feature adoption.
  - Example: Estimating increased database costs for a new analytics feature.

2. Steps to Forecast Costs
- Define Project Scope:
  - Outline the resources required for the project, including compute, storage, and network.
- Identify Cost Drivers:
  - Determine which services contribute most to expenses.
  - Example: High-cost drivers might include machine learning workloads or large-scale data transfers.
- Simulate Scenarios:
  - Use AI tools to simulate best-case, worst-case, and expected scenarios.
- Review and Adjust:
  - Continuously refine forecasts based on real-time data and changing requirements.

6. Challenges in FinOps and How to Overcome Them
Challenge 1: Lack of Visibility
- Solution: Use tagging and dashboards to provide detailed cost breakdowns.

Challenge 2: Resistance to Accountability
- Solution: Foster a culture of cost ownership by aligning spending with team goals.

Challenge 3: Complexity of Multi-Cloud Environments
- Solution: Use third-party tools like CloudHealth to manage costs across providers.

Challenge 4: Unpredictable Usage Patterns
- Solution: Leverage AI forecasting and predictive scaling to handle variability.

Exercises for Readers
- Reflection: Identify the top three cost drivers in your organization's cloud environment. How could FinOps strategies improve their efficiency?
- Hands-On Activity:
  - Use AWS Budgets or Azure Cost Management to create a budget for a specific project.
  - Implement tagging for resources and track spending by department or environment.
- Case Study: Research how a leading company, such as Spotify or Airbnb, implemented FinOps to control cloud costs and improve efficiency.

Cost management and FinOps are not just financial strategies—they are enablers of sustainable innovation in the cloud. By integrating FinOps principles, leveraging AI-driven tools, and adopting proactive budgeting practices, organizations can align cloud spending with business goals while maintaining scalability and performance.

AI Insight:
"FinOps transforms cost management into a collaborative and proactive process, empowering teams to innovate without overspending."

Conclusion:
Cost management in cloud computing is a critical component of financial efficiency and sustainable innovation. This chapter has provided a comprehensive overview of how FinOps strategies, AI-driven tools, and proactive budgeting practices can empower organizations to optimize their cloud spending while achieving their business goals.

Key Takeaways
- Understanding FinOps Principles:
  - FinOps emphasizes visibility, accountability, and optimization, aligning cloud costs with organizational objectives.
  - Collaboration between finance, engineering, and leadership ensures informed decision-making.
- Leveraging AI Tools for Cost Management:
  - AI-powered tools like AWS Cost Explorer, Azure Cost Management, and third-party platforms offer real-time insights, predictive forecasting, and actionable recommendations.
  - Automation and anomaly detection streamline cost tracking and resource allocation.
- Proactive Budgeting and Optimization:
  - Strategies such as tagging resources, setting budget thresholds, and automating cleanups ensure financial control.
  - Forecasting future costs with AI improves budget planning and minimizes surprises.
- Continuous Improvement:
  - Regular audits, ongoing optimization, and scenario modeling allow organizations to adapt to changing workloads and business priorities.

The Bigger Picture
FinOps is more than a cost-management framework—it's a mindset that enables organizations to harness the full potential of the cloud without overspending. By fostering a culture of financial accountability and leveraging advanced tools and strategies, businesses can scale confidently while maintaining control over their budgets. In an era where cloud usage is both a competitive advantage and a financial challenge, FinOps provides the roadmap to balance innovation with efficiency.

Looking Ahead
The next chapter, Disaster Recovery and Backup, explores strategies for safeguarding data and ensuring business continuity in the face of potential disruptions, offering practical solutions for resilient cloud operations.

AI Insight:
"FinOps is the bridge between cloud innovation and financial efficiency, ensuring every dollar spent contributes to business value."

Chapter 16: Hybrid and Multi-Cloud Strategies

In today's diverse cloud computing landscape, organizations often opt for hybrid or multi-cloud strategies to achieve flexibility, scalability, and resilience. Hybrid cloud combines on-premises infrastructure with public or private cloud services, while multi-cloud uses multiple cloud providers to meet specific needs. This chapter explores the benefits, challenges, and tools for hybrid and multi-cloud setups, along with real-world use cases that demonstrate their potential.

1. Benefits and Challenges of Hybrid and Multi-Cloud Setups
A. Benefits of Hybrid Cloud
- Flexibility and Scalability:
  - Hybrid cloud enables organizations to keep sensitive workloads on-premises while scaling non-critical tasks to the public cloud.
  - Example: A financial institution processes customer data on-premises for compliance but uses public cloud resources for analytics.
- Cost Efficiency:
  - Organizations can balance costs by optimizing workloads for cheaper on-premises or cloud environments based on resource needs.
  - Example: Running predictable workloads on-premises to save on cloud computing costs.
- Improved Disaster Recovery:
  - By integrating on-premises infrastructure with cloud backups, hybrid setups enhance business continuity during failures.
  - Example: Backing up critical databases to AWS S3 for off-site redundancy.

B. Benefits of Multi-Cloud
- Avoiding Vendor Lock-In:
  - Multi-cloud strategies prevent dependency on a single provider, giving businesses the freedom to switch or negotiate better terms.
  - Example: Hosting a web application on Azure while using Google Cloud for machine learning workloads.
- Performance Optimization:
  - Organizations can leverage the strengths of each provider to optimize performance for specific workloads.
  - Example: Using AWS Lambda for serverless functions and Google BigQuery for data warehousing.

- Global Reach:
  - Multi-cloud setups take advantage of different providers' global data centers to reduce latency and meet regulatory requirements.
  - Example: Deploying applications in AWS's US region and Azure's Europe region to meet data sovereignty laws.

C. Challenges of Hybrid and Multi-Cloud
- Complexity of Management:
  - Managing multiple environments increases operational complexity, requiring specialized tools and expertise.
- Interoperability Issues:
  - Differences in APIs, services, and configurations across providers can make integration challenging.
- Security and Compliance Risks:
  - Ensuring consistent security policies across environments requires robust monitoring and governance.

AI Insight:
"Hybrid and multi-cloud strategies offer flexibility and resilience, but they demand robust planning and specialized tools to mitigate complexity."

2. Tools for Seamless Integration Between Multiple Providers
Seamless integration between cloud environments is critical for ensuring that hybrid and multi-cloud setups operate efficiently.

A. Cloud-Native Integration Tools
- AWS Outposts:
  - Extends AWS services to on-premises environments for hybrid cloud setups.
  - Use Case: Running latency-sensitive applications on-premises while integrating with AWS's public cloud.
- Azure Arc:
  - Manages resources across hybrid and multi-cloud environments from a single interface.
  - Use Case: Monitoring Kubernetes clusters on both Azure and Google Cloud.
- Google Anthos:
  - A multi-cloud platform for managing Kubernetes clusters and workloads across cloud providers.
  - Use Case: Deploying containerized applications across AWS and Google Cloud seamlessly.

B. Third-Party Multi-Cloud Tools
- VMware Cloud on AWS:
  - Enables organizations to run VMware workloads in the AWS Cloud.

- Use Case: Migrating on-premises VMware virtual machines to the cloud without refactoring.
- HashiCorp Terraform:
  - A multi-cloud Infrastructure as Code (IaC) tool for provisioning and managing resources across providers.
  - Use Case: Automating deployments across AWS, Azure, and Google Cloud.
- Cisco CloudCenter Suite:
  - Provides governance, workload placement, and cost optimization across hybrid and multi-cloud environments.
  - Use Case: Centralizing workload management across on-premises and cloud platforms.

C. AI-Powered Integration Tools
- Aviatrix:
  - AI-driven platform for managing multi-cloud networking, security, and automation.
  - Use Case: Streamlining network traffic between AWS and Azure regions.
- Datadog:
  - Monitors performance and security across hybrid and multi-cloud environments using AI-powered insights.
  - Use Case: Detecting anomalies in traffic patterns between on-premises and cloud resources.
- Splunk Observability Cloud:
  - AI-enhanced tool for monitoring logs, metrics, and traces across multiple cloud providers.
  - Use Case: Correlating performance data from applications hosted on AWS and Azure.

3. Real-World Examples of Hybrid Cloud Use Cases
A. Financial Services
Scenario:
- A bank must comply with stringent data privacy regulations, requiring customer data to remain on-premises while leveraging the public cloud for analytics.
Solution:
- Use AWS Outposts for on-premises data processing and AWS SageMaker for machine learning analytics.
Outcome:
- Achieved compliance while enhancing data-driven decision-making.

B. Healthcare
Scenario:
- A hospital manages sensitive patient records locally but needs cloud resources for telemedicine applications.

Solution:
- Integrate Microsoft Azure Stack with Azure public cloud for secure data storage and scalable telemedicine solutions.

Outcome:
- Improved patient care with secure and scalable infrastructure.

C. Retail
Scenario:
- An e-commerce company operates globally and needs low-latency services across regions.

Solution:
- Use Google Anthos to deploy containerized applications across AWS, Google Cloud, and on-premises data centers.

Outcome:
- Reduced latency and increased customer satisfaction through localized deployments.

Exercises for Readers
- Reflection: Which workloads in your organization could benefit most from a hybrid or multi-cloud setup?
- Hands-On Activity:
  - Deploy a hybrid cloud application using AWS Outposts or Azure Arc.
  - Use HashiCorp Terraform to provision resources across two different cloud providers.
- Case Study: Research how a major company, such as Netflix or General Electric, uses hybrid or multi-cloud strategies to meet its operational goals.

Hybrid and multi-cloud strategies empower organizations to achieve flexibility, scalability, and resilience by leveraging the strengths of multiple environments. While these setups introduce complexity, the right tools and best practices ensure seamless integration and management. By adopting hybrid and multi-cloud approaches, businesses can optimize costs, meet compliance requirements, and enhance performance in a dynamic, global market.

AI Insight:
"Hybrid and multi-cloud strategies offer the best of both worlds—enabling organizations to customize their cloud approach to meet diverse and evolving needs."

Conclusion:

Hybrid and multi-cloud strategies are transformative approaches that empower organizations to combine the strengths of on-premises infrastructure and multiple cloud providers. These strategies address diverse business needs, offering flexibility, scalability, and resilience in a dynamic digital landscape. While hybrid cloud ensures compliance, performance, and integration of legacy systems, multi-cloud solutions provide organizations with the agility to optimize performance, avoid vendor lock-in, and expand globally.

Key Takeaways

1. Hybrid Cloud Benefits and Use Cases:
   - Combines on-premises control with public cloud scalability for optimal workload management.
   - Real-world applications in industries like healthcare, finance, and retail demonstrate its value for compliance and performance.
2. Multi-Cloud Benefits and Use Cases:
   - Leverages the best features of different providers to optimize cost, performance, and availability.
   - Real-world examples show how multi-cloud supports global reach and workload-specific optimization.
3. Tools for Seamless Integration:
   - Solutions like AWS Outposts, Azure Arc, and Google Anthos enable smooth hybrid and multi-cloud operations.
   - Third-party tools such as Terraform and Aviatrix simplify resource provisioning and multi-cloud networking.

The Bigger Picture

Hybrid and multi-cloud strategies represent the future of cloud computing, offering organizations the ability to customize their infrastructure to meet specific operational needs. While these setups require careful planning and robust tools to manage complexity, they deliver unparalleled benefits in terms of flexibility, cost optimization, and resilience. For businesses seeking to thrive in an increasingly interconnected world, hybrid and multi-cloud approaches provide a competitive edge.

Looking Ahead

The next chapter, Disaster Recovery and Backup, explores how to safeguard data and ensure business continuity in the event of system failures or cyberattacks, a critical complement to hybrid and multi-cloud strategies.

AI Insight:

"By adopting hybrid and multi-cloud strategies, businesses can build an infrastructure that is not only resilient but also adaptable to evolving demands."

Chapter 17: AI-Powered Hybrid and Multi-Cloud Management

Managing hybrid and multi-cloud environments is inherently complex, requiring seamless integration, consistent performance, and robust security across diverse platforms. AI-powered tools are transforming this landscape, simplifying workload management, automating resource orchestration, and mitigating vendor lock-in risks. This chapter explores how AI empowers organizations to optimize their hybrid and multi-cloud strategies, providing actionable insights and real-world applications.

1. How AI Simplifies Cross-Cloud Workload Management
AI has become an essential ally in managing workloads across multiple clouds and on-premises systems, helping organizations overcome the complexities of hybrid and multi-cloud setups.
A. The Challenges of Cross-Cloud Workload Management
Resource Distribution:
- Balancing workloads across multiple clouds to optimize performance and costs.
- Example: A workload may need to split data processing between AWS and Azure to meet regulatory requirements.

Performance Consistency:
- Ensuring consistent application performance despite differences in infrastructure or APIs across providers.

Monitoring and Visibility:
- Gaining real-time insights into workloads distributed across platforms.

B. AI's Role in Simplifying Workload Management
Real-Time Insights:
- AI-driven tools monitor workloads across multiple platforms, providing unified dashboards for real-time metrics like CPU usage, latency, and costs.
- Example Tool: Splunk Observability Cloud offers cross-cloud monitoring with AI-powered anomaly detection.

Dynamic Workload Allocation:
- Machine learning algorithms analyze workload demands and automatically allocate resources to the most efficient provider.
- Example: AI redirects traffic between AWS and Google Cloud based on latency or cost factors.

Streamlined Operations:
- AI identifies inefficiencies, such as redundant processes or underutilized resources, and suggests optimizations.
- Example: Recommending workload migration from an underutilized Azure instance to a more cost-effective AWS EC2 instance.

AI Insight:
"AI turns complex cross-cloud management into a streamlined, efficient process, empowering teams to focus on innovation rather than operational hurdles."

2. Automating Resource Orchestration with AI
Resource orchestration ensures that workloads and applications are efficiently deployed, scaled, and managed across hybrid and multi-cloud environments. AI introduces automation into this process, reducing manual effort and improving resource utilization.
A. AI-Driven Orchestration Platforms
- Kubernetes and AI-Powered Extensions:
    ○ Kubernetes provides container orchestration, and AI tools enhance its capabilities by predicting workload demands and optimizing pod placement.
    ○ Example: Kubeflow automates machine learning workflows across hybrid environments.
- Terraform with AI Integration:
    ○ AI-enhanced Terraform modules suggest optimal configurations for multi-cloud deployments.
    ○ Example: AI analyzes resource requirements and generates Infrastructure as Code templates for AWS and Google Cloud.
- Aviatrix Multi-Cloud Networking:
    ○ Automates network provisioning and management across clouds using AI to optimize traffic flows.
    ○ Example: Redirecting traffic between Azure and AWS regions to avoid latency during high-demand periods.

B. Automating Common Orchestration Tasks
- Scaling:
    ○ AI dynamically scales resources up or down based on real-time workload analysis.
    ○ Example: Auto-scaling an application on Azure Kubernetes Service during traffic spikes.
- Deployment Optimization:
    ○ AI selects the best provider and region for deploying workloads based on cost, latency, and compliance factors.
    ○ Example: Deploying a database to an AWS region closest to end-users for reduced latency.
- Disaster Recovery:
    ○ AI monitors resource health and automatically triggers failovers or backups in case of outages.
    ○ Example: Migrating workloads from a failed Google Cloud region to Azure during a regional outage.

3. Reducing Vendor Lock-In Risks Using Intelligent Platforms

Vendor lock-in is a significant concern in multi-cloud strategies, as organizations may become overly reliant on a single provider. AI helps mitigate this risk by enabling seamless migration, integration, and optimization across platforms.

A. How AI Reduces Lock-In Risks
- Cross-Cloud Compatibility:
  - AI tools abstract provider-specific APIs, creating a unified management layer.
  - Example: Anthos allows applications to run on-premises and across AWS, Azure, and Google Cloud without modification.
- Resource Optimization Across Providers:
  - AI compares resource costs and performance across providers, suggesting alternative setups to avoid dependence on a single cloud.
  - Example: AI recommends shifting a batch processing workload from AWS Lambda to Azure Functions for cost savings.
- Automated Migration:
  - AI automates workload migration between providers, minimizing downtime and manual effort.
  - Example: Migrating containerized applications from Google Kubernetes Engine to Azure Kubernetes Service using AI-driven orchestration.

B. Intelligent Platforms for Vendor Independence
- HashiCorp Nomad:
  - Provides multi-cloud workload orchestration, allowing seamless migration and deployment.
  - Use Case: Deploying the same application across AWS, Azure, and on-premises systems.
- VMware Tanzu:
  - Unifies application management across hybrid and multi-cloud environments.
  - Use Case: Running and scaling Kubernetes applications on multiple clouds without vendor dependencies.
- CloudHealth by VMware:
  - Offers multi-cloud cost management and optimization, enabling businesses to evaluate vendor performance.
  - Use Case: Analyzing cost-performance trade-offs between Google Cloud and Azure for a specific workload.

AI Insight:
"AI empowers organizations to adopt a cloud-agnostic approach, unlocking the flexibility to switch providers and avoid lock-in."

Exercises for Readers
- Reflection: Identify potential vendor lock-in risks in your current cloud strategy. How could AI tools help reduce these dependencies?
- Hands-On Activity:
  - Use Kubernetes to deploy a containerized application across two different cloud providers.
  - Experiment with Terraform to create Infrastructure as Code templates for a hybrid deployment.
- Case Study: Research how a company, like Spotify or GE, uses AI to manage workloads across hybrid and multi-cloud environments.

AI-powered tools and platforms are redefining hybrid and multi-cloud management by simplifying workload orchestration, automating resource allocation, and mitigating vendor lock-in risks. By leveraging AI, organizations can transform complex, distributed environments into streamlined, efficient systems that adapt dynamically to workload demands. These strategies not only enhance performance and scalability but also enable businesses to stay agile in a rapidly evolving cloud landscape.

AI Insight:
"With AI, managing hybrid and multi-cloud environments becomes a strategic advantage, enabling organizations to balance flexibility, performance, and cost-effectiveness."

Conclusion:
Managing hybrid and multi-cloud environments is a complex task, but AI-powered tools and platforms are revolutionizing how organizations approach these challenges. By automating workload orchestration, optimizing resource allocation, and mitigating vendor lock-in risks, AI empowers businesses to unlock the full potential of their cloud strategies.

Key Takeaways
- Simplified Cross-Cloud Management:
  - AI tools streamline workload distribution and enhance visibility across diverse environments, reducing operational complexity.
  - Real-time insights and dynamic workload allocation ensure consistent performance and cost-efficiency.

- Automated Resource Orchestration:
  - Platforms like Kubernetes, Terraform, and Aviatrix, enhanced with AI capabilities, enable seamless scaling, deployment, and failover operations.
  - Automated orchestration ensures optimal resource utilization while minimizing manual effort.
- Reduced Vendor Lock-In Risks:
  - AI-driven platforms foster cross-cloud compatibility, simplifying migration and enabling cost-performance optimization across providers.
  - Intelligent tools like Anthos and Nomad promote a cloud-agnostic approach, granting organizations the freedom to adapt to changing needs.

The Bigger Picture
AI-powered management transforms hybrid and multi-cloud environments from a logistical challenge into a strategic advantage. By simplifying operations and enhancing flexibility, AI allows businesses to focus on innovation, scalability, and resilience. These tools not only ensure performance and cost optimization but also future-proof cloud strategies in an ever-evolving technological landscape.

Looking Ahead
The next chapter, Disaster Recovery and Backup, explores how to secure cloud environments against unexpected disruptions and maintain business continuity, a critical complement to AI-powered cloud management.

AI Insight:
"AI is not just a tool for managing hybrid and multi-cloud setups—it's a strategic partner that enables businesses to thrive in complexity."

Chapter 18: Edge Computing and IoT

Role of Edge Computing in IoT Applications
The Internet of Things (IoT) is transforming industries by connecting devices, sensors, and systems to enable real-time data collection and analysis. However, the centralized nature of traditional cloud computing can hinder IoT applications due to latency, bandwidth constraints, and privacy concerns. Edge computing solves these challenges by bringing computation and storage closer to the data source. This section explores the critical role of edge computing in IoT, highlighting its advantages, use cases, and transformative impact.

1. Understanding Edge Computing in the IoT Context
Edge computing refers to the processing and storage of data at or near the source of generation, rather than relying solely on centralized cloud servers. In IoT, this approach ensures faster response times, reduces network dependency, and supports the demands of resource-constrained environments.

Core Concepts
- Local Processing:
  - Data is processed locally at the edge, enabling devices to act on information without needing to communicate with distant servers.
  - Example: A smart thermostat adjusts temperature settings based on sensor inputs without sending data to the cloud.
- Data Reduction:
  - By processing raw data locally, only relevant insights are sent to the cloud, reducing bandwidth usage.
  - Example: A security camera analyzes video streams for motion detection locally and uploads only flagged footage.
- Real-Time Insights:
  - Immediate processing at the edge allows IoT devices to deliver actionable insights with minimal delay.
  - Example: Industrial robots in a factory use edge computing to adjust operations dynamically in response to sensor feedback.

2. Advantages of Edge Computing for IoT

Edge computing overcomes several limitations of cloud-centric IoT architectures, offering significant benefits that enhance performance, reliability, and security.

A. Low Latency

Latency is a critical factor for IoT applications requiring instantaneous responses. Cloud-based architectures introduce delays due to the time needed to transmit data to remote servers and back.

- Edge Computing Solution:
  - By processing data locally, edge computing reduces latency to milliseconds.
  - Use Case: In autonomous vehicles, edge computing enables real-time analysis of sensor data to detect obstacles and make driving decisions instantly.

B. Bandwidth Efficiency

IoT devices generate massive volumes of data, which can overwhelm network bandwidth when transmitted to centralized servers.

- Edge Computing Solution:
  - Local data processing minimizes the amount of data sent to the cloud, conserving bandwidth.
  - Use Case: In smart cities, edge devices analyze traffic patterns locally and only send summary reports to the cloud.

C. Enhanced Privacy and Security

Transmitting sensitive data to the cloud increases the risk of breaches and exposure to cyber threats.

- Edge Computing Solution:
  - Keeping data localized reduces its exposure during transmission and minimizes privacy risks.
  - Use Case: Wearable health devices store and process patient data locally, ensuring privacy while delivering actionable insights to users.

3. Key IoT Applications Powered by Edge Computing
Edge computing has unlocked a wide array of use cases across industries, transforming how IoT applications operate.

A. Industrial IoT (IIoT)
In manufacturing, edge computing plays a pivotal role in optimizing production processes and reducing downtime.
- Predictive Maintenance:
  - Edge devices monitor machinery performance and predict failures before they occur.
  - Example: A factory uses edge sensors to analyze vibration data from equipment, enabling maintenance teams to address issues proactively.
- Process Optimization:
  - Real-time data processing at the edge allows factories to adjust production lines dynamically.
  - Example: Edge systems in a bottling plant regulate conveyor speeds based on sensor feedback.

B. Smart Cities
Edge computing supports the development of smarter, more efficient urban environments.
- Traffic Management:
  - Sensors and cameras process data locally to optimize traffic light timings and reduce congestion.
  - Example: An edge-enabled traffic system adjusts signals based on real-time vehicle counts.
- Environmental Monitoring:
  - Edge devices analyze air quality data and alert authorities about pollution hotspots.
  - Example: A city deploys edge sensors to detect and respond to hazardous gas leaks.

C. Healthcare
Edge computing enhances patient care by enabling real-time monitoring and decision-making.
- Remote Patient Monitoring:
  - Wearable devices process data locally to detect health anomalies and alert healthcare providers.
  - Example: A heart monitor uses edge computing to trigger alerts for irregular heartbeats.
- Medical Imaging:
  - Edge systems analyze medical images at the point of care, reducing diagnosis times.
  - Example: An edge-enabled imaging device provides instant X-ray analysis in rural clinics.

D. Retail
Retailers leverage edge computing to enhance customer experiences and optimize operations.
- In-Store Analytics:
  - Edge devices analyze shopper behavior to provide personalized recommendations.
  - Example: A smart kiosk processes customer interactions locally to suggest products.
- Inventory Management:
  - Sensors at the edge track inventory levels and automate reordering processes.
  - Example: A grocery store uses edge computing to monitor stock and predict demand.

4. Challenges in Edge Computing for IoT
Despite its advantages, edge computing in IoT also presents challenges that must be addressed for successful implementation.

A. Resource Constraints
IoT devices often have limited processing power, memory, and storage, which can restrict the complexity of computations they can perform.
- Potential Solution: Use specialized hardware like NVIDIA Jetson or Google Coral designed for edge AI applications.

B. Interoperability Issues
Integrating devices from different manufacturers and ensuring seamless communication can be challenging.
- Potential Solution: Adopt standardized protocols and platforms, such as MQTT and EdgeX Foundry, to enable interoperability.

C. Security Concerns
While edge computing enhances privacy, edge devices themselves can become targets for cyberattacks.
- Potential Solution: Implement robust security measures, such as encryption and regular firmware updates, to protect edge devices.

5. Future Potential of Edge Computing in IoT
The combination of edge computing and IoT continues to evolve, driven by advancements in hardware, software, and connectivity.

A. AI-Enhanced Edge Systems
As AI algorithms become more efficient, edge devices will handle increasingly complex computations, further reducing dependency on cloud processing.

B. Integration with 5G Networks
The widespread adoption of 5G will amplify the capabilities of edge computing, enabling ultra-low latency and massive IoT deployments.

C. Expanding Use Cases
From agriculture to autonomous systems, edge computing is set to play a central role in powering innovative IoT applications.

Edge computing is revolutionizing IoT by addressing the latency, bandwidth, and privacy challenges associated with centralized cloud processing. By enabling real-time decision-making at the edge, it unlocks transformative applications across industries, paving the way for smarter, faster, and more responsive systems.

AI Insight:
"Edge computing is the linchpin of IoT innovation, bringing the power of real-time intelligence to the devices that shape our connected world."

AI-Powered Solutions for Low-Latency Processing
In the rapidly evolving world of IoT and edge computing, low-latency processing is critical for ensuring real-time responsiveness and seamless user experiences. AI-powered solutions play a pivotal role in achieving this by enabling intelligent data analysis and decision-making directly at the edge. This section explores how AI enhances low-latency processing, the technologies driving these advancements, and the diverse applications across industries.

1. Why Low-Latency Processing is Critical
Low latency—the ability to process and respond to data with minimal delay—is essential for IoT systems that operate in dynamic, high-stakes environments. Applications such as autonomous vehicles, industrial robotics, and smart healthcare demand real-time insights to function effectively.

Challenges of Traditional Architectures
- Network Dependency:
  - Reliance on centralized cloud systems introduces delays due to data transmission and server processing times.
- Scalability Constraints:
  - As the number of IoT devices grows, centralized architectures struggle to handle the sheer volume of data.
- Resource Bottlenecks:
  - Bandwidth limitations and high costs hinder the transmission of large datasets to remote servers.

How AI Addresses These Challenges
AI-powered solutions reduce reliance on centralized processing by enabling localized data analysis. This approach ensures:
- Real-Time Decision-Making: AI models deployed at the edge analyze data instantly, avoiding the latency of round-trip cloud communications.

- Bandwidth Optimization: By processing raw data locally and transmitting only actionable insights, AI reduces the load on networks.
- Scalability: AI tools can handle complex computations across distributed devices, supporting large-scale IoT deployments.

2. Core Technologies Enabling AI at the Edge
AI-powered low-latency processing relies on a combination of hardware, software, and innovative algorithms designed for edge environments.

A. Edge AI Hardware
- NVIDIA Jetson:
  - Purpose-built for AI workloads at the edge, Jetson modules support real-time video analytics, autonomous machines, and smart cities.
  - Example: A retail store uses Jetson-enabled cameras to analyze shopper behavior and optimize displays in real time.
- Google Coral:
  - Provides edge devices with high-speed tensor processing for machine learning tasks.
  - Example: Coral hardware powers IoT sensors in agriculture, detecting soil quality changes instantly.
- Intel Movidius:
  - Specialized for computer vision and deep learning tasks in resource-constrained environments.
  - Example: Drones equipped with Movidius chips analyze aerial images to assess crop health on the fly.

B. Lightweight AI Models
- TinyML:
  - ○ Focuses on running machine learning models on resource-constrained devices, enabling high performance with minimal power consumption.
  - ○ Example: A wearable fitness tracker uses TinyML to detect and analyze physical activity patterns locally.
- Pruned Neural Networks:
  - ○ AI models are optimized by removing redundant connections, reducing computational overhead without sacrificing accuracy.
  - ○ Example: Edge cameras use pruned networks for facial recognition at security checkpoints.
- Federated Learning:
  - ○ Trains AI models across multiple edge devices without transmitting sensitive data to the cloud.
  - ○ Example: Smartphones improve predictive text models by learning from user inputs locally.

3. Applications of AI-Powered Low-Latency Solutions
AI's ability to process data instantly at the edge has revolutionized a variety of industries, enabling applications that were previously unattainable due to latency constraints.

A. Autonomous Systems
- Self-Driving Cars:
  - ○ AI at the edge processes sensor data (e.g., LIDAR, cameras) in real time to detect obstacles, make navigation decisions, and ensure safety.
  - ○ Example: Tesla's autopilot system relies on edge AI to perform lane detection and object recognition with split-second precision.
- Delivery Drones:
  - ○ Edge AI analyzes weather conditions, terrain, and obstacles to optimize flight paths.
  - ○ Example: A delivery drone avoids power lines and adjusts its route dynamically during delivery.

B. Industrial Automation
- Robotics:
  - ○ Factory robots equipped with AI-powered edge systems adjust their operations in real time based on environmental changes.
  - ○ Example: A robotic arm in an automotive plant recalibrates its movements to adapt to new assembly line configurations.

- Predictive Maintenance:
  - AI models deployed at the edge monitor equipment health and predict failures before they occur.
  - Example: Sensors on wind turbines detect anomalies in vibration patterns and trigger maintenance alerts.

C. Smart Healthcare
- Wearable Devices:
  - AI processes biometric data locally to detect anomalies, reducing dependency on cloud systems for critical alerts.
  - Example: A heart monitor triggers an alert for arrhythmias without needing cloud connectivity.
- Point-of-Care Diagnostics:
  - Edge AI devices analyze medical images (e.g., X-rays, MRIs) instantly, accelerating diagnosis and treatment decisions.
  - Example: Portable diagnostic tools in remote clinics provide real-time analysis of patient scans.

D. Smart Retail
- Personalized Recommendations:
  - AI-powered kiosks analyze shopper preferences locally to provide tailored product suggestions.
  - Example: A retail display recommends products based on a customer's browsing history analyzed at the edge.
- Inventory Optimization:
  - Edge devices track stock levels and predict demand, enabling just-in-time restocking.
  - Example: AI sensors in a grocery store reorder perishable items automatically when inventory runs low.

4. Benefits of AI-Powered Low-Latency Processing
AI-driven low-latency solutions unlock significant advantages for businesses and users alike.

A. Enhanced User Experience
- Faster Response Times: Instant data processing ensures smoother interactions with IoT devices.
- Example: A smart home system responds immediately to voice commands, adjusting lighting and temperature.

B. Cost Efficiency
- Reduced Bandwidth Usage: By transmitting only actionable insights, AI minimizes data transfer costs.
- Example: An edge-enabled surveillance system uploads flagged events instead of continuous video streams.

C. Scalability
- Supports Large Deployments: Distributed AI models handle growing numbers of IoT devices without overwhelming centralized resources.
- Example: A citywide network of AI-powered traffic cameras scales seamlessly with urban expansion.

5. Future Potential of AI-Powered Edge Solutions
As AI and edge computing continue to evolve, new possibilities for low-latency processing are emerging.

A. Integration with 5G
5G networks will further enhance low-latency capabilities, enabling more complex and time-sensitive AI applications.
- Example: Smart transportation systems coordinate vehicles, pedestrians, and infrastructure in real time.

B. AI-Enhanced Federated Learning
Future advancements in federated learning will allow edge devices to share insights without compromising privacy.
- Example: Federated AI trains smart home devices to optimize energy usage collectively.

C. Autonomous Edge Networks
AI will power self-managing edge networks that dynamically allocate resources based on workload demands.
- Example: An autonomous network adjusts compute power in a disaster zone to prioritize emergency services.

AI-powered solutions are transforming edge computing by enabling low-latency processing that supports real-time applications across diverse industries. By combining advanced hardware, efficient algorithms, and innovative use cases, AI ensures that IoT systems can operate faster, smarter, and more efficiently. As technologies like 5G and federated learning mature, the potential for AI at the edge will only continue to grow.

AI Insight:
"AI at the edge unlocks real-time responsiveness, making it a cornerstone of future IoT and edge computing innovations."

Future Trends in 5G and IoT-Enabled Cloud Technologies
The rise of 5G technology is reshaping the landscape of IoT and cloud computing. With faster speeds, ultra-low latency, and support for massive device connectivity, 5G enables a new generation of IoT applications. Coupled with advancements in edge computing and AI, 5G allows cloud technologies to operate closer to end-users and devices, driving real-time processing, faster data transfers, and greater system efficiency. This section explores key future trends in 5G and IoT-enabled cloud technologies, with a focus on upcoming innovations and the industries they will transform.

1. The Role of 5G in IoT and Cloud Evolution
5G is not just an upgrade from 4G—it is a technological leap that will enable cloud and IoT solutions to operate more efficiently and reliably.

A. Key Features of 5G Relevant to IoT and Cloud
- Ultra-Low Latency:
  - 5G can achieve latency as low as 1 millisecond, enabling applications that require near-instantaneous decision-making.
  - Example: Autonomous vehicles and remote robotic surgery require real-time responsiveness.
- High Bandwidth:
  - 5G supports speeds up to 10 Gbps, enabling fast data transfers and high-definition video streaming from IoT cameras, drones, and smart devices.
  - Example: A connected manufacturing facility can stream live HD footage from multiple sensors in real time.
- Massive Device Connectivity:
  - 5G networks can support 1 million devices per square kilometer, ideal for large IoT deployments in smart cities, agriculture, and healthcare.
  - Example: Smart cities can use 5G to support millions of connected traffic lights, cameras, and environmental sensors simultaneously.
- Network Slicing:
  - 5G enables network slicing, allowing service providers to create customized "slices" of the network with specific performance characteristics.
  - Example: A smart hospital can reserve a dedicated network slice for emergency medical devices to guarantee low latency and high reliability.

B. How 5G Enhances IoT-Enabled Cloud Technologies
- Edge-to-Cloud Integration:
  - ○ 5G allows seamless data transmission from edge devices to cloud platforms, supporting continuous communication.
  - ○ Example: Edge devices in a wind farm process sensor data locally but send insights to a central cloud for advanced analysis.
- Real-Time Processing:
  - ○ With ultra-low latency, 5G supports real-time processing of data from IoT devices, enabling faster responses.
  - ○ Example: A self-driving car uses edge AI for local decision-making but accesses a centralized cloud for route optimization.
- AI-Powered 5G Networks:
  - ○ AI optimizes 5G networks by predicting data traffic, adjusting bandwidth, and managing device connections.
  - ○ Example: AI-powered network optimization improves video streaming quality on 5G networks.

2. Key Future Trends in 5G and IoT-Enabled Cloud Technologies
The convergence of 5G, IoT, and cloud technologies is driving the following key trends.

A. Autonomous IoT Networks
- What It Is: AI-powered IoT networks that operate with minimal human intervention.
- How It Works: AI algorithms at the edge analyze system health and performance, adjusting network configurations automatically.
- Example: Smart factories with autonomous robots that self-manage their connectivity, switching between 5G and Wi-Fi as needed.
- Industry Impact: Smart manufacturing, logistics, and agriculture will benefit from self-managing IoT networks, reducing operational costs.

B. Decentralized Cloud and Distributed Systems
- What It Is: A move away from centralized cloud models to distributed systems powered by 5G and edge computing.
- How It Works: Cloud services are delivered closer to users, reducing dependency on centralized data centers.
- Example: Cloudflare's distributed cloud network processes data at the edge, reducing the need to transmit data back to a central server.
- Industry Impact: Distributed cloud systems enable faster, location-aware services in sectors like finance, healthcare, and smart cities.

C. 5G-Enhanced Edge Computing

- What It Is: The use of 5G to support advanced edge computing, enabling near-instantaneous processing and decision-making.
- How It Works: Edge AI devices process data locally, while 5G connects them to centralized cloud services for additional processing.
- Example: Autonomous drones use edge AI to navigate in real time but rely on 5G to send data for predictive analysis in the cloud.
- Industry Impact: Autonomous vehicles, smart agriculture, and robotics will experience significant growth due to enhanced edge capabilities.

D. Advanced AR/VR Experiences

- What It Is: Augmented reality (AR) and virtual reality (VR) experiences powered by 5G and cloud-enabled processing.
- How It Works: 5G enables real-time rendering of 3D content and interactive experiences with low-latency data streams.
- Example: AR-guided training in manufacturing allows technicians to see real-time instructions overlaid on machinery.
- Industry Impact: Retail, healthcare, and education will use AR/VR for customer engagement, remote learning, and immersive medical training.

E. Smart Cities and Connected Infrastructure

- What It Is: Entire urban ecosystems connected through 5G, IoT, and edge computing.
- How It Works: IoT sensors and devices collect and analyze environmental data to manage traffic, utilities, and emergency response systems.
- Example: Edge-based traffic management systems powered by 5G dynamically adjust traffic lights to reduce congestion.
- Industry Impact: Cities worldwide are adopting smart infrastructure to reduce pollution, manage public safety, and improve transportation efficiency.

3. Industry Use Cases of 5G and IoT-Enabled Cloud Technologies

A. Healthcare
- Remote Patient Monitoring: Wearable devices use 5G to transmit health data to cloud-based healthcare platforms.
- Remote Surgery: 5G enables robotic surgeries where surgeons control robots remotely with ultra-low latency.

B. Automotive
- Vehicle-to-Everything (V2X) Communication: Cars communicate with other vehicles, traffic signals, and infrastructure using 5G networks.
- Predictive Maintenance: Vehicle data is sent to the cloud for predictive maintenance analysis.

C. Smart Agriculture
- Precision Farming: IoT sensors, combined with 5G, analyze soil conditions in real-time, enabling precise watering and fertilization.
- Autonomous Tractors: Smart tractors connected via 5G can operate autonomously, using AI for navigation.

D. Retail
- Contactless Payments: Retailers leverage 5G for fast, contactless payments and seamless in-store checkout.
- Smart Kiosks: Edge AI kiosks use 5G for personalization and interactive product recommendations.

E. Industrial Automation
- Digital Twins: 5G supports real-time synchronization of physical and digital assets.
- Predictive Maintenance: Sensors relay equipment data to the cloud, where AI models predict failures.

4. Challenges and Risks of 5G-Driven IoT and Cloud Systems

A. Security Risks
- Vulnerabilities in Edge Devices: IoT devices can be hacked, exposing sensitive data.
- Mitigation: Use end-to-end encryption and device authentication.

B. Privacy Concerns
- Data Privacy Risks: Devices generate large amounts of personal data that must be protected.
- Mitigation: Implement privacy-by-design principles for IoT devices.

C. Cost of 5G Infrastructure
- High Deployment Costs: Rolling out 5G networks requires significant infrastructure investment.
- Mitigation: Partner with cloud providers and telecom operators to reduce costs.

The convergence of 5G, IoT, and cloud technologies will drive profound changes in how businesses and cities operate. Ultra-low latency, higher bandwidth, and massive device connectivity will enable new applications in autonomous vehicles, smart cities, healthcare, and beyond. Distributed cloud systems, combined with edge computing, will empower organizations to deliver faster, location-aware services. As 5G networks continue to evolve, the full potential of IoT-enabled cloud technologies is only beginning to be realized.

AI Insight:
"5G isn't just faster internet—it's the foundation for the next generation of IoT and cloud technologies, enabling real-time intelligence at unprecedented scale."

Conclusion:
The future of edge computing, IoT, and cloud technologies is being redefined by the integration of 5G networks, AI-powered solutions, and distributed cloud infrastructures. These advancements are unlocking real-time processing, faster response times, and a new era of hyper-connected devices. By enabling local computation, minimizing latency, and supporting privacy-first approaches, edge computing empowers IoT applications across industries.

Key Takeaways
  1. Role of Edge Computing in IoT:
     o Edge computing processes data at or near the source, enabling faster response times, greater privacy, and bandwidth efficiency.
     o Use cases in healthcare, smart cities, retail, and industrial IoT demonstrate how local processing transforms IoT capabilities.
  2. AI-Powered Low-Latency Solutions:
     o AI enables edge devices to process and act on data instantly, supporting applications like autonomous vehicles, predictive maintenance, and smart healthcare.
     o Key technologies like NVIDIA Jetson, Google Coral, and federated learning models ensure efficient, real-time AI processing.
  3. Impact of 5G on IoT and Cloud Technologies:
     o 5G's ultra-low latency, high bandwidth, and massive device connectivity are revolutionizing IoT and cloud solutions.
     o Emerging trends like distributed cloud systems, autonomous IoT networks, and real-time AR/VR experiences highlight the potential of 5G to transform industries.

The Bigger Picture
Edge computing, AI, and 5G are driving the next wave of innovation in IoT and cloud technologies. By enabling faster, smarter, and more secure data processing at the edge, these technologies are unlocking groundbreaking possibilities in healthcare, autonomous systems, smart cities, and beyond. The future of IoT is one where devices act autonomously, cloud resources are distributed, and AI models learn from local data—all made possible through the convergence of edge computing, AI, and 5G.

AI Insight:
"5G, AI, and edge computing are the catalysts for next-gen IoT, shaping a world where devices don't just collect data—they think, act, and evolve in real time."

Chapter 19: Disaster Recovery and Backup

In a world where data is the backbone of business operations, the ability to recover from disasters quickly is critical. Cloud-based disaster recovery (DR) and backup strategies enable organizations to safeguard their data, maintain continuity, and minimize downtime during unexpected events such as natural disasters, cyberattacks, or system failures. This chapter explores how to plan effective disaster recovery solutions, leverage automation tools, and ensure business continuity through robust cloud strategies.

1. Planning Cloud-Based Disaster Recovery Solutions
Disaster recovery (DR) is the process of restoring data, systems, and applications after a disruptive event. Cloud-based DR shifts the traditional approach from on-premises systems to a cloud-enabled model that offers cost-efficiency, scalability, and flexibility.

A. Key Concepts of Disaster Recovery
- Recovery Time Objective (RTO):
  - The maximum acceptable amount of time for systems to be offline during a disaster.
  - Example: If an e-commerce platform has an RTO of 1 hour, it must be back online within 60 minutes of an outage.
- Recovery Point Objective (RPO):
  - The maximum acceptable data loss measured in time.
  - Example: If an RPO is set to 30 minutes, the company can only afford to lose up to 30 minutes of transaction data.
- High Availability (HA) vs. Disaster Recovery (DR):
  - High availability focuses on preventing downtime, while disaster recovery focuses on recovering from a complete failure.
  - Example: A load-balanced application ensures high availability, while cloud backups facilitate disaster recovery.

B. Cloud-Based Disaster Recovery Models
- Backup and Restore:
  - Data is backed up regularly and restored during a disaster.
  - Use Case: A small business that prioritizes cost efficiency over rapid recovery times.
- Pilot Light:
  - Core services are pre-configured in the cloud but remain dormant until a disaster occurs.
  - Use Case: Retailers that run minimal operations but need rapid scalability during peak events like Black Friday.

- Warm Standby:
  - A scaled-down version of the production environment is always running in the cloud, ready to scale up when needed.
  - Use Case: A financial institution maintains a minimal environment to ensure continuity in case of system failures.
- Multi-Site Active-Active:
  - Production systems run in multiple cloud regions, ensuring no single point of failure.
  - Use Case: Global organizations like Netflix use multi-site active-active to ensure uninterrupted streaming.

C. Steps to Create a Disaster Recovery Plan
- Risk Assessment: Identify potential threats, such as cyberattacks, natural disasters, or hardware failures.
- Define RTO and RPO: Determine acceptable downtime and data loss thresholds.
- Select a DR Model: Choose the most appropriate model based on business needs and budget.
- Data Replication: Ensure data is replicated to cloud environments in real time or near real time.
- Regular Testing: Simulate disaster scenarios and test the effectiveness of the recovery plan.
- Continuous Improvement: Update the DR strategy as infrastructure, applications, and risks evolve.

2. Tools for Backup Automation and Compliance
Manual backups are no longer sufficient for modern cloud environments. Automation tools and compliance standards ensure that organizations maintain consistent, reliable, and audit-ready backups.
A. Backup Automation Tools
- AWS Backup:
  - Centralizes backup automation for AWS services, such as EC2, RDS, and S3.
  - Features: Automated schedules, retention policies, and cross-region backups.
- Azure Backup:
  - Provides secure, scalable backup for on-premises and cloud workloads.
  - Features: Encryption, long-term retention, and integration with Azure Site Recovery for disaster recovery.
- Google Cloud Backup:
  - Offers scheduled and on-demand backups for Google Cloud services, including databases and storage.
  - Features: Granular data restoration and lifecycle management for cost control.

223

- Third-Party Tools:
    - Veeam Backup for AWS, Azure, and Google Cloud: Provides unified management for multi-cloud backups.
    - Commvault: A comprehensive solution for managing backups across on-premises, hybrid, and multi-cloud environments.

B. Key Features of Backup Automation
- Automated Schedules:
    - Set custom schedules for daily, weekly, or phased backups.
    - Example: An e-commerce platform schedules daily backups at midnight to minimize service disruption.
- Retention Policies:
    - Define how long backups should be stored to comply with legal, regulatory, or internal policies.
    - Example: A healthcare provider maintains backups for 7 years to comply with HIPAA requirements.
- Versioning:
    - Retain multiple versions of files and databases to support point-in-time recovery.
    - Example: Cloud storage services like AWS S3 offer versioning to restore previous versions of files.
- Cross-Region Backups:
    - Replicate backups to different cloud regions to ensure redundancy.
    - Example: A SaaS company stores backups in multiple AWS regions to ensure data availability even if one region is down.
- Alerting and Monitoring:
    - Receive alerts when backups fail or storage thresholds are reached.
    - Example: Azure Monitor sends alerts to DevOps teams if a scheduled backup fails.

C. Compliance Considerations
- Regulatory Requirements:
    - Ensure backups meet standards like GDPR, HIPAA, and PCI-DSS.
- Encryption:
    - Encrypt data in transit and at rest to protect against breaches.
- Auditability:
    - Maintain audit logs to track changes and access to backup files.
- Disaster Recovery as a Service (DRaaS):
    - Third-party providers offer end-to-end DR solutions to simplify compliance and security requirements.

3. Ensuring Business Continuity with Cloud Strategies

Business continuity goes beyond disaster recovery. It focuses on ensuring ongoing business operations despite disruptions. By leveraging cloud-based strategies, organizations can maintain availability, reduce downtime, and provide seamless customer experiences.

A. High Availability Strategies
- Load Balancing:
  - Distributes traffic across multiple servers to prevent overloading.
  - Example: AWS Elastic Load Balancer routes requests to healthy instances only.
- Multi-Region Deployments:
  - Deploy applications across multiple cloud regions to avoid single points of failure.
  - Example: A global e-commerce site runs its platform in AWS regions in the U.S., Europe, and Asia.
- Content Delivery Networks (CDNs):
  - Use CDNs like Cloudflare or AWS CloudFront to cache content closer to users.
  - Example: An online media company uses Cloudflare to deliver content quickly to users worldwide.

B. Business Continuity Strategies
- Failover Systems:
  - Automatically switch to secondary systems when the primary system fails.
  - Example: When a cloud database fails, AWS RDS automatically promotes a standby instance to the primary role.
- Disaster Recovery Testing:
  - Test DR plans regularly to identify vulnerabilities.
  - Example: A company runs a quarterly disaster simulation to test system resilience.
- Data Redundancy:
  - Store data in multiple locations, ensuring data remains accessible.
  - Example: AWS S3 stores objects in multiple availability zones by default.

C. Cloud-First Strategy for Business Continuity
- Adopt Cloud-Native Services:
  - Use cloud-native tools like AWS Lambda, Azure Functions, and Google Cloud Run for serverless operations.

- Use Managed Databases:
  - Cloud-managed databases, like AWS RDS, handle failover, patching, and replication automatically.
- Real-Time Monitoring:
  - Use tools like AWS CloudWatch or Azure Monitor to detect issues before they escalate.

Exercises for Readers
- Reflection: What RTO and RPO are realistic for your critical business applications?
- Hands-On Activity:
  - Set up an automated backup with AWS Backup or Azure Backup.
  - Create an alert for failed backups using AWS CloudWatch or Azure Monitor.
- Case Study: Research how a major company, like Netflix or Walmart, implemented cloud-based disaster recovery to ensure business continuity.

Disaster recovery and backup solutions are essential for minimizing downtime, protecting data, and maintaining customer trust. By adopting automated cloud backups, compliance policies, and business continuity strategies, organizations can recover quickly and sustain operations during unexpected disruptions.

AI Insight:
"Disaster recovery isn't just a plan—it's a business imperative. Cloud-based DR ensures that no matter what happens, your business stays online."

Conclusion:
Disaster recovery and backup strategies are essential for modern businesses that rely on continuous data availability and operational resilience. Cloud-based solutions have revolutionized how organizations prepare for and respond to disruptions, providing automated, scalable, and cost-effective alternatives to traditional on-premises systems. This chapter explored how to develop comprehensive disaster recovery plans, leverage automation tools for backups, and ensure business continuity through high-availability cloud strategies.

Key Takeaways
1. Planning Cloud-Based Disaster Recovery Solutions:
   - Disaster recovery models such as Backup and Restore, Pilot Light, Warm Standby, and Multi-Site Active-Active provide varying levels of cost, speed, and efficiency.
   - Setting clear RTO (Recovery Time Objective) and RPO (Recovery Point Objective) ensures businesses recover within acceptable timeframes.
2. Automated Backup Tools and Compliance:
   - Cloud-native tools like AWS Backup, Azure Backup, and Google Cloud Backup offer automated scheduling, cross-region replication, and data versioning.
   - Compliance with regulations like GDPR and HIPAA is achieved through encryption, audit logs, and automated data retention policies.
3. Ensuring Business Continuity with Cloud Strategies:
   - Cloud-first strategies, such as multi-region deployments, load balancing, and failover systems, reduce downtime and keep systems operational during crises.
   - Automation, real-time monitoring, and regular disaster recovery tests help organizations detect vulnerabilities and improve recovery processes.

The Bigger Picture
Cloud-based disaster recovery and backup strategies are no longer optional—they are essential for organizations seeking to ensure business continuity in a digital-first world. From ransomware attacks to natural disasters, businesses must be prepared for any event that threatens their data or operations. By leveraging automated backups, disaster recovery models, and failover strategies, companies can reduce downtime, protect critical data, and maintain customer trust.

AI Insight:
"The best disaster recovery strategy is one that you never have to use—but if you do, cloud-based automation ensures you're back online before customers even notice."

Chapter 20: AI in Disaster Recovery and Resilience

Predictive Tools for Risk Assessment and Mitigation

In the realm of disaster recovery and business resilience, the old adage "prevention is better than cure" has never been more relevant. AI-powered predictive tools enable organizations to identify potential threats before they materialize, providing the foresight to mitigate risks proactively. By analyzing historical data, current system conditions, and real-time events, AI can predict system failures, cyberattacks, and natural disasters. This foresight allows companies to develop preemptive measures, reducing downtime and safeguarding data.

1. The Role of AI in Predictive Risk Assessment

AI-driven predictive risk assessment enables organizations to identify vulnerabilities and impending risks in real time. By analyzing vast datasets from past incidents, real-time telemetry, and environmental data, AI identifies early warning signs of potential disruptions.

A. How Predictive Risk Assessment Works
- Data Collection and Analysis:
  - AI systems collect vast amounts of historical and real-time data from IoT devices, servers, user activity logs, and environmental sensors.
  - Example: Cloud monitoring tools like AWS CloudWatch or Azure Monitor analyze system metrics (CPU usage, network traffic) for anomalies that may signal an impending failure.
- Pattern Recognition:
  - AI uses machine learning models to recognize trends, patterns, and anomalies that deviate from expected behavior.
  - Example: An anomaly detection model identifies abnormal traffic patterns that may signal an impending Distributed Denial of Service (DDoS) attack.
- Risk Scoring:
  - AI assigns a risk score to each potential threat, allowing organizations to prioritize issues that require immediate attention.
  - Example: A predictive AI tool assesses the risk of hardware failure on a cloud server and assigns it a "critical" rating if disk read/write speeds slow down significantly.

- Proactive Alerts and Notifications:
  - AI tools send alerts to DevOps teams when critical thresholds are breached.
  - Example: Azure Monitor sends a warning when memory usage reaches 90%, prompting the team to address the issue before an outage occurs.

B. Types of Predictive Models Used in Risk Assessment
- Anomaly Detection Models:
  - Identify deviations from normal system behavior.
  - Example: AI flags a sudden increase in outbound network traffic that could indicate a data exfiltration attempt.
- Time-Series Forecasting Models:
  - Predict when future events, like failures or surges in demand, will occur.
  - Example: Predictive maintenance systems forecast when cloud infrastructure components, like storage disks, are likely to fail.
- Classification Models:
  - Categorize risks based on severity and potential impact.
  - Example: Classifying threats as "low," "medium," or "high" to help prioritize disaster response efforts.

2. Predictive Tools for Risk Mitigation
Once risks have been identified, AI tools can provide recommendations and automation strategies for mitigation. Instead of reacting to disasters after they occur, predictive mitigation allows organizations to prevent disruptions before they escalate.
A. AI-Driven Risk Mitigation Tools
- Cloud-Specific Tools:
  - AWS Health Dashboard: Offers real-time alerts about AWS service issues, helping organizations mitigate disruptions.
  - Azure Security Center: Uses AI to provide security recommendations and alert DevOps teams to potential threats.
- Third-Party Predictive Analytics Tools:
  - Splunk ITSI (IT Service Intelligence): Uses predictive analytics to detect and prevent outages in hybrid and multi-cloud environments.
  - Datadog AI-Based Monitoring: Offers predictive alerts for infrastructure, application performance, and security.
- Threat Intelligence Platforms (TIPs):
  - AI-enhanced TIPs provide real-time threat intelligence and recommend actions for risk mitigation.

- Example: IBM QRadar uses machine learning to detect security threats in cloud environments and automatically trigger mitigation actions.

B. Predictive Risk Mitigation Strategies
- Preemptive Resource Scaling:
  - AI models predict traffic surges and scale cloud resources accordingly.
  - Example: A retail website scales up its AWS EC2 instances in anticipation of Black Friday traffic spikes, avoiding slow load times or outages.

- Proactive Data Replication:
  - AI identifies at-risk data storage locations and triggers data replication to safe cloud regions.
  - Example: Google Cloud's Multi-Region Storage automatically replicates data to multiple regions to maintain availability.
- Security Hardening:
  - AI analyzes vulnerabilities and suggests configuration changes to reduce attack surfaces.
  - Example: An AI tool scans AWS security groups and identifies overly permissive inbound rules, recommending changes to tighten access.
- Load Balancer Optimization:
  - AI predicts demand shifts and adjusts load balancer configurations to prevent service degradation.
  - Example: AI modifies the load balancer's routing logic to divert traffic to less congested regions during an outage.
- Infrastructure Rightsizing:
  - Predictive analytics tools recommend the optimal size for cloud instances, reducing the risk of over-provisioning or under-provisioning resources.
  - Example: AI recommends downgrading an oversized EC2 instance, saving on costs while maintaining availability.

3. Benefits of Predictive Risk Assessment and Mitigation

The integration of AI into disaster recovery transforms risk management from a reactive process into a proactive strategy. By forecasting risks and taking preemptive actions, organizations can reduce the impact of disasters and improve resilience.

A. Reduced Downtime
- Proactive detection and mitigation of issues prevent unexpected system failures.
- Example: AI detects early signs of disk failure on a cloud database and triggers a failover, preventing downtime.

B. Enhanced Data Security
- Predictive analytics identify security vulnerabilities before they can be exploited.
- Example: A cloud provider uses AI threat intelligence to detect unusual API calls from an unrecognized IP address.

C. Improved Cost Efficiency
- Avoiding downtime and disruptions reduces financial losses caused by outages.
- Example: A predictive maintenance model identifies at-risk resources and automates their replacement, avoiding costly unplanned downtime.

D. Greater Business Resilience
- Organizations can continue operations during system failures, natural disasters, and cyberattacks.
- Example: A multi-cloud strategy, combined with predictive risk assessment, ensures critical workloads failover to backup regions seamlessly.

E. Automation and Efficiency
- Predictive tools automate risk mitigation, reducing reliance on manual intervention.
- Example: If AWS Health detects an issue in a specific region, automation scripts automatically migrate workloads to another region.

4. Case Studies of Predictive Tools in Disaster Recovery

Case Study 1: E-Commerce Retailer
- Problem: High downtime risk during holiday shopping season.
- Solution: The retailer implemented AI-based predictive analytics to anticipate traffic spikes and dynamically scale AWS EC2 instances.
- Outcome: Zero downtime during Black Friday and 25% reduced cloud costs through efficient scaling.

Case Study 2: Financial Institution
- Problem: Data loss due to ransomware attacks.
- Solution: AI-powered anomaly detection flagged unusual file access patterns in AWS S3 storage. The system automatically isolated the affected files to prevent further encryption.
- Outcome: Early intervention prevented a full-scale attack, reducing data loss and enabling a full system restore in 2 hours.

Case Study 3: Cloud Service Provider
- Problem: Region-wide outages affecting customer applications.
- Solution: Predictive models identified risks of power outages, prompting preemptive failover to secondary data centers.
- Outcome: The provider maintained 99.99% uptime, earning industry accolades for business continuity.

AI-driven predictive tools have become a fundamental part of modern disaster recovery strategies. By identifying potential risks, automating threat mitigation, and ensuring business continuity, predictive analytics enable businesses to stay ahead of potential disasters. As cloud environments grow more complex, predictive risk management ensures organizations remain operational, resilient, and secure.

AI Insight:
"Predictive tools turn uncertainty into foresight, allowing businesses to mitigate risks before they become disasters."

Automating Recovery Workflows with AI-Driven Platforms
Automation is a cornerstone of effective disaster recovery (DR). When disaster strikes, the speed and efficiency of the recovery process determine how quickly businesses can resume operations. Traditional recovery workflows are often slow, manual, and prone to human error. AI-driven platforms revolutionize this process by enabling automated, intelligent, and self-healing recovery workflows. These systems detect failures, trigger automated recovery protocols, and restore business operations with minimal intervention.

This section explores how AI-driven platforms automate recovery workflows, the tools and techniques available, and the benefits of automating disaster recovery in modern cloud environments.

1. The Role of AI in Automating Recovery Workflows
AI-driven platforms leverage machine learning, predictive analytics, and intelligent automation to streamline disaster recovery. Traditional recovery workflows required manual input at every stage — from identifying system failures to initiating backups and failovers. AI-driven platforms eliminate this dependency by creating autonomous workflows that react in real time.

A. How AI Powers Workflow Automation
- Anomaly Detection and Alerts:
  - AI models continuously monitor system health and detect abnormal conditions that might signal an impending failure.
  - Example: AWS CloudWatch detects sudden spikes in CPU usage and triggers an automated action to increase server capacity.
- Automated Recovery Triggers:
  - AI tools recognize failure points and trigger pre-configured recovery actions, such as restarting services or migrating workloads.
  - Example: If Azure detects a failed virtual machine, the system automatically restarts it or switches traffic to a backup instance.
- Intelligent Decision-Making:
  - AI-based decision engines select the best course of action based on risk assessments and business priorities.

- Example: If AI identifies that an AWS EC2 instance is nearing capacity, it can trigger an auto-scaling event to launch new instances.
- Orchestration and Workflow Automation:
  - AI-driven platforms orchestrate workflows across multi-cloud and hybrid environments, ensuring seamless failovers and backups.
  - Example: If an AWS region goes offline, an AI-driven orchestration system automatically shifts workloads to another region.

B. Key Capabilities of AI-Driven Recovery Platforms
- Self-Healing Systems:
  - Self-healing systems detect failures, isolate affected components, and restore services automatically.
  - Example: A Kubernetes cluster with AI-based health monitoring will automatically restart pods if container crashes are detected.
- Runbook Automation:
  - Runbooks are predefined steps to recover systems during incidents. AI converts runbooks into automated workflows.
  - Example: If a storage volume reaches 90% capacity, an AI tool follows the runbook to increase volume size automatically.
- Predictive Failure Recovery:
  - Predictive AI models identify potential failures before they occur, allowing for preemptive recovery.
  - Example: If an AI system predicts that an AWS RDS database will experience a failure due to disk health issues, it proactively triggers a database failover to a healthy instance.

2. AI-Driven Tools for Workflow Automation
AI-driven platforms provide organizations with the tools to automate disaster recovery workflows across multi-cloud and hybrid environments. These platforms offer features such as real-time monitoring, failover orchestration, and intelligent decision-making.

A. Cloud-Native AI Recovery Tools
- AWS Elastic Disaster Recovery (AWS DRS):
  - Simplifies disaster recovery by enabling continuous replication of on-premises and cloud resources.
  - Features: Automated failover, self-healing recovery processes, and event-driven triggers.
- Azure Site Recovery (ASR):
  - Provides replication, failover, and failback capabilities for on-premises and cloud-based workloads.
  - Features: Automated failover and failback workflows, application-consistent recovery points, and multi-region replication.
- Google Cloud Backup and DR:
  - Automates backup scheduling and disaster recovery workflows for cloud-native and hybrid workloads.
  - Features: Automated orchestration of failovers and recovery workflows across cloud regions.

B. Third-Party AI-Driven Platforms
- Zerto:
  - Automates disaster recovery and failover workflows with continuous data replication.
  - Features: Orchestration of recovery workflows, ransomware recovery, and automatic failover.
- Veeam Disaster Recovery Orchestrator:
  - Offers automated orchestration for disaster recovery, testing, and failover across hybrid and multi-cloud environments.
  - Features: Workflow automation, compliance reporting, and continuous failover testing.
- Commvault Disaster Recovery:
  - Provides orchestration for backup, recovery, and replication processes.
  - Features: AI-based insights, ransomware protection, and automated workflow triggers.
- Splunk IT Service Intelligence (ITSI):
  - Uses predictive analytics to monitor IT services and trigger automated workflows for system recovery.
  - Features: Real-time anomaly detection, self-healing workflows, and cross-cloud failover orchestration.

3. AI-Driven Disaster Recovery Workflow Examples

AI-driven disaster recovery workflows are used across industries to ensure fast, reliable, and efficient recovery from disruptions. Below are real-world examples of how AI automates recovery workflows.

A. E-Commerce Retailer (Cloud Outage)
- Scenario: An AWS region outage affects e-commerce operations during a flash sale.
- AI Response: The AWS DRS system identifies the outage, triggers the failover to a secondary region, and updates DNS records automatically.
- Outcome: Recovery time is reduced from 2 hours to 10 minutes, maintaining revenue during peak sales periods.

B. Financial Institution (Cyberattack)
- Scenario: A ransomware attack encrypts financial data, threatening to shut down critical services.
- AI Response: AI detects unusual file access patterns, isolates affected VMs, and activates a clean failover to a backup instance.
- Outcome: The business continues uninterrupted while affected resources are quarantined and restored.

C. Healthcare Provider (Data Breach)
- Scenario: A data breach compromises sensitive patient data stored in a cloud environment.
- AI Response: Anomaly detection tools identify unauthorized access, trigger automated shutdown of access points, and activate backup recovery workflows.
- Outcome: Sensitive patient data is restored from backup, and the attack is neutralized within minutes.

4. Benefits of Automating Recovery Workflows with AI-Driven Platforms

Automation, powered by AI, ensures that recovery workflows are consistent, fast, and reliable. Here's how AI benefits the disaster recovery process.

A. Faster Recovery Times
- Before AI: Manual recovery processes could take hours or even days.
- With AI: Failover happens within minutes or seconds through automated triggers.

B. Error Reduction
- Before AI: Manual recovery tasks are prone to human error, such as incorrect file restorations.
- With AI: AI-driven platforms follow pre-configured workflows with precise, error-free execution.

C. Lower Recovery Costs
- Before AI: Companies pay high operational costs for on-site DR infrastructure.
- With AI: Cloud-based failover and serverless disaster recovery workflows reduce infrastructure expenses.

D. Increased Availability and Uptime
- Before AI: Downtime often lasts until recovery teams manually restore systems.
- With AI: AI-driven platforms restore critical services automatically, reducing downtime significantly.

5. Building a Resilient Disaster Recovery Workflow

AI-driven disaster recovery workflows can be customized for any business need. Below is a step-by-step approach to creating a robust DR workflow.

- Risk Assessment:
- Identify potential failure points, such as power outages, server failures, or cyberattacks.
- Define Recovery Objectives (RTO and RPO):
- Set goals for recovery time (RTO) and acceptable data loss (RPO).
- Set Up Automated Triggers:
- Configure AI triggers that detect failures and automatically start failover workflows.
- Orchestrate End-to-End Workflows:
- Design workflows that include backups, failover, DNS updates, and notifications to teams.
- Run Simulations:
- Simulate disaster scenarios to test the effectiveness of automated workflows.

AI-driven platforms are transforming disaster recovery workflows by enabling automation, self-healing systems, and real-time failover responses. From orchestrating failovers to preemptively identifying risks, AI eliminates the manual burden of disaster recovery and ensures rapid, seamless system restoration. As AI technologies evolve, disaster recovery will become faster, more cost-effective, and more resilient.

AI Insight:
"With AI-driven automation, disaster recovery is no longer a manual process—it's a self-healing, always-on solution that restores systems in seconds."

Examples of Disaster Recovery Use Cases

Disaster recovery (DR) use cases span a wide range of industries, each with unique challenges and priorities. From safeguarding critical financial transactions to ensuring uninterrupted healthcare services, disaster recovery strategies are tailored to meet specific needs. AI-driven platforms have further enhanced these strategies by enabling predictive analytics, automated failover, and self-healing workflows. This section highlights key disaster recovery use cases across various industries, illustrating how cloud-based DR and AI-driven platforms ensure continuity and resilience.

1. E-Commerce and Retail Use Case
Scenario: Cloud Outage During Peak Sales (Black Friday)
During high-demand periods, like Black Friday, e-commerce websites experience enormous traffic spikes. A cloud region outage or server overload during this critical time can result in millions in lost revenue.
Challenges
- High Traffic Surges: Demand spikes overwhelm servers, causing slow load times or outages.
- Revenue Loss: Downtime during peak sales events leads to lost transactions and brand reputation damage.

Solution: AI-Driven Failover and Auto-Scaling
- Predictive Scaling: AI models predict traffic surges and trigger the automatic provisioning of additional server capacity.
- Failover Automation: AI-driven failover systems detect failures and redirect traffic to secondary regions or availability zones.

Outcome
- Downtime Reduced: Automated failover redirects traffic to healthy regions, reducing downtime from hours to minutes.
- Revenue Protection: The e-commerce site stays operational during Black Friday, ensuring uninterrupted sales.

2. Financial Services Use Case
Scenario: Cyberattack and Data Breach
Banks and financial institutions face ongoing threats from ransomware, phishing, and malware attacks. If a breach occurs, sensitive customer data may be compromised, and critical financial transactions may be disrupted.

Challenges
- Data Security: Cyberattacks may encrypt customer data or exfiltrate sensitive information.
- Regulatory Compliance: Regulations like GDPR and PCI-DSS impose strict penalties for data breaches.

Solution: AI-Driven Threat Detection and Recovery
- Anomaly Detection: AI identifies unusual network traffic or abnormal access patterns, flagging potential attacks.
- Isolated Recovery Environment (IRE): AI triggers the isolation of infected environments and activates a failover to a clean system.
- Backup Automation: Data is continuously backed up using AWS Backup or Azure Backup to ensure data is recoverable.

Outcome
- Fast Response: AI detects and responds to cyberattacks within seconds, preventing further spread.
- Data Restoration: Backup recovery workflows restore encrypted files from pre-attack backups, ensuring minimal data loss.
- Compliance Assurance: Audit logs and automated workflows demonstrate compliance with GDPR and PCI-DSS requirements.

3. Healthcare and Telemedicine Use Case
Scenario: Outage in Patient Data Systems
Hospitals and healthcare providers rely on electronic health record (EHR) systems to access patient data and deliver care. If an outage occurs, healthcare workers may lose access to critical patient information, delaying care and risking patient safety.

Challenges
- Data Availability: Healthcare providers need uninterrupted access to patient records.
- Patient Safety: Delays in access to EHRs during emergencies can compromise patient care.

Solution: Multi-Site Active-Active Failover
- Active-Active Deployment: EHR systems run simultaneously across multiple cloud regions, ensuring zero-downtime failover.
- Predictive Failure Detection: AI predicts storage failures and triggers preemptive migration of data.
- Data Replication: Patient data is continuously replicated across cloud regions to maintain availability.

Outcome
- Zero Downtime: Active-active failover keeps patient data accessible during outages.
- Continuous Data Access: Doctors and nurses access EHRs even if one cloud region fails.
- Improved Patient Care: Faster access to patient data ensures timely treatment during emergencies.

4. Manufacturing and Industrial IoT (IIoT) Use Case

Scenario: Equipment Failure in a Smart Factory

Factories use Industrial IoT (IIoT) devices and edge computing to automate production lines. If a critical machine fails, production may be halted, leading to lost revenue and downtime.

Challenges
- Unplanned Downtime: Equipment failure disrupts production lines.
- Cost of Repairs: Emergency repairs and unscheduled downtime increase operational costs.

Solution: Predictive Maintenance and Self-Healing Systems
- Predictive Analytics: AI predicts equipment failures before they happen by analyzing sensor data (e.g., vibration, temperature, and pressure).
- Automated Failover: If a critical machine fails, production is automatically shifted to a redundant system or spare machine.
- Edge AI Systems: AI-based edge devices analyze sensor data in real time to prevent failures.

Outcome
- Downtime Avoided: Predictive maintenance ensures repairs are scheduled during non-peak hours.
- Self-Healing Production Lines: AI triggers automated responses to failures, such as switching production to secondary machines.
- Cost Savings: Proactive repairs reduce the cost of emergency repairs and unplanned downtime.

5. Media and Streaming Use Case

Scenario: Service Outage During a Live Event

Media streaming services like Netflix, Hulu, and Twitch deliver live events and on-demand content to millions of viewers. A streaming outage during a live sports event can damage brand reputation and lead to customer churn.

Challenges
- Live Stream Reliability: Delays or interruptions ruin the customer experience.
- Latency and Bandwidth: Delivering high-definition (HD) or 4K video streams requires high bandwidth and low latency.

Solution: AI-Driven Multi-CDN Failover
- Content Delivery Network (CDN) Failover: AI automatically switches traffic to a secondary CDN provider if the primary CDN fails.
- Proactive Scaling: AI predicts peak traffic and preemptively scales up CDN servers and edge caches.
- Regional Failover: Video streams are distributed across multiple cloud regions, ensuring redundancy.

Outcome
- Uninterrupted Streaming: Viewers experience zero buffering during live events due to multi-CDN failover.
- High Customer Satisfaction: Redundant regional streams keep viewers connected even if one region goes offline.
- Cost Control: Proactive scaling reduces infrastructure costs, as additional capacity is only activated when needed.

6. Education and Online Learning Use Case
Scenario: Outage of Online Learning Platforms
Universities and educational institutions use learning management systems (LMS) to facilitate online classes. If an outage occurs during peak exam periods, students are unable to access course materials and exams may be postponed.

Challenges
- Continuous Access: Students require 24/7 access to course materials and exams.
- High Traffic Spikes: Online exams experience sudden spikes in demand, stressing infrastructure.

Solution: AI-Driven Traffic Management
- Load Balancing: AI-based load balancers distribute user requests across multiple servers.
- Predictive Scaling: AI predicts peak usage during exam periods and preemptively scales up cloud resources.
- Failover: If one server fails, AI automatically redirects users to a backup server.

Outcome
- Continuous Access: Students access online exams even during peak usage.
- No Exam Interruptions: AI-driven failover prevents exam disruptions, ensuring continuous access for students.
- Enhanced User Experience: Students experience faster loading times and uninterrupted sessions.

7. Energy and Utilities Use Case

Scenario: Power Grid Disruption
Utilities manage large, distributed networks of smart meters, sensors, and IoT devices to monitor and control power grids. Disruptions caused by storms or cyberattacks can lead to power outages.

Challenges
- Grid Stability: Power grids must maintain a continuous flow of electricity.
- Security Risks: Cyberattacks on utility grids could disrupt power supply for entire regions.

Solution: AI-Powered Grid Recovery
- Automated Grid Recovery: AI detects outages and triggers automated failover to backup power sources.
- Real-Time Monitoring: Edge AI sensors detect fluctuations in electricity supply and send predictive maintenance alerts.
- Cybersecurity: AI identifies suspicious access patterns and isolates at-risk network components.

Outcome
- Faster Recovery: AI-driven failover ensures customers experience minimal power disruptions.
- Improved Resilience: Smart grids maintain stable energy delivery even during outages.
- Proactive Maintenance: AI predicts component failures and schedules preemptive maintenance.

Disaster recovery use cases highlight the importance of AI-driven automation, predictive analytics, and failover workflows. From e-commerce and healthcare to financial services and manufacturing, each industry faces unique challenges that can be solved with cloud-based disaster recovery solutions. By automating these workflows with AI, businesses reduce downtime, improve operational efficiency, and strengthen resilience.

AI Insight:
"Every second of downtime matters. With AI-driven recovery, industries can bounce back from disruption in minutes—not hours."

Conclusion:
AI-driven disaster recovery and resilience strategies are transforming how organizations respond to unexpected disruptions. By leveraging predictive analytics, workflow automation, and real-time response mechanisms, businesses can mitigate risks, reduce downtime, and maintain operational continuity. Traditional manual processes are being replaced by AI-powered platforms capable of self-healing, preemptive failover, and automated decision-making, ensuring faster and more effective disaster recovery.

Key Takeaways
- Predictive Tools for Risk Assessment and Mitigation:
  - AI models predict failures before they happen, enabling organizations to take proactive measures.
  - Anomaly detection, time-series forecasting, and classification models allow businesses to prevent outages, cyberattacks, and hardware failures.
  - By predicting and mitigating risks before they escalate, organizations reduce downtime, minimize financial loss, and protect customer trust.
- Automating Recovery Workflows with AI-Driven Platforms:
  - AI-driven platforms enable automated workflows that handle failovers, backups, and resource scaling without manual intervention.
  - Self-healing systems, automated runbooks, and predictive scaling are key to reducing human error and accelerating recovery times.
  - Cloud-native tools like AWS Elastic Disaster Recovery, Azure Site Recovery, and Google Cloud Backup provide out-of-the-box automation features.
- Disaster Recovery Use Cases Across Industries:
  - Industries such as e-commerce, healthcare, financial services, and manufacturing rely on AI-driven DR strategies to remain resilient.
  - Use cases like e-commerce failovers, healthcare EHR accessibility, and financial data protection demonstrate the power of AI-driven DR automation.
  - Predictive maintenance, proactive scaling, and multi-site active-active setups help businesses maintain continuity in the face of disasters.

The Bigger Picture
AI-driven disaster recovery is no longer a luxury—it is a necessity. In an era where downtime can cost millions of dollars and erode customer trust, the ability to predict, mitigate, and recover from disruptions is a competitive advantage. AI ensures faster, more effective disaster recovery by enabling predictive risk assessment, self-healing systems, and automated failover workflows.

Organizations that embrace AI-driven disaster recovery solutions are better prepared to handle natural disasters, cyberattacks, and system failures. From e-commerce giants to financial institutions and healthcare providers, every industry benefits from faster failovers, lower downtime, and proactive risk mitigation. With AI on their side, businesses can recover from disruptions in minutes, not hours—ensuring uninterrupted service and operational resilience.

AI Insight:
"Disasters may be unpredictable, but with AI-driven automation, your response doesn't have to be. AI ensures that when failure strikes, recovery is swift, seamless, and automatic."

Chapter 21: Cloud Service Level Agreements (SLAs) and Vendor Management

Cloud Service Level Agreements (SLAs) and vendor management play a vital role in ensuring businesses receive consistent, reliable, and high-quality cloud services. A well-structured SLA defines the performance metrics, availability guarantees, and penalties for service failures, while effective vendor management mitigates the risks of lock-in and ensures businesses can maintain control over their cloud strategy. This chapter explores how to negotiate SLAs, manage vendor relationships, and choose the right cloud provider for your business needs.

1. How to Negotiate and Manage SLAs Effectively

A Cloud Service Level Agreement (SLA) is a legally binding document between a cloud provider and its customer that outlines service expectations, performance metrics, and consequences for failing to meet those obligations. Crafting a clear, enforceable SLA ensures that businesses have leverage if a provider's service fails to meet agreed-upon standards.

A. Key Components of an SLA
- Service Availability and Uptime
  - Describes the guaranteed availability of the service, often stated as a percentage (e.g., 99.9% uptime).
  - Example: An SLA may guarantee 99.9% uptime for cloud storage, meaning the system can only be down for 43 minutes per month.
- Response and Resolution Times
  - Specifies how quickly the provider will respond to issues and how long it will take to resolve them.
  - Example: An SLA for AWS Support may guarantee a response within 15 minutes for critical outages.
- Performance Metrics
  - Covers throughput, response time, latency, and other technical performance benchmarks.
  - Example: A content delivery network (CDN) SLA may specify a maximum response time of 300 milliseconds for serving cached content.
- Disaster Recovery and Business Continuity
  - Defines how providers will maintain service continuity during a disaster, such as a natural event or cyberattack.
  - Example: The SLA may specify automatic failover to another availability zone or cloud region.

- Security and Compliance
  - Details the security measures the provider will use to protect data, such as encryption and access controls.
  - Example: Providers like AWS and Azure commit to compliance with standards like GDPR, ISO 27001, and SOC 2.
- Penalties and Compensation
  - Specifies the financial credits, refunds, or other remedies offered if the provider fails to meet SLA commitments.
  - Example: If an SLA guarantees 99.9% uptime and the provider only delivers 99.5%, the customer may be eligible for a 10% refund of that month's service fees.

B. How to Negotiate an SLA
- Define Business Needs
  - Identify critical services and prioritize the most important SLA elements, such as uptime or latency guarantees.
- Push for Customization
  - Most providers offer a "standard SLA," but large customers can negotiate terms tailored to their business.
- Focus on Measurability and Clarity
  - Insist on precise, quantifiable terms. Instead of "high availability," require a specific percentage (e.g., 99.95%).
- Negotiate Penalties and Remedies
  - Request financial credits or penalty clauses if service disruptions affect business operations.
- Review the Terms Regularly
  - As cloud needs evolve, SLAs should be revisited to ensure terms remain relevant.

C. SLA Management Best Practices
- Monitor SLA Performance
  - Use monitoring tools like AWS CloudWatch, Azure Monitor, or Google Cloud Operations Suite to track performance.
- Review SLA Reports
  - Most cloud providers offer monthly SLA performance reports, which should be analyzed for compliance.
- Hold Vendors Accountable
  - If a provider fails to meet SLA obligations, request service credits or compensation as specified in the contract.

2. Mitigating Risks of Vendor Lock-In
Vendor lock-in occurs when an organization becomes too dependent on a single cloud provider, making it difficult or costly to switch providers. This lack of flexibility can lead to higher costs, limited service choices, and reduced innovation.

A. What is Vendor Lock-In?
Vendor lock-in happens when a business relies on proprietary tools, services, or frameworks specific to one cloud provider, making it difficult to migrate to another platform. For example, applications built with AWS Lambda may not easily transfer to Google Cloud Functions without modification.

B. Risks of Vendor Lock-In
- Increased Switching Costs
  - Moving workloads from one cloud provider to another can be expensive due to retooling, migration costs, and compatibility issues.
- Reduced Flexibility
  - Organizations lose the ability to use the best-of-breed tools from other providers.
- Pricing Power Shift
  - Providers may increase prices if they know the customer has limited migration options.

C. Strategies to Mitigate Vendor Lock-In
- Adopt Multi-Cloud Strategies
  - Use multiple cloud providers (e.g., AWS, Azure, and Google Cloud) to ensure operational flexibility.
- Use Open-Source and Cross-Platform Tools
  - Use open-source platforms like Kubernetes, Terraform, and Docker that work across multiple providers.
- Avoid Proprietary APIs
  - Avoid vendor-specific APIs that are not portable. Instead, use standards-based protocols.
- Leverage Cloud-Agnostic Services
  - Opt for cloud-agnostic solutions, such as PostgreSQL databases, which can run on AWS, Azure, and GCP.
- Containerization and Microservices
  - Deploy applications as microservices using containerization tools like Docker, which can be moved easily across cloud providers.

3. Key Considerations When Choosing a Cloud Provider
Selecting a cloud provider is one of the most critical decisions for businesses embarking on a cloud strategy. Each provider has unique offerings, but businesses must consider their operational needs, costs, and technical capabilities.

A. Factors to Consider
- Performance and Uptime Guarantees
  - Review SLA uptime guarantees for each provider (e.g., AWS guarantees 99.99% availability for EC2).
- Service Offerings and Compatibility
  - Ensure the provider offers the services and tools required for your applications (e.g., AI/ML services, serverless computing, or DevOps support).
- Pricing and Cost Structure
  - Compare pricing models (pay-as-you-go, reserved instances, spot instances) to ensure cost efficiency.
- Security and Compliance
  - Check if the provider meets industry compliance standards (GDPR, HIPAA, ISO 27001) and has built-in security tools.
- Customer Support and Incident Response
  - Look for support availability (24/7) and response times for critical outages.
- Data Residency and Sovereignty
  - Ensure data remains within specific regions if subject to local data privacy regulations (like GDPR).

B. Cloud Provider Comparison
When it comes to choosing a cloud provider, AWS, Azure, and Google Cloud (GCP) are the three most prominent options. Each provider has its own strengths, unique features, and target audiences. Here's a breakdown of the key comparisons to help you choose the best provider for your specific needs.

1. Market Position
- AWS: AWS is the largest cloud provider in the world, with the highest market share. As a first-mover in cloud services, AWS remains the leader in terms of customer base, service variety, and global reach. It's widely adopted by startups, enterprises, and government organizations alike.
- Azure: Azure holds the position of the second-largest cloud provider globally. It is known for its strong focus on hybrid cloud solutions and is widely used by enterprises that rely on Microsoft's existing products like Windows Server, Office 365, and Active Directory.

248

- Google Cloud (GCP): GCP is the smallest of the three major providers in terms of market share. However, it is recognized as a leader in AI, machine learning, and big data analytics. Google Cloud is widely used by organizations focused on AI-driven development, data science, and analytics-heavy workloads.

2. Core Strengths
- AWS: Known for having the broadest and most comprehensive catalog of services. AWS offers over 200+ services, including advanced tools for AI/ML, IoT, and developer support. It's also the leader in terms of global reach, with the most availability zones and data centers worldwide.
- Azure: Hybrid cloud leadership is Azure's core strength. Companies that want to run a hybrid infrastructure (mixing on-premise and cloud) often choose Azure because it integrates seamlessly with on-premises data centers. Azure also provides strong integration with Microsoft products like Office 365 and Windows Server.
- Google Cloud (GCP): GCP stands out in the area of AI, machine learning, and data analytics. It offers industry-leading tools like BigQuery, TensorFlow, and Vertex AI, making it the top choice for companies focused on AI, machine learning, and large-scale data processing.

3. Pricing
- AWS: AWS uses a pay-as-you-go pricing model with options for reserved instances, on-demand pricing, and spot instances. While AWS has a wide range of cost-saving options, its pricing is often seen as complex and difficult to predict without tools like AWS Cost Explorer.
- Azure: Similar to AWS, Azure offers pay-as-you-go pricing, reserved instances, and hybrid benefits for users with existing Windows licenses. Companies that already have Microsoft enterprise agreements can get discounts on Azure services, making it cost-effective for businesses heavily invested in Microsoft products.
- Google Cloud (GCP): GCP's pricing is often seen as more transparent and simpler compared to AWS and Azure. GCP offers per-second billing (rather than per-minute or hourly) and provides sustained-use discounts that reduce the cost of instances that run for extended periods. This makes it a popular choice for companies looking for transparent pricing.

4. Service Availability
- AWS: AWS has the largest global infrastructure, with 30+ regions and 90+ availability zones. Its vast reach makes it ideal for companies with customers in multiple regions who need to reduce latency and ensure uptime.
- Azure: Azure also has an extensive global presence, with 60+ regions and 140+ availability zones. It's especially popular in countries with strict data privacy laws (like Europe) due to its sovereign cloud options for government and regulated industries.
- Google Cloud (GCP): GCP operates in 35+ regions and 100+ availability zones. While GCP does not have as many zones as AWS or Azure, it is strategically positioned in key locations to support AI, big data, and analytics-heavy applications.

5. Deployment Models
- AWS: Primarily designed for public cloud deployments, but it also supports hybrid cloud using AWS Outposts, which allows businesses to run AWS services on-premise. AWS also offers GovCloud, a region specifically designed for US government workloads.
- Azure: Hybrid cloud is Azure's specialty, allowing businesses to deploy workloads across on-premises, cloud, and edge locations. Azure Arc extends Azure services to on-premises and multi-cloud environments, making it a preferred option for hybrid deployments.
- Google Cloud (GCP): GCP is typically used as a public cloud provider, but it offers hybrid cloud solutions with Anthos, allowing companies to manage workloads across on-premises and multi-cloud platforms. Anthos supports both Google Cloud and other cloud providers.

6. Security and Compliance
- AWS: AWS follows the shared responsibility model, where AWS secures the cloud infrastructure, and customers are responsible for securing their data, applications, and configurations. AWS offers extensive compliance certifications like SOC 2, PCI-DSS, GDPR, and HIPAA.
- Azure: Azure places a strong focus on government compliance. It provides specialized offerings like Azure Government to serve US government agencies and contractors. Azure is also known for its deep integration with Active Directory for identity management.

- Google Cloud (GCP): GCP emphasizes zero-trust security with its BeyondCorp framework, which ensures that users must authenticate before accessing data. It is also compliant with major certifications like GDPR, ISO 27001, and HIPAA, making it a strong option for industries with privacy and security regulations.

7. Machine Learning and AI
- AWS: AWS offers Amazon SageMaker, a fully managed service to build, train, and deploy machine learning models. It also provides Rekognition (image analysis) and Comprehend (natural language processing). While AWS has solid AI tools, it is not as specialized in AI/ML as GCP.
- Azure: Azure Machine Learning (AML) allows companies to build, deploy, and manage ML models. Azure integrates AI with Microsoft products like Power BI and Dynamics 365, making it appealing for companies already using the Microsoft ecosystem.
- Google Cloud (GCP): GCP is the undisputed leader in AI, machine learning, and big data analytics. It is the home of TensorFlow and offers tools like Vertex AI for advanced model development. If your business is heavily focused on AI, deep learning, or large-scale data analytics, GCP is the clear choice.

8. Developer and DevOps Tools
- AWS: AWS has a robust set of developer tools, including AWS CodePipeline, CodeBuild, and CloudFormation. It allows for Infrastructure as Code (IaC) with AWS CloudFormation, enabling users to deploy infrastructure as easily as writing scripts.
- Azure: Azure integrates tightly with Azure DevOps and GitHub (since Microsoft owns GitHub). It's a preferred choice for developers using GitHub Actions, CI/CD pipelines, and automated releases.
- Google Cloud (GCP): GCP supports Cloud Build and Cloud Deploy for building CI/CD pipelines, but it's not as strong as AWS CodePipeline or Azure DevOps. However, GCP is the birthplace of Kubernetes (GKE), which makes it a preferred choice for companies heavily reliant on containerized applications.

Summary
- AWS: Best for global scalability, enterprise flexibility, and large service catalogs. It is ideal for companies with diverse workloads or those who want multi-region availability and massive scalability.
- Azure: Best for businesses seeking hybrid cloud solutions and enterprises already invested in the Microsoft ecosystem. Azure integrates well with on-premises systems, government workloads, and Windows Server environments.
- Google Cloud (GCP): Best for companies that require AI, machine learning, and big data analytics. GCP offers powerful tools for data science, real-time analysis, and large-scale data processing.

By understanding the strengths, use cases, and differences of AWS, Azure, and GCP, businesses can select the best cloud provider for their unique needs. If your focus is global scalability and service variety, go with AWS. If you need hybrid cloud and seamless Microsoft integration, choose Azure. If your goal is to build AI-driven or data-heavy applications, Google Cloud is the clear winner.

Conclusion:
SLAs and vendor management are crucial components of a successful cloud strategy. SLAs provide accountability and assurance, while vendor management protects against vendor lock-in and pricing risks. By understanding and negotiating SLA terms, businesses can protect their interests and ensure providers meet service commitments. Likewise, multi-cloud and cloud-agnostic strategies provide flexibility and ensure that organizations are never trapped in a single provider's ecosystem.

AI Insight:
"A well-negotiated SLA can be the difference between a minor inconvenience and a multi-million dollar disaster. Always review, negotiate, and hold providers accountable."

Chapter 22: Emerging Technologies in Cloud Computing – Quantum Computing

Quantum computing is no longer a concept reserved for research labs and academic circles. With the rise of cloud-based quantum platforms, businesses, developers, and researchers can now access quantum computing resources remotely. This chapter explores the fundamentals of quantum computing in the cloud, highlights current advancements, and examines its future potential. Finally, we explore practical use cases in AI, optimization, and scientific research.

1. Introduction to Quantum Computing in the Cloud
Quantum computing represents a radical shift from classical computing. Instead of relying on bits (0s and 1s), quantum computers use qubits, which can exist in multiple states simultaneously due to the principles of superposition and entanglement. While classical computers handle logical operations sequentially, quantum computers can solve certain problems exponentially faster.

A. Key Concepts of Quantum Computing
- Qubits (Quantum Bits):
    - Qubits are the basic units of information in quantum computing, similar to classical bits but with the ability to exist in multiple states at once.
    - Example: While a classical bit is either 0 or 1, a qubit can be 0, 1, or both at the same time (superposition).
- Superposition:
    - Qubits exist in multiple states simultaneously until observed. This allows quantum computers to process multiple possibilities at once.
    - Example: Instead of trying password combinations one at a time, a quantum computer can analyze multiple combinations at once.
- Entanglement:
    - When qubits are entangled, their states are linked, even when separated by large distances.
    - Example: If one entangled qubit changes, its partner qubit changes instantly, allowing for faster information transfer.
- Quantum Gates:
    - Quantum gates control how qubits interact and change states, similar to logical gates in classical computers.

B. How Cloud Providers Offer Quantum Computing
- Quantum-as-a-Service (QaaS):
  - Cloud providers now offer Quantum-as-a-Service, allowing developers to access quantum computing power via APIs.
  - Example Providers:
    - AWS Braket: AWS Braket offers access to quantum devices from D-Wave, IonQ, and Rigetti.
    - IBM Quantum Experience: IBM provides cloud access to quantum computers, enabling developers to run quantum algorithms.
    - Google Quantum AI: Google Cloud offers access to quantum simulations and hybrid quantum-classical computing tools.
- Hybrid Quantum-Classical Systems:
  - Since most real-world problems aren't purely quantum, providers offer hybrid systems that combine classical and quantum computing.

C. Benefits of Cloud-Based Quantum Computing
- Accessibility: Anyone can access quantum computing via platforms like AWS Braket, even without owning quantum hardware.
- Cost-Efficiency: Companies avoid the massive costs of quantum hardware by paying only for what they use.
- Innovation Acceleration: Startups, researchers, and universities can now test quantum algorithms without significant investment.

2. Current Advancements and Future Potential
Quantum computing is advancing rapidly, and cloud platforms are driving adoption by making this cutting-edge technology accessible to businesses and researchers. Current advancements include breakthroughs in hardware, hybrid computing, and the development of quantum programming languages.

A. Current Advancements in Quantum Computing
- Improved Quantum Hardware
  - Providers like IBM and Google are developing more stable and error-resistant qubits.
  - Example: IBM's "Eagle" 127-qubit processor marks a significant leap in computational capacity.
- Error Correction Techniques
  - Quantum systems are highly error-prone, but error-correction algorithms like surface codes and repetition codes are improving stability.

- Hybrid Cloud-Quantum Solutions
  - Hybrid quantum-classical solutions allow classical computers to handle less complex tasks while quantum machines focus on more challenging computations.
  - Example: A hybrid system can use classical resources for pre-processing data and hand over the most challenging problems to quantum resources.
- New Quantum Programming Languages
  - Providers like IBM and Microsoft are releasing quantum programming languages to make quantum development more accessible.
  - Example: Microsoft Q# and IBM Qiskit allow developers to write quantum algorithms using familiar programming syntax.

B. The Role of Cloud Providers in Advancing Quantum Technology
- AWS Braket:
  - Offers access to hardware from multiple quantum providers, allowing comparisons of performance.
- IBM Quantum:
  - Provides free access to IBM's quantum processors, allowing developers to experiment with quantum algorithms.
- Google Quantum AI:
  - Focuses on hybrid quantum-classical systems, enabling developers to leverage both systems in tandem.

C. The Future of Quantum Cloud Computing
- Quantum Supremacy:
  - Quantum supremacy occurs when a quantum computer performs a calculation that would be infeasible for classical computers. Google achieved this in 2019, but the real-world applications of quantum supremacy are still being explored.
- Decentralized Quantum Networks:
  - As edge computing becomes more common, researchers are exploring how quantum networks could enable decentralized quantum computing.
- Advancements in Qubit Stability:
  - Future quantum processors may use error-resistant qubits, allowing for longer computations and reduced failure rates.
- Quantum Encryption (Post-Quantum Cryptography):
  - Since quantum computers can crack current encryption algorithms, post-quantum cryptography will be essential for securing cloud data.

- Commercial Use of Quantum Computing:
  - Today, quantum computing is experimental, but its future role in financial modeling, pharmaceutical discovery, and climate prediction is undeniable.

3. Use Cases in AI and Scientific Research

The unique capabilities of quantum computing position it as a game-changer for industries that require complex computation, like AI, pharmaceuticals, and climate modeling.

A. AI and Machine Learning
- Accelerated Model Training
  - Quantum systems can speed up model training by reducing computational time for large datasets.
  - Example: AI models for autonomous vehicles may train significantly faster on a quantum platform than on classical GPUs.
- Solving Optimization Problems
  - Quantum optimization algorithms (like QAOA) can identify optimal solutions to problems like route optimization or supply chain logistics.
  - Example: An e-commerce company could use quantum computing to optimize delivery routes in real time.
- Quantum-Enhanced Feature Selection
  - Selecting the best features for AI/ML models is time-consuming. Quantum computers can rapidly determine the most relevant features.

B. Scientific Research
- Drug Discovery and Pharmaceuticals
  - Quantum computing can simulate molecular structures to speed up drug discovery.
  - Example: Quantum computers model drug interactions, accelerating drug discovery timelines for pharmaceutical companies.
- Climate Modeling and Weather Prediction
  - Current climate models are limited by classical computing power, but quantum computing allows for more accurate simulations.
  - Example: Quantum computers simulate climate change models, enabling governments to better predict extreme weather events.
- Materials Science and Chemistry
  - Quantum systems can predict the behavior of complex molecules, enabling breakthroughs in battery technology and superconductors.

C. Business Use Cases
- Financial Modeling
  - Quantum computing optimizes risk analysis, portfolio selection, and financial forecasting for investment firms.
- Cybersecurity and Cryptography
  - Post-quantum cryptography will protect data from quantum decryption attacks. Cloud providers are already testing quantum-resistant encryption.
- Supply Chain Optimization
  - Quantum algorithms optimize supply chains, shipping routes, and inventory management to reduce costs.

Conclusion:
Quantum computing is set to revolutionize the cloud industry by offering unparalleled computational power. Through cloud platforms like AWS Braket, Google Quantum AI, and IBM Quantum, businesses and researchers can access quantum computing resources on demand. These advancements have the potential to transform industries like pharmaceuticals, AI, and financial modeling. While still in its early stages, quantum computing in the cloud is laying the groundwork for future breakthroughs.

AI Insight:
"Quantum computing will redefine the limits of cloud performance, making once-impossible tasks routine. With cloud access to quantum systems, even small startups can wield this immense power."

Chapter 23: AI and Data Sovereignty in the Cloud

Data sovereignty is one of the most critical issues facing modern businesses that operate in a global, cloud-connected world. As organizations expand their reach across borders, they must comply with local data protection regulations like GDPR (General Data Protection Regulation), CCPA (California Consumer Privacy Act), and other regional standards. Cloud providers play a significant role in maintaining data compliance, but managing cross-border data flows requires more than geographic data centers. AI-driven systems are transforming how companies manage compliance, security, and data accessibility in the cloud.

This chapter explores how organizations ensure data sovereignty, the role of AI in managing cross-border data challenges, and how businesses balance security and accessibility in global cloud operations.

1. Ensuring Compliance with Regional Data Regulations
Data sovereignty refers to the principle that data is subject to the laws and regulations of the country in which it is stored or processed. For companies with a global presence, ensuring compliance with local data protection laws is essential for avoiding legal penalties and preserving customer trust.

A. Key Data Sovereignty Regulations
- General Data Protection Regulation (GDPR) – Europe
    - Scope: Applies to all companies processing personal data of EU citizens, regardless of company location.
    - Key Provisions: Right to be forgotten, data access requests, breach notifications, and data minimization.
    - Penalties: Fines up to €20 million or 4% of global turnover, whichever is higher.
- California Consumer Privacy Act (CCPA) – USA
    - Scope: Applies to companies that process the personal data of California residents.
    - Key Provisions: Right to know, right to delete, right to opt out of sales, and data security measures.
- Personal Information Protection Law (PIPL) – China
    - Scope: Similar to GDPR but specific to the personal data of Chinese citizens.
    - Key Provisions: Data localization, cross-border transfer restrictions, and explicit user consent.

- Data Sovereignty in Other Regions
  - Brazil (LGPD): Focuses on user rights, consent, and data processing rules.
  - India (DPDP Bill): Proposed regulations on how businesses collect, store, and process Indian citizens' data.

B. How Cloud Providers Ensure Compliance
- Data Residency and Data Localization
  - Cloud providers like AWS, Azure, and Google Cloud maintain region-specific data centers to ensure data is stored within specific geographic locations.
  - Example: AWS has data centers in Frankfurt to ensure GDPR compliance for European customers.
- Data Encryption and Tokenization
  - Encryption ensures that even if data is transferred across borders, it remains unreadable without a decryption key.
  - Example: Google Cloud encrypts data both in transit and at rest, allowing businesses to comply with regional privacy laws.
- Compliance Certifications and Audits
  - Cloud providers undergo audits to achieve compliance certifications like GDPR, SOC 2, ISO 27001, and PCI DSS.
- Legal Agreements and Data Processing Addendums (DPAs)
  - Many providers offer Data Processing Addendums (DPAs) to ensure customers remain compliant when using cloud-based services.
  - Example: An EU-based business may sign a DPA with AWS to ensure data stored in the EU remains compliant with GDPR.

C. How Businesses Maintain Data Sovereignty
- Data Mapping
  - Businesses track where data is stored, transferred, and accessed to ensure it stays within compliant regions.
- Geofencing Cloud Storage
  - Data geofencing restricts where customer data can be stored or processed.
  - Example: A multinational bank restricts customer data for European accounts to remain within the EU.
- Data Residency Policies
  - Companies develop policies to ensure specific categories of data (like customer PII) stay within country borders.

2. How AI Manages Cross-Border Data Challenges

Managing cross-border data transfers is one of the most complex aspects of data sovereignty. AI-driven solutions play a key role in tracking, classifying, and controlling the flow of sensitive data.

A. AI-Driven Data Classification
- Data Tagging and Metadata Analysis
  - AI analyzes and labels data based on content, context, and regulatory requirements.
  - Example: An AI tool scans a cloud storage system to classify files as "Personal Data," "Financial Data," or "Public Data."
- PII (Personally Identifiable Information) Detection
  - AI detects personal data such as names, phone numbers, and email addresses in datasets.
  - Example: AWS Macie uses machine learning to identify and protect PII stored in Amazon S3 buckets.
- Data Sensitivity Levels
  - AI assigns sensitivity levels to data (e.g., "Public," "Confidential," or "Restricted") to determine the appropriate security controls.

B. AI-Powered Data Flow Management
- Automated Data Routing
  - AI automatically routes data to the most appropriate storage region based on compliance needs.
  - Example: A financial company routes EU customer data to Frankfurt, while U.S. data is sent to Virginia.
- Data Masking and Anonymization
  - AI automatically anonymizes PII, ensuring data can be processed across borders without breaching privacy laws.
  - Example: Machine learning models used for training customer service AI are fed anonymized data that has been stripped of PII.
- Dynamic Access Control
  - AI dynamically controls user access based on roles, locations, and other risk factors.
  - Example: If an employee from the U.S. tries to access customer data stored in the EU, AI-based geofencing blocks access.

C. AI-Driven Compliance Monitoring
- Automated Compliance Audits
  - AI continuously audits cloud environments to ensure data sovereignty rules are enforced.
  - Example: An audit tool identifies files stored outside of allowed geographic regions and issues compliance alerts.
- Real-Time Alerts and Incident Response
  - AI tools like AWS Config send alerts when files are moved outside of compliant storage zones.
- Regulatory Change Monitoring
  - AI tracks changes in regional regulations and adapts data compliance protocols accordingly.
  - Example: AI flags new GDPR rules that impact cross-border data transfers and recommends configuration updates.

3. Balancing Security and Accessibility in Global Operations
Balancing security and accessibility is one of the biggest challenges for companies operating across multiple countries. Data sovereignty laws impose restrictions on where data can be stored, while businesses must still provide employees with access to critical resources.

A. Key Security Measures for Global Operations
- Encryption and Key Management
  - Data is encrypted at rest and in transit, with encryption keys stored locally.
  - Example: Azure Key Vault manages encryption keys for multi-region deployments.
- Identity and Access Management (IAM)
  - Role-based access control (RBAC) restricts user access to specific data based on location, role, or device.
- Zero-Trust Security Model
  - Users and devices are continuously verified before being granted access to sensitive data.

B. Global Data Accessibility Techniques
- Cloud Content Delivery Networks (CDNs)
  - Content is cached locally and delivered from regional edge locations.
  - Example: A media company stores large files on a U.S. CDN but serves it locally to users in the EU.
- Distributed Cloud Systems
  - Multi-region cloud deployments ensure data remains accessible to users in every country while staying compliant.

- Data Tokenization
  - Replace sensitive data with "tokens" to process data while avoiding storage of PII.

Conclusion:
Data sovereignty and cross-border data compliance are critical for businesses operating in the cloud. Compliance requires businesses to adhere to GDPR, CCPA, and other global regulations, while AI-driven tools simplify the process of managing data transfers, geofencing, and data privacy. AI-powered classification, access control, and monitoring systems allow organizations to achieve compliance without sacrificing efficiency or data accessibility.

AI Insight:
"AI is the compliance officer of the future. It enforces regional regulations, manages data flows, and ensures that no sensitive data crosses borders unlawfully."

Chapter 24: Cross-Platform Integration and APIs

Leveraging APIs and Middleware for Seamless Integrations

In a multi-cloud and hybrid-cloud environment, seamless integration between platforms, applications, and services is crucial for business efficiency. This is where Application Programming Interfaces (APIs) and middleware play a pivotal role. APIs act as the communication bridge between different applications, while middleware provides a connective layer that allows disparate systems to work together harmoniously. The combination of these technologies enables cloud platforms, SaaS applications, and on-premises systems to interoperate.

This section explores how APIs and middleware enable seamless integrations, the role of cloud-native API gateways, and how businesses can design and manage API-first architectures to ensure scalability and agility.

1. What are APIs and Middleware?

A. APIs (Application Programming Interfaces)

An API is a set of defined rules that allow different software systems to communicate with one another. It enables applications to request and exchange data, which is essential for cross-platform integrations.

- Types of APIs:
    - REST APIs (Representational State Transfer) – Most commonly used in modern cloud platforms.
    - SOAP APIs (Simple Object Access Protocol) – Often used in legacy systems with higher security needs.
    - GraphQL APIs – Used for more flexible and efficient queries, especially in front-end applications.
    - Webhooks – Event-driven APIs that trigger actions in real time.
- Example Use Case:
    - A payroll system (like Workday) integrates with a financial system (like QuickBooks) using an API to automatically transfer payment data.

B. Middleware

Middleware is the connective layer that facilitates communication between different applications, platforms, and services. It acts as a "broker" that standardizes data, handles formatting, and ensures messages are transmitted correctly.

- Types of Middleware:
    - Message Brokers (like RabbitMQ) – Handle the queuing and delivery of messages between applications.

- Enterprise Service Bus (ESB) – A centralized system that facilitates message routing, data transformation, and security between multiple platforms.
- API Gateways – Middleware tools that expose APIs to external users while managing security, rate limiting, and request transformation.
- Example Use Case:
  - An e-commerce platform uses middleware to connect its front-end website with back-end inventory, shipping, and payment systems.

2. Role of APIs in Cross-Platform Integration

APIs are essential for enabling cross-platform integration in cloud computing. They enable applications, tools, and services to interact with cloud platforms, whether they are on AWS, Azure, Google Cloud, or a private cloud.

A. How APIs Enable Integration
- Application Integration
  - APIs allow cloud applications like Slack, Zoom, and Salesforce to exchange data in real-time.
  - Example: A CRM system (like Salesforce) can use an API to pull customer order data from an ERP system (like SAP) to provide customer support agents with up-to-date order information.
- Data Synchronization
  - APIs ensure data remains synchronized across multiple cloud and on-premises systems.
  - Example: A company can sync user profiles between a Human Resources (HR) system and an Identity Provider (IdP) like Okta, ensuring employee data is consistent.
- Process Automation
  - APIs automate business processes by linking systems and triggering workflows.
  - Example: A customer filling out an online form triggers an API call to a backend CRM, automatically creating a customer profile.

B. Cloud-Native API Gateways
API gateways are essential for managing and exposing APIs to internal and external users. These gateways provide security, request routing, and monitoring.
- What an API Gateway Does:
  - Handles API requests and routes them to the appropriate backend service.
  - Applies security policies like rate limiting, authentication, and authorization.

264

- Monitors API usage and generates analytics for performance optimization.
- Popular API Gateway Providers:
  - AWS API Gateway – Simplifies API creation, management, and monitoring for AWS services.
  - Azure API Management – Enables multi-cloud API management and developer portal creation.
  - Google Cloud Endpoints – Offers serverless API management to expose APIs securely.
- Example Use Case:
  - A company exposes its API to third-party developers via an AWS API Gateway, allowing them to integrate with its product catalog.

C. API-First Design Approach

An API-first approach means that APIs are designed as reusable assets before the actual software or applications are developed. This method ensures that APIs are at the center of product development, enabling reusability, modularity, and consistency.

- Benefits of API-First Design:
  - Faster Time-to-Market – Developers can reuse APIs across multiple applications.
  - Consistency – Ensures that all microservices follow a common API standard.
  - Scalability – New products can be built by reusing existing APIs instead of developing from scratch.
- How API-First Design Works:
  - Design APIs First – API requirements are written before any application code is written.
  - Create Reusable APIs – APIs are designed for use in multiple applications.
  - Document and Share – API documentation is created for developers to consume.

3. Role of Middleware in Cross-Platform Integration

Middleware plays a vital role in ensuring that different platforms can "talk" to each other, especially when the systems have different data formats, protocols, or operating environments.

A. How Middleware Supports Integration

- Data Transformation
  - Middleware transforms data formats (like XML to JSON) to ensure compatibility.
  - Example: A payment processor sends payment data in XML format, but the CRM expects it in JSON. Middleware transforms XML into JSON.

- Message Routing
  - Middleware determines where to route incoming requests and responses.
  - Example: An e-commerce site sends an order request to the shipping API, which routes it to the appropriate shipping provider (FedEx, UPS, or DHL) based on location.
- Queue Management
  - Middleware can store and manage message queues, ensuring no message is lost, even if the recipient is temporarily unavailable.
  - Example: RabbitMQ manages a queue of shipping requests and retries failed requests until they are processed.

B. Tools for Middleware Integration
- Message Brokers (for Asynchronous Communication)
  - RabbitMQ, Apache Kafka, and Amazon SQS handle asynchronous message queues.
- Enterprise Service Bus (ESB)
  - MuleSoft and Dell Boomi provide ESBs for data integration between cloud, on-premises, and SaaS platforms.
- Cloud-Native Middleware
  - AWS Step Functions, Azure Logic Apps, and Google Cloud Workflows provide orchestration for complex business workflows.

4. Best Practices for API and Middleware Integration
To ensure a smooth integration process, companies must design APIs and middleware with scalability, security, and reusability in mind.

A. Best Practices for API Integration
- Use RESTful APIs – They are lightweight, fast, and scalable for most integration needs.
- Implement OAuth Authentication – Secure APIs with OAuth to ensure only authorized users can access them.
- Rate Limiting – Prevent abuse by controlling the number of requests users can make to an API.
- Detailed API Documentation – Tools like Swagger and Postman help developers understand API functionality.

B. Best Practices for Middleware Integration
- Use Centralized Monitoring – Tools like AWS CloudWatch and Azure Monitor provide insights into middleware performance.
- Ensure Fault Tolerance – Design middleware with retry logic and failover capabilities.

- Data Transformation Efficiency – Minimize the transformation steps to avoid latency issues.
- Version Control for APIs – Track changes in APIs and support multiple versions to avoid breaking existing integrations.

APIs and middleware are essential for cross-platform integration. APIs provide a unified way to access cloud services, enabling seamless communication between applications. Middleware, on the other hand, provides a bridge that facilitates compatibility, message routing, and workflow orchestration. Together, they create a modern, interconnected, and scalable system that supports hybrid and multi-cloud environments.

AI Insight:
"With APIs, applications talk. With middleware, they understand each other. Together, they power the next generation of cloud integration."

Building Scalable, Cross-Platform Applications

Building scalable, cross-platform applications is essential for modern cloud-native development. As businesses seek to support users on multiple devices, operating systems, and cloud platforms, developers must ensure that applications remain performant, secure, and adaptable. Cloud platforms like AWS, Azure, and Google Cloud, combined with modern development frameworks, enable the creation of cross-platform applications that scale dynamically with user demand.

This section explores the key principles, architectural considerations, and best practices for building scalable, cross-platform applications. You'll learn about essential tools, cloud-native development techniques, and how AI enhances scalability and cross-platform compatibility.

1. What are Cross-Platform Applications?

Cross-platform applications are applications that can run on multiple operating systems, devices, and cloud environments with minimal or no modification to the source code. They are designed to provide a consistent experience across platforms, whether they are web-based, mobile, or desktop applications.

A. Types of Cross-Platform Applications
- Web Applications
  - Web applications are browser-based apps that work on any device with a web browser.
  - Example: Gmail, Trello, and Google Docs are cross-platform web applications.

- Mobile Applications
  - Mobile apps can be developed using frameworks like React Native, Flutter, and Xamarin to work on iOS, Android, and Windows devices.
  - Example: Instagram and Facebook use cross-platform development frameworks to ensure consistency on iOS and Android.
- Desktop Applications
  - Desktop apps, like Zoom, use platforms like Electron and .NET MAUI to run on macOS, Windows, and Linux.
- Cloud-Native Applications
  - Cloud-native apps are designed to run in cloud environments, supporting multiple cloud providers (AWS, Azure, GCP) without the need for re-engineering.
  - Example: Serverless apps built with AWS Lambda or Azure Functions can run in multi-cloud environments.

B. Characteristics of Cross-Platform Applications
- Code Reusability
  - Write once, deploy everywhere. Developers can reuse most of the source code across platforms.
- Platform Independence
  - Apps run on any device, operating system, or cloud platform.
- Consistent User Experience (UX)
  - UI/UX remains consistent across devices and platforms, ensuring familiarity for users.
- Cloud Scalability
  - Apps can scale dynamically to handle millions of users across different regions and devices.

2. How to Build Scalable, Cross-Platform Applications
Creating scalable, cross-platform applications requires strategic planning, technical knowledge, and the right development tools. Key elements like architecture, programming frameworks, testing, and deployment play a critical role in ensuring smooth scalability and cross-platform functionality.

A. Key Architectural Considerations
- Microservices Architecture
  - Break the application into smaller, loosely coupled services that can be developed, deployed, and scaled independently.
  - Example: E-commerce applications often separate user authentication, product catalogs, payments, and notifications into individual microservices.

- Containerization with Docker and Kubernetes
  - Use containers to package applications with all dependencies, making them portable across platforms and clouds.
  - Example: Docker containers ensure an app running on AWS can be redeployed on Azure or Google Cloud without reconfiguration.
- Serverless Design
  - Write applications as serverless functions (like AWS Lambda, Azure Functions, and Google Cloud Functions) that run in response to events.
  - Example: A file upload to an S3 bucket triggers a serverless function to process and resize images.
- Event-Driven Architecture
  - Design applications to respond to real-time events like user actions, system alerts, or IoT device triggers.
  - Example: An order management system processes customer purchases in real time using event-driven messaging with AWS SNS and AWS SQS.

B. Essential Tools and Frameworks
- Development Frameworks
  - React Native: Used to build cross-platform mobile apps for iOS and Android.
  - Flutter: Allows for cross-platform app development with a single codebase.
  - Xamarin: Ideal for building cross-platform mobile apps in C#.
- Containerization and Orchestration
  - Docker: Packages apps into containers for platform independence.
  - Kubernetes: Manages containers for high availability and scalability.
- Cloud-Native Services
  - AWS Lambda, Azure Functions, Google Cloud Functions: Ideal for serverless cross-platform functions.
  - Cloud Load Balancers: Balance traffic for scalable, cross-platform apps to maintain performance during traffic spikes.
- API Gateways and Middleware
  - AWS API Gateway, Azure API Management, Google Cloud Endpoints: Securely expose APIs to allow other platforms to communicate with your application.

C. Design Patterns for Scalability
- Horizontal Scaling
  - Add more instances of an application to support increased load.
  - Example: During a flash sale, AWS Auto Scaling launches multiple instances of an e-commerce application to meet user demand.
- Load Balancing
  - Distribute traffic across multiple instances of an application to prevent overload.
  - Example: AWS Elastic Load Balancer directs requests to the instance with the least load.
- Data Caching
  - Cache frequently requested data to reduce latency and improve speed.
  - Example: A news app caches top headlines to serve users instantly instead of querying the database repeatedly.
- Database Sharding
  - Split large databases into smaller, faster parts to improve read/write performance.
  - Example: A social media platform shards user profiles based on user location to improve query speed.

3. AI's Role in Building Scalable Cross-Platform Applications

AI plays a crucial role in building scalable, cross-platform applications. From automating testing and performance optimization to ensuring cross-platform compatibility, AI-driven tools make it easier to develop and manage cloud-native applications.

A. AI-Powered Testing and QA
- Automated Testing
  - AI testing tools like TestComplete and Selenium automate cross-platform testing to detect compatibility issues.
  - Example: AI-driven testing identifies and fixes rendering issues on iOS, Android, and desktop browsers.
- Visual Regression Testing
  - Detects visual differences between application versions to ensure consistent UI/UX across platforms.
  - Example: If a button alignment is incorrect in iOS, AI testing flags it for correction.
- API Testing with AI
  - AI tools like Postman AI automate testing API responses for different platforms.
  - Example: If an API request produces a different response on Android vs. iOS, AI detects the inconsistency.

B. AI-Driven Scalability and Load Management
- Predictive Scaling
  - AI analyzes user traffic to predict when additional resources will be needed.
  - Example: AI scales up server capacity before a flash sale begins, ensuring no downtime occurs.
- Intelligent Load Balancing
  - AI adjusts how traffic is routed between application instances in real time.
  - Example: AI moves users from slow regions to less congested areas to maintain app performance.
- Failure Prediction and Auto-Healing
  - AI detects signs of system failure (e.g., CPU spikes) and automatically restarts failing components.
  - Example: Google Cloud Operations detects slow response times and spins up additional resources to stabilize performance.

Building scalable, cross-platform applications requires a combination of architectural foresight, modern frameworks, and automation. By using containers, APIs, and microservices, companies can create apps that run on any device, anywhere. AI further enhances scalability by enabling predictive scaling, auto-healing, and cross-platform testing. With this approach, businesses can ensure smooth operations, fast response times, and consistent user experiences across platforms.

AI Insight:
"Scalability isn't just about handling growth—it's about staying ahead of it. AI-driven automation ensures that your app scales before your users even know it needs to."

AI's Role in Simplifying Integrations
In today's multi-cloud and hybrid-cloud environments, integrations between platforms, applications, and services have become increasingly complex. Traditional manual approaches to integration require custom coding, data mapping, and manual troubleshooting, which are time-consuming and error-prone. AI-driven integration tools simplify these processes, making it easier to connect cloud platforms, on-premises systems, and third-party applications.

AI introduces automation, predictive analytics, and self-learning capabilities that accelerate the speed and accuracy of integrations. With AI, businesses can achieve seamless, cross-platform integrations with minimal manual intervention. This section delves into AI's role in simplifying integrations, the key AI-powered tools available, and how AI enhances API management, middleware, and system orchestration.

1. How AI Simplifies Integration Workflows
AI transforms how organizations manage integration workflows by automating repetitive tasks, predicting errors, and providing intelligent recommendations. Instead of manually coding integrations, developers can now rely on AI to detect issues, optimize data flows, and handle routine updates.

A. AI-Driven Automation
- Automated API Discovery and Integration
  o AI tools can automatically detect APIs from third-party services, generate API calls, and create integration workflows.
  o Example: Tools like MuleSoft Anypoint and Zapier allow users to integrate thousands of APIs automatically with little manual intervention.
- Data Mapping and Transformation
  o AI automatically maps data fields between source and target systems, eliminating the need for manual field mapping.
  o Example: When integrating an e-commerce platform with a shipping service, AI tools automatically match "Order ID" in the e-commerce system to "Tracking ID" in the shipping system.
- AI-Powered Orchestration
  o AI enables the orchestration of workflows across multiple platforms. Instead of configuring manual workflows, AI-powered orchestration platforms create event-driven, dynamic workflows.
  o Example: AWS Step Functions and Azure Logic Apps allow businesses to automate multi-step workflows, such as processing an e-commerce order, updating inventory, and notifying customers.
- Automated Error Resolution
  o When integrations fail, AI tools analyze logs, detect patterns, and suggest corrective actions.
  o Example: If a payment API fails to process a transaction, AI can identify the cause (like an expired API key) and offer a recommended fix.

B. Predictive Integration Management
- Failure Prediction and Prevention
  - AI tools analyze historical data to predict when an integration might fail, allowing businesses to prevent outages.
  - Example: If a third-party API shows slow response times, AI-based observability tools like AWS CloudWatch or Splunk alert the integration manager to switch to a backup API.
- Dynamic Load Balancing
  - AI dynamically adjusts traffic flows to avoid overloading a single service endpoint.
  - Example: If API requests to a payment service increase, AI redirects traffic to alternative endpoints to prevent overload.
- Performance Optimization
  - AI analyzes integration performance in real-time and suggests optimizations, such as caching data or reducing API call frequency.
  - Example: An AI tool might detect slow response times from a CRM API and recommend increasing the caching interval to reduce dependency on the live API.

C. AI-Enhanced Security and Compliance
- Data Privacy and Compliance Checks
  - AI checks data flows for compliance with privacy regulations like GDPR and CCPA. It flags data transfers to unauthorized regions or the use of personal data without consent.
  - Example: If customer data from the EU is being transferred to a data center in the U.S., AI compliance tools alert the user to a potential GDPR violation.
- AI-Driven Access Control
  - AI enforces dynamic access controls for API endpoints, ensuring only authorized users and systems can access sensitive data.
  - Example: If an unusual request comes from an unfamiliar IP address, the AI tool might automatically block the request or require multi-factor authentication.

2. AI-Powered Tools for Integration
There are numerous AI-powered tools that make cross-platform integration seamless. These tools use machine learning models to identify bottlenecks, automate data transformation, and maintain service continuity.

A. AI-Powered Integration Platforms
- MuleSoft Anypoint
  - An integration platform that connects SaaS, legacy systems, and cloud-native applications.
  - AI Capabilities: Automated data mapping, intelligent API design, and auto-generated API documentation.
- Zapier and Make (formerly Integromat)
  - No-code platforms for connecting applications like Google Sheets, Slack, and Trello.
  - AI Capabilities: Predictive workflow suggestions and AI-generated integration templates.
- Dell Boomi
  - Cloud-native middleware that connects cloud, SaaS, and on-premises applications.
  - AI Capabilities: Data mapping suggestions, process intelligence, and anomaly detection for workflow failures.
- AWS Step Functions
  - A cloud-based orchestration service for managing multi-step workflows.
  - AI Capabilities: Automated event handling, workflow error detection, and automatic retries for failed tasks.

B. AI-Powered API Management Tools
- AWS API Gateway
  - AI Capabilities: Detects high-volume traffic spikes and automatically scales API capacity.
- Azure API Management
  - AI Capabilities: Uses AI to enforce security policies, rate limits, and request throttling.
- Google Cloud Endpoints
  - AI Capabilities: Monitors API traffic and detects anomalies in API usage patterns.
- Postman with AI Testing
  - Postman provides AI-based API testing that automatically generates test cases.
  - AI Capabilities: Uses machine learning to recommend test scenarios, predict API failures, and identify common errors.

3. Benefits of AI-Driven Integration
By leveraging AI, businesses can achieve faster, more reliable, and cost-effective cross-platform integrations. Here's a summary of the key benefits.

A. Speed and Efficiency
- Faster Time-to-Value
  - AI eliminates manual development work, enabling faster integrations.
  - Example: Integrating an e-commerce platform with a payment gateway can be done in minutes using no-code AI platforms like Zapier or Dell Boomi.
- Reduced Development Time
  - Automated API generation and documentation speed up the development process.
- Automated Data Mapping
  - AI detects data fields and automatically maps source-to-destination connections.

B. Improved Scalability and Flexibility
- Dynamic Scaling
  - AI scales API endpoints and connections dynamically in response to usage spikes.
  - Example: AWS API Gateway increases capacity automatically during a product launch.
- Multi-Cloud Compatibility
  - With AI, companies can deploy integrations that work across AWS, Azure, and Google Cloud.
- Cross-Platform Orchestration
  - AI orchestration allows businesses to manage workflows that span multiple cloud providers.

C. Enhanced Reliability and Resilience
- Self-Healing Workflows
  - AI-powered workflows automatically retry failed steps and recover from outages.
  - Example: AWS Step Functions detect a failed API call and re-execute the task without human intervention.
- Error Prediction and Anomaly Detection
  - AI detects and resolves issues before they affect workflows.
  - Example: Google Cloud Operations predicts an API endpoint failure and re-routes traffic to an alternate API.
- Automated Backup and Failover
  - AI detects when an API service is down and switches to a backup endpoint.

AI is transforming cross-platform integration, offering automation, error prediction, and dynamic scaling. Instead of manually mapping data fields or coding custom integrations, AI-powered tools like MuleSoft Anypoint, AWS Step Functions, and Postman simplify the process, allowing faster time-to-market and more resilient workflows. AI-driven orchestration platforms enable seamless communication between cloud providers, APIs, and on-premises systems. With AI, integrations become smarter, more scalable, and more secure.

AI Insight:
"AI doesn't just connect platforms—it teaches them how to work together, anticipate failures, and fix themselves before you even know there's a problem."

Conclusion:
Cross-platform integration is essential in today's interconnected, cloud-driven world. APIs and middleware form the backbone of these integrations, enabling seamless communication between cloud services, on-premises applications, and third-party platforms. The role of AI in cross-platform integration has revolutionized this process, automating data mapping, optimizing workflows, and enabling dynamic load balancing to ensure peak performance. This chapter highlighted how businesses can leverage APIs, middleware, and AI-driven solutions to streamline integrations. From using API gateways to securely expose APIs to middleware orchestration tools like AWS Step Functions and AI-powered platforms like MuleSoft and Dell Boomi, companies now have access to a robust toolkit for integration success.

Key Takeaways
1. APIs and Middleware Enable Seamless Cross-Platform Integration
   - APIs facilitate communication between applications, enabling real-time data exchange.
   - Middleware acts as the bridge that connects disparate systems, managing message routing, data transformation, and security.
   - Together, APIs and middleware allow businesses to link SaaS tools, cloud services, and legacy systems into a unified ecosystem.

2. Building Scalable, Cross-Platform Applications
- Modern applications must be designed to run on multiple platforms (mobile, desktop, and cloud) with minimal code changes.
- Using containers (Docker, Kubernetes), serverless functions (AWS Lambda, Azure Functions), and cross-platform frameworks (React Native, Flutter), developers can ensure applications remain scalable and device-agnostic.
- Event-driven architecture and microservices further enhance scalability, allowing applications to adapt to fluctuating user demands.

3. AI's Role in Simplifying Integration
- AI-driven tools simplify cross-platform integration by automating API discovery, data mapping, and error detection.
- Platforms like Postman AI and AWS Step Functions automate workflows, while MuleSoft and Dell Boomi provide low-code tools for integration.
- AI-driven predictive analytics enable businesses to detect and prevent failures before they occur, improving system reliability and performance.

Why This Chapter Matters
With the rise of multi-cloud and hybrid-cloud strategies, businesses need agile, flexible, and future-proof integration solutions. APIs and middleware ensure smooth communication between diverse systems, but manual integration is time-consuming, expensive, and error-prone. AI-driven platforms have emerged as the answer, automating the design, monitoring, and optimization of integration workflows.

This chapter empowers businesses to:
- Integrate faster using pre-built APIs and middleware tools.
- Build smarter with AI-enhanced orchestration and automation.
- Scale globally with containerized, serverless, and multi-cloud-ready applications.

As cloud adoption accelerates, companies that master cross-platform integration will gain a competitive edge. AI isn't just simplifying the process — it's redefining how integrations are built, managed, and optimized.
AI Insight:

"Integration isn't just about connecting systems. It's about connecting possibilities. AI ensures every system, app, and platform can work together in ways that weren't possible before."

Chapter 25: Industry Use Cases for Cloud Computing

Cloud computing has revolutionized the way industries operate by enabling flexible, scalable, and cost-effective solutions. From healthcare to finance and gaming, businesses leverage cloud infrastructure to enhance efficiency, accelerate innovation, and improve customer experience. The role of AI in cloud computing has only heightened its transformative impact, allowing organizations to automate processes, predict outcomes, and deliver personalized experiences at scale.

This chapter explores real-world examples of cloud computing in healthcare, finance, and gaming. It also highlights AI-driven innovations that are transforming entire industries and provides practical applications across multiple sectors.

1. Real-World Examples of Cloud Computing in Key Industries

A. Healthcare: Cloud-Enabled Patient Care and Medical Research
Healthcare organizations are using cloud platforms to improve patient care, enable telemedicine, and accelerate medical research. The cloud facilitates the secure storage and analysis of large datasets, enabling the development of predictive models for disease prevention and personalized treatment plans.

Key Use Cases:
- Electronic Health Records (EHR) Management
  - Problem: Traditional on-premises EHR systems are costly to maintain, and data sharing between hospitals is complex.
  - Solution: Cloud-based EHRs (like AWS HealthLake) store patient records securely, enabling easy access and sharing across healthcare providers.
  - Impact: Doctors can access patient histories from any location, speeding up diagnosis and improving patient outcomes.
- Telemedicine and Remote Patient Monitoring
  - Problem: The COVID-19 pandemic accelerated the need for remote healthcare services.
  - Solution: Telemedicine platforms like Amwell and Teladoc Health use AWS and Azure cloud services to offer secure video consultations and collect patient data remotely.
  - Impact: Patients can receive medical care from home, while hospitals reduce the strain on in-person services.

- Medical Research and Genomics
    - Problem: Genomic analysis requires massive computational power to process terabytes of DNA sequence data.
    - Solution: Cloud platforms like Google Cloud Genomics and AWS Bioinformatics allow researchers to perform large-scale genetic analysis in the cloud.
    - Impact: Faster genomic analysis accelerates the discovery of treatments for diseases like cancer and COVID-19.

B. Finance: Cloud-Powered Banking, Risk Analysis, and Fraud Detection
Financial institutions are rapidly adopting cloud solutions to improve customer experience, enhance risk assessment, and strengthen fraud detection. The cloud enables banks to analyze massive amounts of data in real time, supporting predictive analytics, customer insights, and regulatory compliance.

Key Use Cases:
- Banking-as-a-Service (BaaS)
    - Problem: FinTech startups need a fast way to create banking services without building infrastructure from scratch.
    - Solution: AWS Banking-as-a-Service and Google Cloud Financial Services enable companies like Chime and N26 to offer banking apps without owning physical servers.
    - Impact: Startups reduce development costs and bring digital banking apps to market faster.
- Fraud Detection and Prevention
    - Problem: Traditional fraud detection models rely on historical patterns and fail to detect new threats.
    - Solution: AI-powered fraud detection tools, like AWS Fraud Detector, use machine learning to detect suspicious activity in real time.
    - Impact: Banks detect fraudulent transactions faster and prevent revenue loss, while customers receive instant fraud alerts.
- Risk Management and Regulatory Compliance
    - Problem: Financial institutions must comply with strict regulations like GDPR and SOX while managing risk.
    - Solution: Cloud-based GRC (Governance, Risk, and Compliance) platforms allow banks to track compliance in real time, automatically document audit trails, and monitor financial risks.
    - Impact: Banks reduce operational risks, avoid regulatory penalties, and ensure data compliance across global markets.

C. Gaming: Cloud-Powered Streaming and Real-Time Multiplayer Games

Gaming has undergone a massive transformation with the rise of cloud gaming, where games are streamed directly from the cloud to devices, eliminating the need for expensive consoles or gaming PCs. Companies like Google Stadia, NVIDIA GeForce NOW, and Microsoft Xbox Cloud Gaming rely on cloud platforms to deliver low-latency, high-fidelity game streaming.

Key Use Cases:
- Cloud Gaming and Game Streaming
  - Problem: Gamers want to play high-end games without purchasing expensive hardware.
  - Solution: Cloud gaming platforms like Google Stadia, Xbox Cloud Gaming, and NVIDIA GeForce NOW use GPU-accelerated cloud servers to stream games to low-end devices.
  - Impact: Gamers play AAA titles on smartphones, tablets, and smart TVs without the need for expensive gaming hardware.
- Real-Time Multiplayer Gaming
  - Problem: Online multiplayer games require ultra-low latency to ensure smooth gameplay.
  - Solution: Game developers use Amazon GameLift and Google Cloud Game Servers to host multiplayer games with low latency and real-time synchronization.
  - Impact: Games like Call of Duty and Fortnite offer seamless multiplayer experiences by hosting regional game servers in cloud data centers.
- Player Analytics and Personalized Experiences
  - Problem: Game studios need to understand player behavior to optimize gameplay and improve engagement.
  - Solution: Cloud AI platforms like Google Cloud BigQuery analyze player interactions, predict churn, and deliver personalized in-game content.
  - Impact: Games tailor difficulty levels, offer personalized rewards, and create engaging in-game experiences.

2. AI-Driven Innovations in Cloud-Powered Industries
AI-driven innovations are revolutionizing industries that rely on cloud computing. By leveraging machine learning, natural language processing, and predictive analytics, cloud platforms offer industry-specific AI tools that transform business models.

A. AI-Powered Healthcare Innovations
- AI-Powered Virtual Health Assistants (e.g., Babylon Health) – Virtual assistants help patients with basic health inquiries using AI chatbots.
- AI-Driven Drug Discovery – AI models predict how potential drugs interact with the human body, accelerating drug development.

B. AI in Finance
- Robo-Advisors – AI-driven investment advisors (like Wealthfront) automatically manage portfolios for clients.
- Real-Time Anomaly Detection – AI systems flag suspicious financial transactions in real time, ensuring rapid fraud detection.

C. AI-Powered Gaming
- AI-Enhanced NPCs (Non-Player Characters) – AI creates realistic NPCs with lifelike decision-making.
- AI-Driven Procedural Content Generation – AI generates new maps, quests, and in-game environments dynamically.

3. Practical Applications Across Multiple Sectors
AI-driven cloud innovations are being applied in several other industries, including:
- Retail: AI-driven recommendation engines and smart checkout systems.
- Manufacturing: AI-based predictive maintenance powered by cloud IoT sensors.
- Education: Remote learning platforms with AI-powered personalized learning paths.
- Logistics: Real-time shipment tracking and route optimization using cloud GPS and machine learning.

Conclusion:
Cloud computing has become an essential driver of innovation across industries. In healthcare, it powers telemedicine, EHRs, and genomic analysis. In finance, it facilitates banking-as-a-service, fraud detection, and compliance. In gaming, it enables cloud gaming, multiplayer game hosting, and player analytics.

The introduction of AI-powered tools has further accelerated industry transformation. By automating workflows, predicting outcomes, and enabling real-time decision-making, AI enhances operational efficiency and customer experience. The impact of cloud computing on industries is undeniable, and with AI's help, future innovations will be even more groundbreaking.

Key Takeaways
- Industry Impact: Cloud computing is driving innovation in healthcare, finance, and gaming, with industry-specific applications transforming operations.
- AI-Driven Transformation: AI-powered tools enhance healthcare diagnosis, financial fraud detection, and game personalization, offering smarter, data-driven solutions.
- Practical Application: From remote work to AI chatbots and predictive maintenance, cloud-based solutions are reshaping entire industries.

AI Insight:
"Industries aren't just adopting the cloud — they're being reshaped by it. With AI as the driving force, entire sectors are transforming faster than ever before."

Chapter 26: AI in Cloud Learning and Skill Development

The rapid adoption of cloud computing has created a demand for skilled professionals who can design, manage, and optimize cloud-based systems. To meet this demand, educational platforms, certification bodies, and training providers have turned to AI-powered learning tools. These tools offer personalized learning experiences, real-time feedback, and tailored career guidance, making it easier for learners to master essential cloud skills.

This chapter explores how AI is transforming cloud learning, highlights the most sought-after cloud certification programs, and explains how learners can use AI to build their skills, prepare for certifications, and boost their cloud computing careers.

1. AI Tools for Personalized Learning and Skill-Building
AI has revolutionized the way cloud skills are taught and learned. Unlike traditional, one-size-fits-all learning approaches, AI-driven personalized learning platforms create customized learning paths based on each learner's pace, strengths, and areas for improvement. This approach ensures that learners acquire skills faster, retain more knowledge, and achieve better outcomes.

A. Personalized Learning Paths
- Adaptive Learning Systems
  - AI-driven learning platforms adjust the difficulty and content of lessons in real time, ensuring the learner receives content that matches their level of knowledge.
  - Example: If a learner struggles with cloud networking concepts, the platform may assign simpler lessons or offer additional explanations.
  - AI Tools: Coursera, edX, and AWS Skill Builder use adaptive learning systems.
- Skill Gap Analysis
  - AI tools analyze student progress and identify knowledge gaps, offering targeted lessons to fill those gaps.
  - Example: An AI system may identify that a learner has a weak understanding of AWS IAM (Identity and Access Management) and recommend focused practice in this area.
- Learning Recommendations
  - AI suggests courses, articles, and practice exams tailored to the learner's goals.
  - Example: If a student is preparing for the AWS Solutions Architect exam, AI might recommend AWS Labs on IAM policies, EC2 instance design, and CloudFront integration.

B. AI-Powered Practice and Assessment
- Real-Time Feedback Systems
  - AI tracks a learner's responses to practice exams and provides feedback on where they went wrong and how to improve.
  - Example: When taking a cloud certification mock exam, AI can identify patterns in incorrect answers (e.g., confusion with VPC concepts) and offer tailored explanations.
  - AI Tools: Cloud Academy and Whizlabs provide real-time feedback for AWS, Azure, and Google Cloud certifications.
- Intelligent Practice Exams
  - AI generates dynamic practice exams that change each time, ensuring no two tests are identical.
  - Example: After a learner scores poorly on serverless architecture questions, the system increases the number of serverless-related questions in the next test attempt.
- Automated Code Review
  - For cloud development training (like serverless functions or IaC), AI tools review submitted code for correctness and suggest improvements.
  - Example: AWS Cloud9 uses AI-assisted linting to identify syntax errors, potential security issues, and inefficiencies in Infrastructure as Code (IaC) scripts.

C. Gamification and Microlearning
- Gamification of Cloud Skills
  - AI-powered platforms offer badges, leaderboards, and progress milestones, turning learning into a rewarding, game-like experience.
  - Example: Learners on Trailhead by Salesforce earn badges for completing cloud-related projects, which can be showcased on LinkedIn profiles.
- Microlearning with AI
  - AI creates bite-sized learning sessions (5–15 minutes) that maximize engagement and knowledge retention.
  - Example: After a student watches a 10-minute AWS video tutorial, the platform serves short quizzes to reinforce learning.

2. Exploring Certification Programs and Career Paths
Cloud computing certifications validate a learner's expertise and boost their career prospects. Certifications from AWS, Azure, and Google Cloud are among the most sought-after credentials in the tech industry. With AI's help, learners can create structured learning plans, practice exam questions, and receive personalized guidance on which certifications to pursue.

A. Most Popular Cloud Certifications
- AWS Certifications
  - AWS Certified Cloud Practitioner – Entry-level certification for cloud concepts and AWS services.
  - AWS Solutions Architect – Associate – Validates the ability to design AWS-based solutions.
  - AWS Certified DevOps Engineer – Advanced certification focused on CI/CD, automation, and infrastructure as code.
- Microsoft Azure Certifications
  - Azure Fundamentals (AZ-900) – Entry-level certification for understanding Azure services.
  - Azure Solutions Architect Expert (AZ-305) – Validates advanced skills in solution design and Azure architecture.
- Google Cloud Certifications
  - Google Cloud Associate Engineer – Entry-level certification for managing Google Cloud deployments.
  - Google Cloud Professional Data Engineer – Validates the ability to design and manage data solutions.

B. Career Paths in Cloud Computing
- Cloud Engineer
  - Role: Builds and maintains cloud environments using tools like AWS, Azure, and GCP.
  - Certifications: AWS Solutions Architect, Azure Associate Engineer.
- Cloud Solutions Architect
  - Role: Designs cloud solutions for business needs, often working with DevOps teams.
  - Certifications: AWS Solutions Architect – Professional, Azure Solutions Architect Expert.
- DevOps Engineer
  - Role: Manages CI/CD pipelines, automation, and Infrastructure as Code (IaC) tools.
  - Certifications: AWS DevOps Engineer, Azure DevOps Engineer Expert.

- AI/ML Engineer
  - Role: Builds AI-driven cloud solutions and works with tools like AWS SageMaker and Azure ML.
  - Certifications: AWS Certified Machine Learning – Specialty, Google Cloud Professional ML Engineer.

3. Leveraging AI for Real-Time Training and Feedback

AI-driven feedback is one of the most effective ways to ensure learners stay engaged, motivated, and continuously improve. AI identifies where learners struggle and provides immediate corrective guidance.

A. AI for Personalized Coaching
- AI Tutors and Chatbots
  - Chatbots like edX AI Mentor answer questions and guide learners in real time.
  - Example: A learner struggling to understand how AWS EC2 pricing works can ask the AI tutor for an explanation, which is tailored to their learning style.
- Real-Time Course Adjustments
  - If a student fails multiple attempts on IAM-related questions, AI can assign additional videos, hands-on labs, and articles on IAM.

B. AI-Driven Labs and Hands-On Exercises
- Interactive Cloud Labs
  - Platforms like AWS Skill Builder offer hands-on labs for deploying EC2 instances, configuring VPCs, and launching serverless apps.
  - AI tracks student performance, identifies errors, and recommends corrections in real time.
- Live Simulations and Hackathons
  - AI-based "simulators" provide real-world scenarios, like responding to an AWS outage or resolving a security breach.
- Automated Hands-On Lab Feedback
  - If a student misconfigures a security group or VPC, AI provides guidance on what went wrong.
  - Example: A Cloud Guru provides immediate lab feedback, allowing learners to retry tasks and correct mistakes.

Conclusion:
AI has become a transformative force in cloud learning and skill development. From adaptive learning systems to real-time feedback, AI allows learners to acquire cloud skills faster, smarter, and with greater precision. Personalized learning paths, automated practice exams, and hands-on labs ensure that students are equipped to master essential cloud concepts.

As the demand for cloud certifications grows, learners can rely on AI-driven platforms to track their progress, identify gaps, and prepare them for AWS, Azure, and Google Cloud certification exams. Career paths like Cloud Engineer, Solutions Architect, and DevOps Engineer are within reach for learners who leverage AI to accelerate their learning journey.

Key Takeaways
- Personalized Learning: AI adapts learning paths and provides instant feedback for faster progress.
- Skill Development: AI identifies skill gaps and provides targeted lessons on key cloud concepts.
- Career Impact: AI-guided career paths help learners achieve certifications and job-ready skills.

AI Insight:
"AI isn't just your tutor — it's your career coach. From building your first EC2 instance to earning your AWS certification, AI ensures you learn smarter, not harder."

Chapter 27: Cloud Governance and Compliance

Cloud governance and compliance are essential for businesses operating in the cloud, especially as regulations like GDPR, CCPA, and SOX impose strict rules on data privacy, security, and operational transparency. Without a clear governance framework, organizations risk non-compliance, security breaches, and potential financial penalties.

This chapter covers how organizations establish effective cloud governance, the role of AI in automating governance tasks, and the essential tools for auditing, reporting, and maintaining compliance in multi-cloud and hybrid cloud environments.

1. Frameworks for Maintaining Compliance with Global Regulations

Compliance frameworks provide the structure and guidelines businesses use to meet regulatory requirements. Each industry and country has specific data privacy and security mandates, and cloud providers play a key role in ensuring compliance.

A. Key Compliance Regulations
- General Data Protection Regulation (GDPR) – Europe
  - Purpose: Protects the privacy of EU citizens and regulates how personal data is collected, processed, and stored.
  - Cloud Implications: Companies must store EU customer data in EU-compliant data centers. Cloud providers like AWS, Azure, and Google Cloud offer Data Residency features to store data in specific regions.
  - Example: If a U.S.-based e-commerce company collects data from EU customers, GDPR requires the company to follow strict guidelines for data protection and breach notifications.
- California Consumer Privacy Act (CCPA) – USA
  - Purpose: Gives California residents the right to know, access, and delete personal data collected by businesses.
  - Cloud Implications: Cloud platforms must offer features like Right to Delete and Data Subject Access Requests (DSARs).
  - Example: If a customer from California requests to delete their account information, companies must have processes to delete cloud-stored data from AWS, Azure, or Google Cloud.
- Health Insurance Portability and Accountability Act (HIPAA) – USA
  - Purpose: Governs the security of Protected Health Information (PHI) for healthcare providers.

- Cloud Implications: Healthcare apps on AWS, Azure, and Google Cloud must encrypt PHI and limit access to authorized users only.
  - Example: A healthcare app that uses AWS for patient records must sign a Business Associate Agreement (BAA) with AWS to ensure compliance with HIPAA.
- Other Regional Regulations
  - Brazil (LGPD): Data privacy laws similar to GDPR.
  - China (PIPL): Requires that Chinese citizen data remain within China's borders.
  - India (DPDP): Data Protection Bill governing personal data collected from Indian citizens.

B. Cloud Governance Frameworks
Cloud governance frameworks ensure businesses maintain security, privacy, and regulatory compliance. These frameworks outline policies, standards, and best practices for managing multi-cloud and hybrid cloud environments.
- Control Objectives for Information and Related Technologies (COBIT)
  - Focuses on IT governance, risk management, and control processes.
  - Use Case: Helps organizations align cloud security and compliance with business goals.
- ISO 27001 – Information Security Management
  - Focuses on information security risk management for cloud environments.
  - Use Case: Ensures organizations establish an Information Security Management System (ISMS) to control cloud security risks.
- NIST Cybersecurity Framework (NIST CSF)
  - Focuses on managing cybersecurity risk.
  - Use Case: Helps cloud teams define access control, data protection, and incident response strategies.
- Cloud Security Alliance (CSA) Cloud Controls Matrix (CCM)
  - Specifically designed for cloud providers and consumers to evaluate cloud security risks.
  - Use Case: Provides a detailed mapping of cloud security controls to other compliance frameworks like ISO 27001, GDPR, and PCI DSS.

2. Role of AI in Automating Governance Tasks

AI plays a crucial role in cloud governance by automating audits, ensuring real-time compliance, and simplifying the enforcement of regulatory controls. AI not only identifies compliance gaps but also offers recommendations on how to address them. This automation reduces the need for manual intervention and enables businesses to maintain continuous compliance.

A. AI for Real-Time Compliance Monitoring
- Continuous Compliance Monitoring
  - AI tracks cloud resource changes (like misconfigured storage buckets) and identifies risks in real time.
  - Example: AWS Config tracks infrastructure changes, and if an S3 bucket is set to "public," AI-based monitoring flags it as a compliance violation.
- Automated Policy Enforcement
  - AI enforces governance rules automatically, ensuring all resources meet compliance requirements.
  - Example: Azure Policy automatically applies encryption rules to Azure SQL databases.
- Dynamic Risk Scoring
  - AI assigns risk scores to cloud configurations and offers remediation advice.
  - Example: AWS Security Hub provides a risk score for non-compliant AWS resources and suggests steps for remediation.

B. AI-Driven Audit and Reporting
- Automated Audit Logs
  - AI generates audit logs for all cloud activity (user logins, data access, resource modifications).
  - Example: AWS CloudTrail tracks changes made to AWS resources and generates audit logs to meet GDPR and CCPA data access requirements.
- Anomaly Detection in Audits
  - AI detects unusual patterns in audit logs (like access from suspicious IP addresses) and triggers security alerts.
  - Example: If an AWS administrator logs in from an unfamiliar country, AI flags it as suspicious activity and sends an alert.
- Audit Report Automation
  - AI generates regulatory audit reports that document compliance with ISO 27001, SOC 2, and GDPR.
  - Example: Splunk generates audit compliance reports for SOC 2 and GDPR requirements using machine learning to detect anomalies.

C. Remediation and Self-Healing
- Self-Healing Cloud Systems
  - AI detects misconfigurations (like public storage buckets) and automatically fixes them.
  - Example: If a developer accidentally makes an S3 bucket public, AI can automatically revert it to private.
- Proactive Threat Detection
  - AI predicts compliance failures before they happen.
  - Example: AWS GuardDuty uses machine learning to detect unusual access patterns that could signal a potential compliance violation.
- Automated Incident Response
  - AI triggers incident response workflows when policy violations occur.
  - Example: If sensitive PII is accessed by an unauthorized user, an automated incident response system quarantines the affected files.

3. Tools for Auditing and Reporting
Modern cloud environments generate massive amounts of log data. To remain compliant, businesses must analyze, report, and store this data. AI-powered tools make auditing and reporting more efficient by analyzing audit logs, generating reports, and recommending improvements.

A. Cloud Provider Tools
- AWS Config – Tracks AWS resource changes and compliance.
- Azure Policy – Enforces governance rules across Azure resources.
- Google Cloud Security Command Center – Centralizes compliance data for Google Cloud.

B. Third-Party Tools
- Splunk – Collects, analyzes, and visualizes cloud compliance logs.
- Datadog – Monitors cloud infrastructure for compliance issues.
- Sumo Logic – Offers continuous compliance monitoring for cloud applications.

C. AI-Powered Auditing Tools
- AWS Security Hub – AI-powered compliance checks for AWS.
- CloudCheckr – Monitors compliance for multi-cloud environments.
- Prisma Cloud – AI-driven compliance and security platform for AWS, Azure, and GCP.

Conclusion:
Cloud governance and compliance are critical for organizations operating in a multi-cloud environment. Without proper governance, companies risk violating data privacy regulations like GDPR and CCPA, leading to financial penalties and reputational damage. By using AI-driven tools, businesses can automate compliance audits, generate reports, and maintain continuous compliance.

AI's Role in Governance:
- Continuous Monitoring: AI tracks cloud resources 24/7 and flags non-compliance in real time.
- Policy Enforcement: AI applies compliance rules automatically, reducing manual intervention.
- Audit Automation: AI generates audit logs, compliance reports, and audit evidence for regulatory standards like ISO 27001 and SOC 2.

As cloud environments grow in complexity, organizations must ensure compliance across AWS, Azure, and GCP. With AI-driven governance, companies can automate compliance, reduce operational risk, and stay ahead of evolving global regulations.

AI Insight:
"AI is your compliance assistant, audit manager, and security guard all in one. It never sleeps, never forgets, and always enforces the rules."

Chapter 28: Ethics and Sustainability in Cloud Computing

As the world becomes increasingly dependent on cloud computing, the ethical and environmental impacts of this technology come under greater scrutiny. From the energy consumption of massive data centers to the ethical implications of AI-driven decision-making, cloud ethics and sustainability have become critical areas of focus.

This chapter examines how organizations can balance cloud innovation with environmental responsibility, addresses key ethical concerns related to AI and cloud usage, and highlights green initiatives aimed at reducing the environmental footprint of data centers and cloud operations.

1. Balancing Cloud Innovation with Environmental Responsibility

The demand for cloud services continues to rise, with companies relying on cloud platforms to store, process, and analyze massive amounts of data. However, this demand has a direct impact on energy consumption and carbon emissions. Balancing innovation with environmental sustainability is now a strategic priority for cloud providers and their customers.

A. Environmental Impact of Cloud Computing
- Data Center Energy Consumption
  - Data centers require enormous amounts of electricity to power servers, networking equipment, and cooling systems.
  - Example: It is estimated that global data centers consume about 1% of the world's total electricity usage, and this percentage is growing.
- Carbon Emissions from Cloud Operations
  - Energy used to power cloud data centers often comes from non-renewable energy sources like coal and natural gas, leading to high carbon emissions.
  - Example: A large data center in a region dependent on coal-fired power plants produces significantly more CO_2 emissions than a center powered by renewable energy.
- E-Waste from Cloud Infrastructure
  - As hardware ages, it is discarded, creating large volumes of electronic waste (e-waste).
  - Example: Hard drives, GPUs, and servers from decommissioned data centers are often sent to landfills unless recycled properly.

B. Strategies for Reducing Cloud's Environmental Impact
- Energy-Efficient Data Centers
  - Data centers use energy-efficient cooling systems, such as liquid cooling and direct-to-chip cooling, to reduce energy consumption.
  - Example: Google Cloud's data centers use AI-driven cooling systems to reduce energy usage by 30%, as the AI constantly monitors and adjusts temperatures.
- Shift to Renewable Energy
  - Cloud providers are investing in renewable energy (solar, wind, hydro) to power data centers.
  - Example: AWS has committed to powering its global infrastructure with 100% renewable energy by 2025, and Microsoft Azure aims to be carbon negative by 2030.
- Server Virtualization and Optimization
  - Virtualization allows multiple virtual machines (VMs) to run on a single server, reducing the total number of physical machines required.
  - Example: Cloud providers use serverless computing to dynamically allocate computing resources only when needed, reducing wasteful "always-on" consumption.

C. Business Benefits of Sustainable Cloud Practices
- Cost Reduction
  - Companies that optimize cloud resources consume less energy, reducing cloud bills.
  - Example: Serverless architectures (like AWS Lambda) allow companies to pay only for what they use, rather than paying for idle servers.
- Positive Brand Image
  - Customers prefer to engage with companies that prioritize sustainability.
  - Example: Companies that achieve sustainability goals, like carbon neutrality, can market themselves as "green brands," increasing customer trust.
- Regulatory Compliance
  - Some regions, like the European Union, have energy consumption regulations that cloud providers must follow.
  - Example: Companies storing data in the EU must comply with energy efficiency regulations under the European Green Deal.

2. Ethical Concerns in AI and Cloud Usage

The ethical use of cloud computing extends beyond sustainability. The use of AI-driven decision-making systems raises important ethical questions related to bias, privacy, and transparency. As cloud providers and AI systems become more embedded in society, organizations must adopt a more ethical approach to cloud usage.

A. Key Ethical Concerns in Cloud and AI
- Data Privacy and Ownership
  - Companies that store sensitive user data in the cloud must protect it from breaches, unauthorized access, and misuse.
  - Example: If a healthcare app stores patient records on AWS, it must comply with HIPAA regulations to ensure that patient data is protected.
- AI Bias and Fairness
  - AI models trained on biased data may produce discriminatory outcomes.
  - Example: An AI recruitment tool that is trained on historical hiring data may prefer male candidates, especially if the data reflects past hiring biases.
- Algorithmic Transparency and Explainability
  - Businesses using black-box AI models (like neural networks) must ensure decision-making processes are transparent and explainable.
  - Example: If a cloud-based AI model denies a customer's loan application, the customer has the right to know how the decision was made.
- Surveillance and Mass Data Collection
  - Governments and corporations may use cloud platforms to conduct mass surveillance on citizens.
  - Example: "Data scraping" occurs when businesses extract publicly available information (like social media posts) and store it in the cloud, raising ethical concerns about privacy.

B. Ethical Best Practices in Cloud and AI Usage
- Privacy-First Design
  - Companies should adopt privacy-by-design principles, ensuring data protection is built into cloud applications.
- Ethical AI Development
  - Use fairness testing tools like AI Fairness 360 to detect and mitigate bias in AI models.
- Transparent AI Models
  - Use explainable AI (XAI) techniques to make AI decision-making processes clear to users.
- Data Minimization
  - Avoid collecting unnecessary data and delete user data once it's no longer needed.

3. Green Initiatives in Data Centers and Cloud Operations

Cloud providers like AWS, Google Cloud, and Microsoft Azure are making significant efforts to build greener data centers and sustainable cloud operations. These green initiatives aim to reduce power consumption, cut emissions, and promote circular economies for hardware.

A. Green Initiatives from Cloud Providers
- 100% Renewable Energy Commitments
  - Major cloud providers are committed to using 100% renewable energy by specific target dates.
  - AWS: 100% renewable energy by 2025.
  - Google Cloud: Carbon-free operations 24/7 by 2030.
  - Microsoft Azure: Carbon negative by 2030.
- Carbon Offsetting and Carbon Removal
  - Providers purchase carbon offsets to balance out the emissions they can't avoid.
  - Example: Microsoft funds projects that remove CO_2 from the atmosphere to compensate for emissions.
- Circular Economy for Cloud Hardware
  - Providers refurbish, resell, or recycle old cloud hardware.
  - Example: Google reuses server parts from old hardware, reducing waste.

B. Sustainable Design for Data Centers
- Water Conservation
  - Data centers rely on water for cooling, but new cooling systems reduce water usage.
  - Example: Google Cloud uses a closed-loop cooling system that recycles water instead of consuming fresh water.
- AI-Powered Energy Management
  - AI systems like DeepMind analyze data center cooling and power consumption to make energy use more efficient.
  - Example: Google's AI-powered cooling system reduced energy usage by 40% in some data centers.

Conclusion:
The rapid expansion of cloud computing brings with it profound ethical and environmental challenges. From energy consumption and carbon emissions to data privacy and AI bias, companies must adopt responsible governance strategies to balance cloud innovation with sustainability. Cloud providers like AWS, Azure, and Google Cloud are leading the charge toward greener data centers and AI-powered compliance tools.

What Can Companies Do?
- Adopt Sustainable Cloud Practices: Use virtualization, serverless architecture, and workload optimization.
- Monitor AI Ethics: Ensure AI models are explainable, fair, and privacy-respecting.
- Demand Accountability from Cloud Providers: Work with providers that have strong environmental and ethical commitments.

AI Insight:
"AI doesn't just make the cloud smarter — it makes it greener. By automating cooling, reducing emissions, and protecting privacy, AI ensures the cloud works for the planet and its people."

Chapter 29: AI and Cloud Sustainability

The shift to cloud computing has brought significant benefits to businesses, such as scalability, flexibility, and cost reduction. However, this growth comes with environmental costs, as massive cloud data centers consume large amounts of energy and produce substantial carbon emissions. To address this challenge, cloud providers and organizations are turning to AI-driven sustainability initiatives.

AI is transforming sustainability in cloud computing by optimizing energy consumption, reducing the carbon footprint of data centers, and enabling the development of future green initiatives. This chapter explores how AI tools promote cloud sustainability, provides real-world examples of green cloud initiatives, and discusses future trends that will define sustainable cloud operations.

1. AI Tools for Optimizing Energy Consumption and Carbon Footprints

One of the biggest concerns with cloud computing is the energy consumption required to power large-scale data centers. Data centers operate 24/7, requiring continuous power for servers, networking equipment, and cooling systems. AI-driven energy optimization tools are revolutionizing how cloud providers and companies reduce their carbon footprints and achieve sustainability goals.

A. AI-Driven Energy Optimization
- AI-Powered Cooling Systems
  - Challenge: Data centers require massive amounts of energy to cool servers, especially in hot climates.
  - AI Solution: AI predicts temperature fluctuations in data centers and adjusts cooling in real time to reduce energy use.
  - Example: Google's AI-driven cooling system (powered by DeepMind) reduced its cooling energy consumption by 40%. The AI continuously monitors temperature, humidity, and airflow to make precise cooling adjustments.
- Predictive Load Balancing
  - Challenge: Data centers experience fluctuating workloads, leading to uneven server utilization.
  - AI Solution: AI-based load balancing algorithms predict future workload demands and distribute the load across multiple servers.
  - Example: AWS Auto Scaling ensures that only the required servers are running during peak and off-peak periods, reducing idle server power consumption.

- Dynamic Resource Allocation
  - Challenge: Virtual machines (VMs) and containerized applications often run continuously, even when idle.
  - AI Solution: AI tools predict when cloud resources (like EC2 instances) will be idle and shut them down automatically.
  - Example: Google Cloud's Active Assist automatically recommends underutilized VM instances that can be scaled down or terminated, reducing unnecessary power usage.

B. Carbon Footprint Analysis Using AI
- Real-Time Carbon Tracking
  - Challenge: Companies struggle to track and quantify the carbon footprint of their cloud usage.
  - AI Solution: AI-powered carbon tracking dashboards monitor CO_2 emissions in real time, allowing businesses to visualize their environmental impact.
  - Example: Microsoft Sustainability Calculator tracks emissions from Azure services, showing companies how much CO_2 their cloud usage generates and how it can be reduced.
- Carbon Footprint Reporting
  - Challenge: Companies face pressure to produce ESG (Environmental, Social, and Governance) reports on their sustainability efforts.
  - AI Solution: Cloud providers like AWS and Google Cloud use AI to provide detailed reports on carbon emissions.
  - Example: AWS offers Sustainability Pillar Reports through the AWS Well-Architected Framework, showing how companies can reduce their carbon footprint.
- Predictive Sustainability Analytics
  - Challenge: Organizations struggle to predict future sustainability goals.
  - AI Solution: Predictive analytics powered by AI simulate future carbon footprint reductions.
  - Example: AI models can predict that switching to serverless functions instead of virtual machines will reduce emissions by 50%, encouraging companies to shift to serverless architectures.

C. AI-Powered Sustainable Design for Cloud Apps
- Green Software Design
  - Challenge: Cloud applications consume excessive power due to inefficient code and software design.
  - AI Solution: AI-powered code analyzers identify inefficient code and offer suggestions for optimization.

- Example: Microsoft Green Software Foundation promotes the development of "green software" that consumes less energy.
- Sustainable Serverless Architectures
  - Challenge: Traditional monolithic cloud apps remain active even when idle.
  - AI Solution: AI recommends serverless architectures like AWS Lambda or Azure Functions, which only consume resources when invoked.
  - Example: An app that runs 24/7 on a VM can be refactored into event-driven serverless functions, saving energy.

2. Examples of Green Cloud Initiatives
Major cloud providers like AWS, Google Cloud, and Microsoft Azure are leading efforts to make cloud operations more sustainable. These green initiatives aim to reduce carbon emissions, increase the use of renewable energy, and minimize e-waste from cloud hardware.

A. AWS Sustainability Initiatives
- 100% Renewable Energy by 2025
  - Goal: AWS has pledged to power its global infrastructure with 100% renewable energy by 2025.
  - Action: AWS is building wind and solar farms and purchasing renewable energy credits.
  - AI Use Case: AWS uses AI to predict peak energy usage and determine optimal renewable energy usage times.
- AWS Sustainability Pillar
  - AWS provides companies with a Sustainability Pillar in its Well-Architected Framework, helping them track and reduce cloud energy consumption.

B. Google Cloud Sustainability Initiatives
- Carbon-Free Energy by 2030
  - Google Cloud has pledged to operate on 100% carbon-free energy 24/7 by 2030.
  - AI Use Case: Google uses DeepMind's AI to reduce cooling system energy usage in data centers by 40%.
- Carbon Footprint Tool
  - Google Cloud provides a tool that allows customers to track their carbon emissions.
  - Use Case: Businesses using Google Cloud can visualize their carbon footprint and make decisions to reduce energy use.

C. Microsoft Azure Sustainability Initiatives
- Carbon Negative by 2030
  - Microsoft aims to remove more CO2 from the atmosphere than it emits by 2030.
  - Action: Investments in carbon capture technology and support for global reforestation projects.
- Sustainable AI Development
  - Microsoft has introduced Green AI initiatives to develop AI models that consume less energy and run on renewable energy sources.

3. Future Trends in Sustainable Cloud Computing
As companies and cloud providers continue to seek more sustainable solutions, several trends will shape the future of green cloud computing.

A. AI-Driven Green Data Centers
- Autonomous Data Centers
  - Future data centers will be fully autonomous, relying on AI to handle server cooling, resource allocation, and server maintenance.
  - Example: Edge data centers use AI robots to install and maintain servers, reducing travel-related emissions from human technicians.
- AI-Powered Energy Grids
  - AI will predict energy consumption needs for cloud data centers and dynamically allocate energy from renewable sources.
  - Example: Cloud providers could prioritize the use of wind or solar power during sunny or windy days.

B. Circular Economy for Cloud Hardware
- Hardware Recycling and Refurbishment
  - Used server hardware will be refurbished, resold, or recycled.
  - Example: Google recycles 19% of its server components to build new servers.
- Sustainable Materials for Server Hardware
  - Companies will develop biodegradable electronics to reduce the e-waste impact of decommissioned servers.

C. Zero-Carbon Cloud Computing
- Zero-Carbon Cloud Services
  - Future cloud offerings will be certified carbon-free, allowing companies to choose net-zero hosting services.
  - Example: Customers will be able to select "Green Hosting" services for AWS EC2 or Azure VMs.
- AI Carbon Management Systems
  - AI will automate carbon credit trading and emissions offsetting for companies using the cloud.

Conclusion:
Cloud sustainability is no longer optional — it's a critical part of cloud strategy. By leveraging AI to optimize energy usage, manage carbon footprints, and enable autonomous operations, companies can achieve a balance between innovation and sustainability.

What Can Companies Do?
- Use AI-powered sustainability dashboards to track carbon emissions.
- Shift to serverless architectures to reduce idle compute resources.
- Optimize workloads with AI-based predictive scaling to minimize energy use.

AI Insight:
"AI doesn't just make the cloud smarter — it makes it greener. With AI-driven energy optimization and predictive analytics, cloud sustainability is no longer a distant goal but an achievable reality."

Chapter 30: Cloud Gaming and Media Streaming

The cloud has revolutionized gaming and media streaming industries, offering seamless access to high-quality content on demand. With cloud gaming platforms like Google Stadia, Microsoft Xbox Cloud Gaming, and NVIDIA GeForce NOW, users can play high-end video games on low-spec devices. Similarly, media streaming platforms like Netflix, YouTube, and Spotify rely on cloud infrastructure to deliver smooth, uninterrupted streaming to millions of users worldwide.

The role of AI in cloud gaming and streaming is transformative. AI optimizes latency, personalizes user experiences, and enhances content delivery. In this chapter, we'll explore how the cloud is shaping the future of gaming and streaming services, how AI plays a role in user experience and network optimization, and what future trends are on the horizon for immersive media technologies.

1. Role of Cloud in Revolutionizing Gaming and Streaming Services

The rise of cloud gaming and media streaming has removed the need for consumers to own powerful hardware. Instead, users can stream games, movies, and music directly to their devices with minimal setup. This shift has unlocked new opportunities for accessibility, cost reduction, and on-demand entertainment.

A. Cloud Gaming: From Consoles to the Cloud
- How Cloud Gaming Works
  - Cloud gaming platforms host games on powerful remote servers.
  - Gamers connect to these servers via the internet and stream game content to their devices in real-time.
  - Example: Services like Google Stadia and Xbox Cloud Gaming allow users to play AAA games on devices like smartphones and smart TVs.
- Benefits of Cloud Gaming
  - No Expensive Hardware: Users don't need gaming consoles or high-end PCs.
  - Instant Access: No downloads or updates are required. Players can launch games instantly.
  - Cross-Platform Play: Users can play games on laptops, smartphones, and smart TVs with no performance loss.
- Challenges in Cloud Gaming
  - Latency Issues: Delays between a player's input and the game response can impact gameplay.
  - Bandwidth Requirements: Players need fast, stable internet connections for smooth streaming.

- Server Load: Hosting massive numbers of concurrent players increases server demands.

B. Media Streaming: From Discs to On-Demand Content
- How Cloud Media Streaming Works
    - Content (like videos, music, and live streams) is hosted on cloud servers.
    - Streaming platforms like Netflix and Spotify deliver content on demand via Content Delivery Networks (CDNs).
    - Example: Netflix uses AWS and Google Cloud to stream movies and TV shows to millions of users worldwide.
- Benefits of Media Streaming
    - On-Demand Access: Users can access vast libraries of movies, TV shows, and music at any time.
    - Global Reach: Cloud infrastructure allows platforms to deliver content worldwide.
    - Content Personalization: AI-driven recommendations suggest new shows, movies, and songs.
- Challenges in Media Streaming
    - Bandwidth Usage: Streaming 4K video requires substantial bandwidth.
    - Global Load Balancing: Streaming platforms must ensure content is available in multiple regions.
    - Piracy and Content Protection: Protecting streamed content from piracy and unauthorized access is crucial.

2. AI's Contribution to Latency Reduction and User Experience
AI is the backbone of modern cloud gaming and media streaming. From reducing latency in gaming to curating personalized recommendations for streaming, AI transforms how users engage with content. Companies like Netflix, Twitch, and Microsoft use AI to deliver smooth, personalized, and lag-free experiences.

A. Reducing Latency with AI in Cloud Gaming
- Predictive Input Systems
    - Problem: Latency occurs when a user's input is delayed due to network lag.
    - AI Solution: Predictive AI anticipates user inputs (like movements or button presses) and pre-renders game frames.
    - Example: Google Stadia employs predictive AI to forecast player inputs, ensuring smooth gameplay even when network delays occur.
- Network Optimization with AI
    - Problem: Server overload and network congestion cause latency spikes.

- AI Solution: AI-based load balancers distribute network traffic across multiple servers to reduce congestion.
- Example: AWS Global Accelerator optimizes routing paths for game data packets, reducing ping times for gamers.
- Edge Computing for Low-Latency Gaming
  - Problem: Players far from cloud servers experience higher latency.
  - AI Solution: AI-powered edge computing ensures game data is processed closer to the player.
  - Example: AWS Wavelength deploys servers at the edge of 5G networks, reducing the distance between players and cloud servers.

B. Enhancing the Streaming Experience with AI
- Content Personalization
  - Problem: Users want personalized content recommendations.
  - AI Solution: AI algorithms analyze user behavior to recommend movies, shows, and songs.
  - Example: Netflix's AI recommendation engine personalizes content for each user based on watch history and search behavior.
- Dynamic Streaming Quality (Adaptive Bitrate Streaming)
  - Problem: Bandwidth fluctuations can cause video buffering or pixelation.
  - AI Solution: AI-powered adaptive bitrate streaming adjusts video quality in real time based on available bandwidth.
  - Example: YouTube and Netflix dynamically reduce video resolution when bandwidth drops, preventing buffering.
- Real-Time Content Moderation
  - Problem: Live-streamed content can contain harmful, illegal, or inappropriate material.
  - AI Solution: AI uses natural language processing (NLP) and image recognition to flag inappropriate content.
  - Example: Twitch uses AI to moderate chat comments in real time and block offensive language.

3. Future Trends in Immersive Media Technologies

As the cloud continues to power gaming and media streaming, the future will bring even more immersive experiences. The combination of AI, 5G, and XR (extended reality) will reshape how users interact with games, movies, and live streams.

A. Cloud-Powered Virtual Reality (VR) and Augmented Reality (AR)

- Cloud XR Platforms
  - Cloud XR enables streaming of VR and AR content from the cloud to lightweight devices like AR glasses.
  - Example: NVIDIA CloudXR allows users to stream VR experiences to AR/VR headsets.
- VR Streaming for Gaming and Education
  - As VR headsets become lighter and more affordable, cloud-powered VR streaming will enable educational simulations, training, and entertainment.
- 5G-Enabled AR/VR Streaming
  - 5G allows low-latency AR/VR streaming, making it possible to experience immersive, cloud-powered virtual reality in real time.

B. AI-Generated Content in Games and Streaming

- AI-Generated Storylines in Games
  - AI systems will create procedurally generated quests and stories for cloud-based games.
  - Example: Future games could offer unique, AI-generated missions tailored to individual players.
- AI-Powered Virtual Characters
  - NPCs (Non-Player Characters) will be powered by AI, giving them human-like behaviors and responses.
  - Example: AI-powered characters in The Elder Scrolls VI could react to player decisions in new and unique ways.

C. Interactive and Social Streaming Experiences

- Interactive Streaming Shows
  - Viewers will influence live-action shows in real time, selecting plot points and character decisions.
  - Example: Netflix's Black Mirror: Bandersnatch allowed viewers to make choices that influenced the storyline.
- Live Shopping Streams
  - Platforms like YouTube will integrate live shopping experiences, allowing viewers to buy products while watching.
- Immersive Watch Parties
  - Users will be able to watch movies with friends remotely in a shared virtual cinema experience.

Conclusion:
The cloud has revolutionized gaming and media streaming, removing the need for expensive hardware and providing users with on-demand entertainment. Cloud platforms like Google Stadia and Netflix have enabled users to stream high-quality content on any device, anywhere in the world. AI-driven latency reduction, personalized content recommendations, and adaptive bitrate streaming are enhancing the experience for users globally.

As 5G and XR (extended reality) evolve, immersive gaming and media streaming experiences will become even more realistic and interactive. From VR streaming to AI-generated storylines, the future is one of endless possibility.

AI Insight:
"AI is the game master, the streaming host, and the referee all rolled into one. It guarantees seamless, immersive, and personalized entertainment — wherever, whenever."

Chapter 31: AI and the Future of Decentralized Cloud Computing

The traditional cloud computing model relies on centralized data centers operated by large providers like AWS, Google Cloud, and Microsoft Azure. While this model offers efficiency and scalability, it also raises concerns about data privacy, vendor lock-in, and single points of failure. Decentralized cloud computing aims to address these issues by using a blockchain-enabled, peer-to-peer model where no single entity controls the network.

AI plays a pivotal role in enhancing decentralized cloud platforms. It enables automated resource allocation, self-healing systems, and intelligent data distribution. This chapter explores the fundamentals of decentralized cloud computing, how AI enhances its capabilities, and the emerging applications for secure, distributed data systems.

1. Introduction to Blockchain-Enabled Cloud Models
Decentralized cloud computing is powered by technologies like blockchain, distributed ledgers, and peer-to-peer (P2P) storage networks. Instead of relying on a single cloud provider, users leverage a distributed network of nodes to store, manage, and access their data.

A. What is Decentralized Cloud Computing?
- How It Works
  - In a decentralized cloud, data is broken into smaller pieces and stored across multiple nodes or "peer devices" on the network.
  - The system uses blockchain-based smart contracts to facilitate trust and transparency between users and storage providers.
  - Example: Instead of relying on AWS to store a file, it is encrypted, split into fragments, and stored on multiple user-operated nodes in a network like Storj or Filecoin.

Difference Between Centralized and Decentralized Clouds

When it comes to cloud infrastructure, businesses can choose between centralized clouds and decentralized clouds. Each approach offers distinct benefits and trade-offs depending on factors like security, control, and scalability. Here's a breakdown of the key differences.

1. Control and Ownership
   - Centralized Cloud: In a centralized cloud, a single provider controls the infrastructure. Services like AWS, Azure, and Google Cloud operate on this model, where a centralized authority manages the servers, updates, and security protocols. Users "rent" access to storage, compute power, and cloud resources from a central source.
   - Decentralized Cloud: Unlike a centralized cloud, no single authority controls the infrastructure. Instead, resources are distributed across multiple peer-to-peer (P2P) nodes. Each participant in the network owns a piece of the infrastructure, which is shared and accessed collectively. Examples include Filecoin and Storj, where users contribute their unused storage to form a shared cloud network.

2. Data Location
   - Centralized Cloud: Data is stored in specific data centers owned by the cloud provider. For example, AWS or Azure may store your data in a specific availability zone or region (like "US-East-1" for AWS). The data is controlled and secured by the provider, and users have little visibility into where, specifically, the data is stored.
   - Decentralized Cloud: Data is fragmented and distributed across multiple nodes worldwide. Instead of being in one location, data is stored in pieces (like shards) on multiple participant nodes. This makes data location unpredictable but provides added redundancy and privacy. Filecoin and Sia are examples where data is stored across a decentralized network of participants.

3. Security and Privacy
   - Centralized Cloud: Security is managed by the cloud provider, and users must trust the provider to maintain data privacy, encrypt files, and protect against breaches. Providers like AWS, Azure, and Google Cloud adhere to GDPR, HIPAA, and SOC 2 compliance, but the risk of a centralized breach remains. If the central provider is hacked, all customer data is at risk.

- Decentralized Cloud: Privacy is inherently stronger in decentralized clouds because data is encrypted and distributed. Since data is fragmented across multiple nodes, no single party has complete access to the full dataset. Even if a single node is hacked, only a small fragment of the data is exposed. This makes decentralized clouds more resilient against attacks like ransomware and breaches.

4. Cost
- Centralized Cloud: Pricing for centralized clouds is based on pay-as-you-go, subscription, and reserved instance models. Users pay for the compute, storage, and bandwidth used. While centralized providers like AWS offer cost-saving options (like reserved instances and spot instances), the pricing can still be high for large-scale data usage.
- Decentralized Cloud: Decentralized cloud pricing is often more affordable and flexible. Since storage is pooled from multiple users (instead of a single company managing the servers), pricing is competitive. Platforms like Storj and Filecoin operate on a model where users rent storage space directly from contributors, reducing operational costs.

5. Scalability
- Centralized Cloud: Centralized clouds like AWS, Azure, and Google Cloud have near-unlimited scalability. Businesses can scale up or down with the click of a button because the provider has a large pool of resources. This makes centralized clouds ideal for enterprises that need dynamic scaling for high-traffic workloads.
- Decentralized Cloud: Scalability depends on network participation. As more users join the decentralized network and share their storage or compute power, the cloud scales accordingly. However, since the system relies on community contributions, scalability may not be as fast or as seamless as with AWS, Azure, or Google Cloud.

6. Availability and Uptime
- Centralized Cloud: Uptime depends on the cloud provider's infrastructure, and large providers like AWS offer 99.9% to 99.99% uptime guarantees. However, single points of failure (like region-wide outages) can disrupt services. For instance, if AWS US-East-1 goes down, businesses relying on that region can experience downtime.

- Decentralized Cloud: Decentralized clouds rely on distributed nodes. Since there is no single point of failure, availability is typically higher. If one node fails, the system can rebuild the data from other nodes, ensuring uptime. This approach is seen as more fault-tolerant and resilient against natural disasters or data center failures.

7. Transparency and Trust
- Centralized Cloud: Users must trust the cloud provider (like AWS or Azure) to handle data securely, maintain uptime, and keep backups. Customers have little visibility into what happens behind the scenes, such as how security patches are applied or where data is stored.
- Decentralized Cloud: Transparency is a core principle of decentralized clouds. Data storage, encryption, and replication processes are often verifiable through blockchain technology. Decentralized storage platforms (like Filecoin) allow users to see exactly how their data is stored and audit the data availability.

8. Fault Tolerance
- Centralized Cloud: If a specific availability zone goes offline (like AWS US-East-1), users relying solely on that zone may face service disruptions. However, larger companies use multi-zone deployments to prevent downtime. AWS, Azure, and Google Cloud all have built-in failover systems, but this requires extra planning.
- Decentralized Cloud: In decentralized clouds, there is no single point of failure. Data is replicated across multiple nodes. If one node fails or goes offline, data can be reconstructed from other nodes. This approach offers stronger redundancy and disaster recovery compared to centralized clouds.

9. Use Cases
- Centralized Cloud: Centralized clouds are best for enterprises, startups, and businesses that prioritize convenience, support, and compliance. They are used for web hosting, software development, machine learning, and enterprise applications. For companies that need complete support, training, and enterprise-grade guarantees, centralized providers like AWS, Azure, and Google Cloud are the best option.

- Decentralized Cloud: Decentralized clouds are better suited for companies that need enhanced privacy, data redundancy, and lower costs. It's ideal for applications where data privacy is a top priority (like blockchain projects, DeFi, and Web3 apps). Decentralized clouds like Storj, Filecoin, and Sia are also used in content distribution networks (CDNs) and secure file storage.

Summary
- Centralized Cloud: Run by a single company (like AWS, Azure, or GCP) with a focus on convenience, scalability, and managed services. Best for enterprises, startups, and businesses that prioritize support and compliance.
- Decentralized Cloud: Distributed across peer-to-peer nodes with no single authority. Provides better privacy, redundancy, and transparency, making it ideal for blockchain, Web3, and secure file storage.

By understanding the strengths and trade-offs between centralized clouds and decentralized clouds, companies can choose the right cloud approach. If you need enterprise support, full-service cloud capabilities, and on-demand scalability, stick with AWS, Azure, or Google Cloud. If you prioritize privacy, security, and fault tolerance, decentralized platforms like Filecoin, Sia, or Storj are strong alternatives.

- Benefits of Decentralized Cloud Models
  - Data Privacy & Sovereignty: Users retain full control of their data, reducing privacy risks.
  - Resilience & Redundancy: Since data is distributed across multiple nodes, outages at one location do not affect availability.
  - Lower Costs: Users pay only for what they use, with fewer fees than traditional providers.
  - Increased Security: Data is encrypted, broken into chunks, and stored on multiple nodes, making it harder for hackers to access.

B. Key Blockchain-Enabled Cloud Models
- Filecoin
  - How It Works: Filecoin allows users to rent out unused hard drive space. Data is encrypted, stored in fragments, and distributed across many users.
  - AI Role: AI algorithms predict storage demand, ensuring optimal resource allocation and preventing overuse of any one storage node.

- Storj
  - How It Works: Storj offers decentralized file storage using encryption and node-based storage. Companies can store files at a fraction of the cost of AWS S3.
  - AI Role: AI tracks node availability and storage usage to ensure smooth file retrieval and uptime.
- Siacoin
  - How It Works: Similar to Filecoin, Sia allows users to rent out unused disk space, and users pay with Siacoin tokens.
  - AI Role: AI helps optimize which nodes store specific files based on redundancy, storage size, and retrieval times.

2. How AI Enhances Decentralized Platforms

While blockchain ensures security, transparency, and immutability, AI brings intelligence and automation to decentralized cloud computing. Without AI, managing millions of distributed nodes, storage demands, and user requests would be inefficient and slow. Here's how AI drives efficiency in decentralized cloud networks.

A. AI for Smart Data Distribution
- Data Sharding and Placement
  - Problem: When a file is split into pieces, where should each piece be stored?
  - AI Solution: AI determines the optimal placement of data shards to reduce latency, maximize redundancy, and ensure security.
  - Example: If a file is split into 10 parts, AI chooses to store 3 parts on nearby nodes and 7 parts on nodes across different geographies, ensuring global availability.
- AI-Optimized Load Balancing
  - Problem: Which storage nodes should handle incoming data requests?
  - AI Solution: AI-based load balancers analyze current node traffic and storage availability to route requests to the least busy node.
  - Example: During a high-traffic event (like a viral video upload), AI load balancers direct data storage and retrieval requests to underutilized nodes, maintaining smooth performance.
- Redundancy and Failover
  - Problem: If a node storing file fragments fails, data could be lost.
  - AI Solution: AI tracks node health and predicts node failures in advance. When a node becomes unavailable, the system triggers self-healing by copying file fragments to new nodes.

○ Example: Storj or Filecoin detect a storage node going offline and automatically transfer stored data to healthy nodes.

B. AI-Driven Network Optimization
- Predictive Network Traffic Management
  ○ AI Role: Predicts demand spikes and allocates storage bandwidth accordingly.
  ○ Example: Before Black Friday, AI predicts traffic spikes and pre-loads content onto edge nodes close to users, ensuring fast access.

- Latency Reduction with Edge AI
  ○ AI Role: Edge AI nodes process data closer to users, reducing latency and ensuring smooth video playback, gaming, and app performance.
  ○ Example: Decentralized gaming services could run game logic at edge nodes, reducing the lag caused by long-distance server communication.
- AI-Powered Content Caching
  ○ AI Role: Caches frequently accessed files on nodes near users.
  ○ Example: If 100 users request a popular video, AI predicts user demand and places the video on nodes in close geographic proximity, reducing download time.

3. Applications in Secure, Distributed Data Systems
Decentralized cloud models combined with AI are used in several innovative ways. Here are a few real-world use cases where blockchain, AI, and the cloud intersect.

A. Decentralized Identity Management
- Problem: Centralized identity providers (like Google or Facebook) control user logins.
- AI Solution: Decentralized identity platforms (like Microsoft ION) use blockchain to provide self-sovereign identities. AI ensures user credentials are verified in real-time.

B. Decentralized Media Storage
- Problem: Centralized streaming platforms (Netflix, YouTube) control which content stays online.
- AI Solution: Decentralized platforms like Theta and Livepeer offer blockchain-based media storage. AI-based predictive caching places popular videos on nearby nodes.

C. Decentralized Supply Chains
- Problem: Supply chains face trust issues and delays in tracking shipments.
- AI Solution: Blockchain creates transparent supply chain records, while AI predicts shipping delays and optimizes delivery routes.
- Example: Walmart uses blockchain to track food shipments, ensuring product freshness. AI-based route optimization reduces delays.

Conclusion:
Decentralized cloud computing offers a glimpse into the future of secure, private, and resilient cloud infrastructure. By moving from centralized to decentralized systems, users gain more control over their data, avoid vendor lock-in, and achieve better fault tolerance. Blockchain enables decentralization, while AI enhances intelligence and automation, ensuring optimal load balancing, predictive node failures, and self-healing systems.

AI's Role:
- AI enables predictive storage by placing file fragments on optimal nodes.
- Load balancing AI ensures smooth data access during high-traffic events.
- Self-healing AI automatically replaces failed storage nodes to maintain data availability.

With the rapid rise of blockchain-enabled cloud storage platforms like Filecoin and Storj, and the growing role of AI automation, the future of decentralized cloud computing looks incredibly promising.

AI Insight:
"AI turns a collection of decentralized nodes into an intelligent, self-healing cloud. No more vendor lock-in, no single points of failure—just a network that's smart, self-repairing, and always on."

Chapter 32: Cloud Migration Strategies

As organizations seek to modernize their infrastructure, moving from on-premises data centers to the cloud has become a key initiative. Cloud migration offers benefits like scalability, reduced operational costs, and increased flexibility. However, successful cloud migration requires careful planning, a clear strategy, and the right execution methodology.

In this chapter, we'll explore the essential steps to plan and execute a smooth cloud migration, the widely adopted "6 Rs" migration framework, and how to avoid common mistakes that can lead to cost overruns, delays, and operational downtime.

1. Planning and Executing On-Premises to Cloud Migrations

Migrating on-premises infrastructure to the cloud is a complex process that requires alignment across business, IT, and DevOps teams. Without proper planning, organizations face risks like system downtime, data loss, and inflated costs. This section highlights how to create an effective migration plan and avoid these challenges.

A. Key Phases of Cloud Migration
- Assessment and Readiness Check
  - Objective: Evaluate the current on-premises environment to understand application dependencies, network topology, and security risks.
  - Steps:
    - Identify which apps are cloud-ready and which require refactoring.
    - Use Cloud Migration Assessment Tools like AWS Migration Hub or Azure Migrate to evaluate the complexity of the migration.
    - AI Tools: AI can analyze dependencies between applications and predict migration difficulty.
- Migration Strategy Selection
  - Objective: Decide on the best migration approach (using the 6 Rs strategy).
  - Steps:
    - Determine which apps should be rehosted, refactored, or retired.
    - Use AI decision models to identify which migration path is most cost-effective.

- Migration Execution
  - Objective: Migrate data, applications, and workloads while maintaining business continuity.
  - Steps:
    - Use data replication tools (like AWS DMS, Azure Data Migration Service) to move large datasets.
    - Set up failover and fallback systems to ensure business continuity during migration.
    - Conduct migration tests on staging environments before going live.
- Post-Migration Validation
  - Objective: Test the success of the migration, ensure performance goals are met, and validate security and compliance.
  - Steps:
    - Run performance tests to check system response times.
    - Validate security settings (IAM roles, access controls, encryption).
    - Conduct AI-driven anomaly detection to identify issues with application performance.

B. Roles and Responsibilities
- Cloud Architects – Design the cloud migration strategy, select tools, and ensure smooth execution.
- DevOps Engineers – Automate CI/CD pipelines, build cloud-native applications, and maintain uptime.
- IT Security Teams – Review security compliance, IAM roles, and data encryption policies.
- Data Engineers – Migrate data while ensuring no loss or corruption occurs.

2. The "6 Rs" of Migration Methodology
The 6 Rs is a well-established framework for cloud migration. It outlines six possible strategies to move workloads from on-premises to the cloud. Choosing the right approach for each application is crucial for success.

Deep Dive into Each "R"
- Rehost (Lift-and-Shift)
  - How It Works: Move an application "as-is" to the cloud with minimal changes.
  - When to Use: When you have legacy apps or need to migrate quickly.
  - Example: Moving a Linux web server running Apache from on-premises to an AWS EC2 instance.
  - Tool: Use AWS Application Migration Service for fast rehosting.
- Replatform (Lift-Tinker-and-Shift)
  - How It Works: Make small modifications (like using managed cloud services) to improve performance.
  - When to Use: When you want to reduce maintenance without a complete rewrite.
  - Example: Migrating a MySQL database to Amazon RDS instead of running it on a VM.
  - Tool: Use AWS Database Migration Service (DMS) for database migration.
- Refactor (Re-Architect)
  - How It Works: Rebuild applications to be cloud-native.
  - When to Use: When you want to fully modernize an app to use serverless or microservices.
  - Example: Rebuilding a monolithic app into a microservices architecture.
  - Tool: Use AWS Lambda or Azure Functions for serverless computing.
- Retire (Decommission)
  - How It Works: Identify and remove obsolete apps that no longer provide value.
  - When to Use: When certain apps are no longer needed.
  - Example: Deleting an old HR system that's been replaced by Workday.
- Retain (Keep On-Premises)
  - How It Works: Keep certain apps on-premises.
  - When to Use: For apps that can't be migrated due to compliance or latency requirements.
  - Example: An on-prem database used for secure government work.

- Repurchase (Switch to SaaS)
  - How It Works: Replace an existing app with a modern SaaS solution.
  - When to Use: When better SaaS options exist.
  - Example: Replacing an on-prem CRM with Salesforce or HubSpot CRM.

3. Avoiding Pitfalls During Cloud Transitions

Even with the best strategies in place, cloud migrations can fail due to cost overruns, data loss, or poor planning. Here's how to avoid common mistakes.

A. Top Mistakes to Avoid
- Poor Cost Management
  - Problem: Cloud costs balloon due to resource mismanagement.
  - Solution: Use AI cost tracking tools like AWS Cost Explorer to track cloud expenses.
- Insufficient Security Controls
  - Problem: Migrating apps without applying IAM roles or access controls can lead to data breaches.
  - Solution: Use AWS IAM Access Analyzer to check for misconfigured roles and permissions.
- Inadequate Testing
  - Problem: Skipping migration tests results in system downtime.
  - Solution: Conduct migration tests in a staging environment to simulate production scenarios.
- Data Loss During Migration
  - Problem: Large datasets can be corrupted or lost during transfer.
  - Solution: Use AWS DataSync to ensure data integrity during migration.
- Not Considering Dependencies
  - Problem: Applications are interdependent, but teams migrate them in isolation.
  - Solution: Use dependency analysis tools like AWS Migration Hub to analyze dependencies between apps.

B. Best Practices for a Successful Migration
- Start with a Proof of Concept (PoC) – Before moving everything, test with a small, non-critical workload.
- Automate with Infrastructure as Code (IaC) – Use Terraform or AWS CloudFormation to automate resource provisioning.
- Use Change Management Tools – Log every change using tools like AWS CloudTrail.
- Leverage AI to Track Progress – Use AI-powered tools like AWS Migration Evaluator to estimate migration costs and identify risks.

Conclusion:
Migrating to the cloud requires careful planning, the right strategy, and effective execution. By following the 6 Rs migration framework, companies can choose the right approach for each application. With the help of AI-powered migration tools, organizations can avoid costly mistakes and streamline data transfers.

AI Insight:
"Migration is not just a technical shift — it's a strategic transformation. AI-driven assessment tools, self-healing systems, and predictive risk analysis ensure every migration stays on track."

Chapter 33: Future Trends in Cloud Computing

Cloud computing has already transformed how businesses, developers, and consumers interact with technology. But the future promises even more groundbreaking changes. From quantum cloud computing to AI-driven automation and metaverse development, the next wave of cloud technologies will redefine what's possible.

In this chapter, we explore future trends in cloud computing, including emerging developments in quantum cloud computing, green initiatives, and federated learning. We'll also discuss AI's role in shaping these trends and the possibilities unlocked by metaverse development.

1. Predictions for Quantum Cloud Computing and Green Initiatives

Cloud providers like AWS, Google Cloud, and IBM are leading the race to offer quantum computing capabilities to businesses. At the same time, growing awareness of environmental sustainability has led to green cloud initiatives aimed at reducing the environmental impact of data centers.

A. Quantum Cloud Computing
Quantum computing is on the brink of commercial viability, and cloud providers like AWS, Google, and IBM have started offering Quantum-as-a-Service (QaaS). Unlike classical computers, which process bits as 0s and 1s, quantum computers use qubits, enabling exponentially faster calculations.

- How Quantum Cloud Works
  - Cloud providers allow developers to write quantum algorithms and run them on quantum simulators or quantum processors.
  - Example: IBM offers quantum access through IBM Q Experience, where users can run quantum circuits on real quantum hardware.
- Key Use Cases for Quantum Cloud
  - Drug Discovery: Simulate complex molecular interactions, accelerating pharmaceutical research.
  - Cryptography: Quantum computers can break existing cryptographic algorithms, forcing the shift to post-quantum encryption.
  - AI Model Training: Quantum AI may accelerate machine learning training times.

- AI's Role in Quantum Cloud
  - AI-Driven Simulations: AI models predict the behavior of quantum algorithms before they run on real hardware, reducing computational costs.
  - Error Correction: Quantum computers are error-prone. AI-driven error correction algorithms help stabilize qubit states.
- Cloud Providers Offering Quantum Services
  - AWS Braket – Quantum computing service on AWS.
  - Google Quantum AI – Google's approach to offering quantum processors in the cloud.
  - IBM Quantum – Provides access to real quantum computers through the IBM Cloud.

B. Green Cloud Initiatives

Cloud providers are under pressure to reduce the environmental impact of their data centers. Green initiatives aim to minimize carbon emissions, improve energy efficiency, and promote sustainable practices.

- Carbon-Neutral and Net-Zero Goals
  - AWS aims for 100% renewable energy by 2025.
  - Google Cloud plans for 100% carbon-free energy 24/7 by 2030.
  - Microsoft Azure aims to become carbon-negative by 2030.
- AI's Role in Sustainability
  - Energy Optimization: AI predicts and reduces energy usage in data centers by controlling cooling systems. Google's DeepMind has reduced cooling system energy usage by 40%.
  - Carbon Footprint Analysis: AI tools track energy consumption and offer actionable steps to reduce usage. Google Cloud's Carbon Footprint Tool shows users their cloud-related CO_2 emissions.
- Innovative Green Technologies
  - Liquid Cooling Systems: Use liquid instead of air to cool data centers, reducing energy waste.
  - Circular Economy Initiatives: Reuse and recycle old cloud hardware, reducing e-waste.

2. AI's Influence on the Next Wave of Cloud Technologies
As cloud environments become more intelligent and autonomous, AI will continue to be the driving force behind automation, self-healing systems, and workload optimization. Cloud providers are building AI-powered features into every layer of their services.

A. Autonomous Cloud Systems
Autonomous cloud systems self-manage, self-heal, and self-optimize without human intervention. AI-powered cloud operations (AIOps) enable predictive automation and incident response.
- How It Works
  - Self-Healing Systems: When an outage occurs, AI automatically detects and fixes the issue.
  - Predictive Maintenance: AI forecasts when a system component (like a server) will fail, allowing proactive action.
- Examples of AI-Driven Cloud Automation
  - AWS Fault Injection Simulator simulates outages, and AI learns how to recover from failures.
  - Google Cloud Operations Suite (formerly Stackdriver) uses AI to analyze logs and detect anomalies before they cause downtime.
- Impact of Autonomous Cloud Systems
  - Faster Recovery Times: Outages that previously required hours to resolve can now be fixed automatically in minutes.
  - Reduced Downtime: Self-healing features prevent system-wide outages, improving uptime.

B. AI-Powered Cost Optimization
Cloud billing can be complex, especially when managing multi-cloud or hybrid cloud setups. AI-based cost management identifies cost-saving opportunities, automates rightsizing of instances, and reduces overall cloud bills.
- Dynamic Cost Optimization
  - AI tracks underutilized instances and suggests shutdowns or instance downgrades.
  - Example: AWS Cost Explorer uses AI to identify "zombie instances" (idle VMs) and recommend termination.
- Predictive Cost Forecasting
  - AI predicts future cloud costs, helping companies budget more effectively.
  - Example: AWS Budgets offers forecasting tools that predict costs for the month based on prior usage trends.

3. Emerging Trends in Federated Learning and Metaverse Development

Federated learning and the metaverse are two of the most exciting developments in cloud computing. Both require massive data processing and cloud-scale infrastructure. Here's how the cloud will support these emerging fields.

A. Federated Learning in the Cloud

Federated learning allows AI models to be trained on distributed data without moving that data to a central server. This approach is critical for data privacy and compliance.

- How It Works
  - Instead of sending raw data to the cloud, devices train AI models locally.
  - These local models are sent back to the cloud, and an aggregate model is built.
- Use Cases of Federated Learning
  - Healthcare: Train AI on private patient records while preserving data privacy.
  - Finance: Build AI fraud detection models using local transaction data from banks.
- AI's Role in Federated Learning
  - AI coordinates local training tasks, aggregates results, and ensures that no raw data is shared.
  - Example: Google's Federated Learning is used to train predictive text models for Gboard.

B. Metaverse Development with Cloud Computing

The metaverse is a persistent, shared, 3D virtual world where users can interact using AR/VR devices. Cloud infrastructure and edge computing are essential for making the metaverse seamless, fast, and interactive.

- Cloud's Role in Metaverse Development
  - The metaverse requires vast computing resources, with millions of users accessing 3D assets simultaneously.
  - Cloud providers (AWS, Google, Microsoft) host the metaverse's backend, streaming 3D environments, user data, and physics simulations.
- AI-Driven Metaverse Features
  - AI-Generated Worlds: AI generates custom 3D worlds in real-time.
  - AI NPCs: Non-playable characters (NPCs) powered by AI interact with users in a realistic, human-like manner.
  - Personalized Avatars: AI builds digital avatars that look, sound, and move like real people.

- Cloud Providers Powering the Metaverse
  - NVIDIA Omniverse – Uses NVIDIA's cloud to build and render real-time 3D simulations.
  - AWS Wavelength – Reduces latency for metaverse AR/VR devices by placing edge nodes closer to users.

Conclusion:
The future of cloud computing is driven by quantum computing, AI-enhanced cloud services, and the development of the metaverse. Quantum cloud computing will allow previously "impossible" problems to be solved in seconds. Federated learning will train AI models without moving private data, and metaverse development will give rise to persistent 3D worlds hosted on cloud platforms.

AI Insight:
"AI will drive every future trend in cloud computing — from powering quantum breakthroughs to optimizing metaverse infrastructure. The cloud isn't just smart — it's becoming sentient."

Chapter 34: Building a Cloud-Native Career Path

The demand for cloud computing professionals is skyrocketing as companies migrate their operations to the cloud. But standing out in this field requires more than just technical skills. It requires certifications, practical experience, and ongoing learning to stay ahead of evolving technologies like AI, DevOps, and quantum computing.

This chapter serves as a career roadmap for aspiring cloud professionals. We'll explore essential certifications, provide guidance on career pathways, and highlight the best tools and resources to accelerate your journey to becoming a cloud expert.

1. Certifications and Skill-Building Strategies
Certifications are the gold standard for proving cloud expertise. Earning a certification demonstrates your ability to configure, secure, and manage cloud environments. In this section, we'll explore the most recognized certifications, how to prepare for them, and skill-building strategies to increase your job market value.

A. Essential Cloud Certifications
For anyone looking to build a career in cloud computing, obtaining industry-recognized certifications is one of the most effective ways to demonstrate your skills and increase job prospects. These certifications validate knowledge in areas like cloud architecture, DevOps, security, and machine learning. Here's an overview of the most essential cloud certifications from AWS, Azure, and Google Cloud (GCP).

1. AWS Certifications
AWS Certified Solutions Architect (Associate)
- What It Covers: This is one of the most popular cloud certifications, focusing on how to design scalable, cost-efficient, and secure AWS solutions. It covers key AWS services, architecture principles, and best practices for cloud design.
- Ideal For: Cloud Architects, Solutions Architects, and IT professionals responsible for designing cloud infrastructure.
- Difficulty: Intermediate-level certification. Basic cloud experience is recommended before attempting.
- Why It Matters: It is one of the most in-demand cloud certifications and is a must-have for cloud architects and technical leads.

AWS Certified Cloud Practitioner
- What It Covers: This certification provides a broad understanding of AWS cloud concepts, terminology, billing models, and support services. It focuses on high-level knowledge without going too deep into technical specifics.
- Ideal For: Business professionals, managers, and non-technical roles who want a general understanding of cloud concepts.
- Difficulty: Beginner-level certification. No prior cloud experience is required.
- Why It Matters: It is a great starting point for beginners who want to understand cloud fundamentals before pursuing more technical certifications.

AWS Certified DevOps Engineer (Professional)
- What It Covers: This certification validates knowledge of CI/CD (Continuous Integration/Continuous Delivery) pipelines, automation, and infrastructure as code (IaC). It focuses on DevOps practices and automation using AWS tools like AWS CodePipeline, AWS CloudFormation, and AWS CodeBuild.
- Ideal For: DevOps Engineers, Site Reliability Engineers (SREs), and Systems Administrators.
- Difficulty: Advanced-level certification. Hands-on experience with DevOps pipelines is essential.
- Why It Matters: This certification proves expertise in DevOps automation, continuous delivery, and cloud infrastructure deployment — skills that are in high demand for modern cloud development roles.

2. Microsoft Azure Certifications
Microsoft Certified: Azure Fundamentals (AZ-900)
- What It Covers: This certification introduces the fundamental concepts of cloud computing and Azure services, covering security, privacy, and pricing models.
- Ideal For: Beginners, business managers, and non-technical stakeholders looking to learn the basics of Azure.
- Difficulty: Entry-level certification. No prior experience with Azure is required.
- Why It Matters: It provides a foundational understanding of Azure services and can lead to more advanced certifications. It's often required for entry-level roles like Cloud Support Associate.

Microsoft Certified: Azure Solutions Architect Expert (AZ-305)
- What It Covers: This is a comprehensive certification that tests knowledge of designing and architecting solutions on Microsoft Azure. It includes topics like networking, identity management, and security in the Azure cloud.
- Ideal For: Cloud Architects, IT Consultants, and Solutions Architects responsible for designing and implementing Azure solutions.
- Difficulty: Advanced-level certification. Candidates need hands-on experience with Azure infrastructure, cloud networking, and hybrid solutions.
- Why It Matters: It's the most sought-after certification for Azure cloud architects, as it validates a candidate's ability to design, secure, and manage large-scale Azure infrastructure.

Microsoft Certified: Azure DevOps Engineer Expert (AZ-400)
- What It Covers: This certification validates knowledge of DevOps principles, CI/CD, and automation using Azure DevOps tools and services. It focuses on integrating development and operations workflows.
- Ideal For: DevOps Engineers, Site Reliability Engineers (SREs), and Cloud Engineers.
- Difficulty: Advanced-level certification. Candidates need hands-on experience with DevOps workflows and Azure tools like Azure Pipelines and Azure Repos.
- Why It Matters: It demonstrates expertise in DevOps automation, infrastructure as code (IaC), and CI/CD pipelines. It's a valuable credential for companies using Azure DevOps pipelines.

3. Google Cloud (GCP) Certifications
Google Cloud Digital Leader
- What It Covers: This certification validates knowledge of Google Cloud services, digital transformation, and cloud strategy. It's designed to help non-technical stakeholders understand cloud technology.
- Ideal For: Business leaders, managers, and non-technical professionals working on cloud transformation projects.
- Difficulty: Beginner-level certification. No prior experience is required.
- Why It Matters: It provides foundational knowledge of Google Cloud services and is ideal for people who want to understand the cloud from a business perspective.

Google Cloud Professional Cloud Architect
- What It Covers: This certification covers designing, managing, and securing Google Cloud infrastructure. It requires knowledge of GCP services like Compute Engine, Cloud Storage, and Kubernetes Engine.
- Ideal For: Cloud Architects, IT Professionals, and Solutions Architects working with Google Cloud.
- Difficulty: Advanced-level certification. Candidates need hands-on experience with GCP infrastructure, IAM, and cloud networking.
- Why It Matters: It is one of the most in-demand cloud certifications and ranks as one of the highest-paying IT certifications globally.

Google Cloud Professional Data Engineer
- What It Covers: This certification focuses on data engineering, data analytics, and big data processing. It covers BigQuery, Dataflow, Pub/Sub, and machine learning pipelines.
- Ideal For: Data Engineers, Data Analysts, and Machine Learning Engineers working with large-scale data processing and analytics.
- Difficulty: Advanced-level certification. Experience with GCP's data tools and ETL (Extract, Transform, Load) processes is essential.
- Why It Matters: As companies rely more on data-driven decision-making, demand for data engineers is skyrocketing. This certification validates expertise in managing big data, analytics, and machine learning pipelines.

4. Other Essential Certifications
- CompTIA Cloud+
- What It Covers: This vendor-neutral certification focuses on multi-cloud management, security, and performance optimization. It is not tied to any specific provider like AWS, Azure, or GCP.
- Ideal For: IT generalists, Cloud Engineers, and Network Administrators who manage multi-cloud or hybrid cloud environments.
- Difficulty: Intermediate-level certification. Basic knowledge of cloud fundamentals is required.
- Why It Matters: If you work with multi-cloud setups, this certification is ideal because it's vendor-neutral. It demonstrates knowledge of how to manage multiple cloud providers like AWS, Azure, and GCP.

Certified Cloud Security Professional (CCSP)
- **What It Covers:** This certification focuses on cloud security, identity management, risk management, and regulatory compliance. It is not specific to AWS, Azure, or GCP but provides best practices for securing cloud applications and infrastructure.
- **Ideal For:** Cybersecurity Professionals, Cloud Security Analysts, and IT Security Consultants.
- **Difficulty:** Advanced-level certification. Candidates need a solid background in security, privacy, and data governance.
- **Why It Matters:** With the rise of cyber threats targeting cloud infrastructure, this certification validates cloud security expertise. It's one of the most respected certifications for cloud security professionals.

Summary
- **AWS Certifications:** Best for roles like Cloud Architects, DevOps Engineers, and Cloud Practitioners. Popular certifications include AWS Solutions Architect and AWS DevOps Engineer.
- **Azure Certifications:** Best for roles like Cloud Architects, Azure DevOps Engineers, and Solutions Architects. Popular certifications include Azure Solutions Architect Expert (AZ-305) and Azure DevOps Engineer (AZ-400).
- **Google Cloud Certifications:** Best for roles like Cloud Architects, Data Engineers, and Machine Learning Engineers. Popular certifications include Google Cloud Professional Cloud Architect and Google Cloud Data Engineer.
- **Other Certifications:** For multi-cloud expertise, consider CompTIA Cloud+. For cloud security, pursue Certified Cloud Security Professional (CCSP).

By earning these essential cloud certifications, you can enhance your career prospects, increase earning potential, and demonstrate your expertise in cloud infrastructure, DevOps, and security. Whether you want to become a Cloud Architect, DevOps Engineer, or Data Engineer, these certifications open the door to higher-paying roles and new opportunities.

B. Choosing the Right Certification
- Role-Based Selection
  - Cloud Architect? Go for AWS Solutions Architect or Google Cloud Professional Cloud Architect.
  - DevOps Engineer? Get Kubernetes (CKA) certification or AWS DevOps Engineer certification.
  - Security Specialist? Focus on Certified Cloud Security Professional (CCSP).
- Beginner's Path
  - Start with AWS Certified Cloud Practitioner or Microsoft Azure Fundamentals if you're a beginner.
- Advanced Path
  - After mastering fundamentals, pursue role-specific certifications (like AWS Solutions Architect) or specialized certifications (like Kubernetes or CCSP for security).

C. Skill-Building Strategies
- Hands-On Learning
  - Use free-tier cloud accounts (AWS, Azure, GCP) to practice creating VMs, configuring IAM roles, and automating deployments.
  - Example: Deploy a serverless function on AWS Lambda or launch a Kubernetes cluster with GCP's Kubernetes Engine.
- Use Online Learning Platforms
  - A Cloud Guru – On-demand cloud training with certification paths.
  - Cloud Academy – Practice labs for AWS, Azure, and Google Cloud.
  - Coursera / edX – Comprehensive cloud courses from Google and AWS.
- Practice Labs and Sandboxes
  - AWS Cloud Quest gamifies cloud learning, making it fun and interactive.
  - Google Qwiklabs offers hands-on labs to practice GCP skills.
- Join Cloud Communities
  - Cloud Certifications Reddit – Discussions, exam tips, and industry news.
  - LinkedIn Learning Groups – Join community discussions on cloud certifications.

2. Career Pathways in Cloud Computing and AI
The cloud computing field offers a wide range of career opportunities, from entry-level support roles to high-paying architect positions. But what roles are available, and how do you build a pathway to success? This section outlines potential career pathways and provides actionable advice for each.

A. Cloud Career Roles and Salaries
As the demand for cloud computing professionals continues to grow, so do the job opportunities and salaries. Cloud careers span multiple roles, from entry-level support positions to senior-level architects and DevOps engineers. Here's an overview of the most important cloud career roles, what they do, and their earning potential.

1. Cloud Engineer
- Role Description: Cloud Engineers are responsible for designing, deploying, and managing cloud infrastructure. They configure cloud services, automate deployments, and ensure systems run efficiently.
- Core Skills: Cloud platforms (AWS, Azure, GCP), automation (Terraform, CloudFormation), and scripting (Python, Bash).
- Responsibilities:
  - Set up and manage cloud-based virtual machines, databases, and storage.
  - Create Infrastructure as Code (IaC) templates to automate deployments.
  - Monitor cloud resources to ensure availability, performance, and cost efficiency.
- Average Salary: $95,000 - $135,000 per year (depending on experience and location).
- Why It Matters: Cloud Engineers are essential for building and managing cloud infrastructure, especially in DevOps environments where infrastructure must be deployed and scaled on demand.

2. Cloud Architect
- Role Description: Cloud Architects design the overall cloud strategy, system architecture, and technical roadmap for cloud-based solutions. They decide which services (like compute, storage, and networking) are used and how they fit together.
- Core Skills: Cloud architecture design (AWS, Azure, GCP), hybrid cloud strategies, and security frameworks.

- Responsibilities:
  - Design scalable, secure cloud solutions that support business goals.
  - Identify which cloud services (like AWS EC2, Azure VMs, or GCP Compute) should be used.
  - Create technical blueprints, disaster recovery plans, and multi-cloud strategies.
- Average Salary: $120,000 - $160,000 per year (depending on experience and certifications).
- Why It Matters: Cloud Architects play a strategic role in enterprise cloud adoption. They make critical decisions that impact performance, security, and long-term operational costs.

3. DevOps Engineer
- Role Description: DevOps Engineers focus on CI/CD pipelines, automation, and continuous deployment of software in cloud environments. They ensure that development and operations teams work together seamlessly.
- Core Skills: CI/CD tools (Jenkins, GitHub Actions), Infrastructure as Code (IaC) with Terraform, and scripting (Python, Bash, Shell).
- Responsibilities:
  - Set up and maintain CI/CD pipelines to automate software releases.
  - Write scripts to automate infrastructure deployments using IaC tools.
  - Monitor cloud environments for system health and performance issues.
- Average Salary: $110,000 - $150,000 per year.
- Why It Matters: DevOps Engineers are vital to companies practicing agile development. By automating the software release process, they reduce errors, increase speed, and support rapid deployments.

4. Cloud Security Engineer

- Role Description: Cloud Security Engineers focus on securing cloud environments. They manage IAM (Identity and Access Management), encrypt sensitive data, and protect against breaches, data leaks, and cyberattacks.
- Core Skills: Cloud security (AWS IAM, Azure AD), threat detection, vulnerability management, and incident response.
- Responsibilities:
    - Implement security policies for IAM, encryption, and firewalls.
    - Detect and respond to security threats and incidents.
    - Set up automated security tools like AWS GuardDuty and Azure Sentinel.
- Average Salary: $115,000 - $160,000 per year.
- Why It Matters: As cloud adoption grows, so do security threats. Cloud Security Engineers ensure data privacy, regulatory compliance, and protection from ransomware attacks.

5. Cloud Consultant

- Role Description: Cloud Consultants help companies plan, strategize, and execute cloud migration projects. They work closely with clients to design and implement tailored cloud solutions.
- Core Skills: Cloud migration, project management, and multi-cloud strategy.
- Responsibilities:
    - Assess current on-premises infrastructure and recommend migration paths.
    - Design cost-effective, scalable cloud migration plans.
    - Advise on tools, platforms, and cloud service providers (AWS, Azure, GCP).
- Average Salary: $100,000 - $140,000 per year.
- Why It Matters: Many companies struggle with cloud migration, so Cloud Consultants provide guidance on moving workloads efficiently while reducing risks and costs.

6. Site Reliability Engineer (SRE)
- Role Description: Site Reliability Engineers (SREs) ensure that cloud-based applications are highly available, stable, and performant. They focus on reliability engineering and incident response.
- Core Skills: Monitoring and alerting (Datadog, New Relic), incident response, and disaster recovery.
- Responsibilities:
  - Develop systems for error detection, failover, and disaster recovery.
  - Implement tools for uptime monitoring and alerting.
  - Respond to outages and ensure 99.9% or higher uptime.
- Average Salary: $115,000 - $150,000 per year.
- Why It Matters: Downtime costs businesses millions. SREs ensure systems are always available, which is essential for e-commerce, financial services, and media streaming platforms.

7. Data Engineer
- Role Description: Data Engineers build pipelines and workflows to process and store large datasets in the cloud. They support big data processing, ETL (Extract, Transform, Load), and analytics.
- Core Skills: Data warehouses (BigQuery, Redshift), data lakes, SQL, and ETL tools.
- Responsibilities:
  - Design and build data pipelines to process large datasets.
  - Set up data warehouses and data lakes on AWS, Azure, or GCP.
  - Ensure data is clean, secure, and accessible for analytics teams.
- Average Salary: $105,000 - $145,000 per year.
- Why It Matters: Data Engineers power big data analytics, AI, and machine learning pipelines. Without them, companies can't make sense of large datasets, impacting decision-making.

8. Cloud Product Manager
- Role Description: Cloud Product Managers work with engineering, sales, and marketing teams to create cloud-based products and services. They own the product roadmap and development strategy.
- Core Skills: Product development, market research, agile methodology, and cloud knowledge.
- Responsibilities:
  - Lead product development for cloud services and tools.
  - Define the product roadmap and release schedule.
  - Work with engineers to ensure the product meets market needs.
- Average Salary: $120,000 - $150,000 per year.
- Why It Matters: As companies shift to SaaS and cloud-based software, Product Managers define the vision for new cloud services, ensuring competitive positioning.

9. Cloud Support Specialist
- Role Description: Cloud Support Specialists provide technical support for users and clients using cloud services. They troubleshoot issues with cloud tools, apps, and platforms.
- Core Skills: Technical support, customer service, and knowledge of AWS, Azure, or GCP.
- Responsibilities:
  - Help users resolve issues with cloud platforms.
  - Provide technical support for cloud services like AWS S3, Azure AD, or GCP Compute.
  - Escalate complex problems to senior engineers.
- Average Salary: $70,000 - $100,000 per year.
- Why It Matters: Support Specialists ensure customers have a positive experience with cloud platforms, reducing churn and keeping businesses running smoothly.

Summary of Roles and Salaries
- Cloud Engineer: $95K - $135K
- Cloud Architect: $120K - $160K
- DevOps Engineer: $110K - $150K
- Cloud Security Engineer: $115K - $160K
- Cloud Consultant: $100K - $140K
- Site Reliability Engineer (SRE): $115K - $150K
- Data Engineer: $105K - $145K
- Cloud Product Manager: $120K - $150K
- Cloud Support Specialist: $70K - $100K

These roles offer high salaries, career growth, and job stability, making cloud computing one of the most lucrative fields today. Whether you want to become an architect, engineer, or consultant, there are opportunities for every level of experience.

B. How to Choose a Cloud Career Path
- Technical Roles (Engineer, DevOps, Architect)
  - If you love technical work, coding, and system design, aim for Cloud Engineer, DevOps Engineer, or Cloud Architect.
- Advisory Roles (Consultant, Cloud Analyst)
  - If you like business strategy and consulting, go for roles like Cloud Consultant or Cloud Cost Analyst.
- Security Roles (Cloud Security, Compliance)
  - If you have a passion for security, ethical hacking, or risk management, become a Cloud Security Engineer or Compliance Specialist.
- AI/ML Roles (AI Cloud Specialist, Data Engineer)
  - If you love AI and machine learning, go for AI Cloud Specialist roles that involve working with SageMaker, TensorFlow, or GCP Vertex AI.

C. How to Gain Experience
- Freelance Projects
  - Sites like Upwork and Fiverr offer freelance gigs for cloud migration and AWS tasks.
- Build Your Portfolio
  - Launch a GitHub portfolio with projects like "Create a cloud-based CI/CD pipeline with AWS" or "Build a Kubernetes cluster on GCP."
- Internships
  - Apply for cloud internships at AWS, Google, Microsoft, or companies like Accenture and Deloitte.

3. Tools and Resources for Professional Growth
Building a successful cloud career requires access to the right tools, resources, and guidance. This section provides a curated list of the best platforms, training resources, and certification prep materials.

A. Learning Platforms
If you want to learn cloud computing, there are several popular learning platforms that offer courses, certifications, and hands-on practice. Each platform caters to different learning styles, from beginner-friendly tutorials to advanced, hands-on labs. Here's a breakdown of the most popular cloud learning platforms and what makes each unique.

1. AWS Skill Builder
- What It Offers: Official AWS training platform with on-demand courses, hands-on labs, and certification exam prep. AWS Skill Builder focuses on AWS certifications like Solutions Architect, DevOps, and Cloud Practitioner.
- Ideal For: Beginners to advanced learners looking for AWS certification prep or hands-on practice with AWS tools.
- Key Features:
  - Interactive hands-on labs and sandbox environments.
  - Learning paths for AWS certifications like AWS Solutions Architect and AWS Cloud Practitioner.
  - Access to live instructor-led classes and self-paced online courses.
- Why It Matters: Since AWS is the largest cloud provider, mastering its platform can significantly increase job opportunities. AWS Skill Builder is an official resource, making it one of the most trusted platforms for AWS learning.

2. Microsoft Learn

- **What It Offers**: Official learning platform for Microsoft Azure, offering free, self-paced courses and role-based learning paths for certifications like Azure Fundamentals (AZ-900) and Azure Solutions Architect (AZ-305).
- **Ideal For**: Beginners, developers, and IT professionals looking to earn Azure certifications.
- **Key Features**:
  - Free self-paced modules with interactive, browser-based sandboxes for hands-on labs.
  - Tracks for certifications like AZ-900, AZ-104, and AZ-400 (DevOps).
  - Interactive exercises and knowledge checks after each module.
- **Why It Matters**: As the second-largest cloud provider, Azure certifications are in high demand, especially for companies that use Microsoft products like Office 365 and Windows Server. Microsoft Learn offers free, accessible learning paths for all skill levels.

3. Google Cloud Skills Boost

- **What It Offers**: Official Google Cloud learning platform with courses, hands-on labs, and role-based certification tracks like Cloud Engineer, Data Engineer, and Cloud Architect.
- **Ideal For**: Learners interested in Google Cloud certifications or careers in AI, data analytics, and machine learning.
- **Key Features**:
  - Hands-on labs with Google Cloud environments to practice skills in real time.
  - Role-based learning paths for Google Cloud certifications.
  - Quests and Challenges that reward users with badges for completing learning tracks.
- **Why It Matters**: Google Cloud is a leader in AI, machine learning, and big data analytics. If you're interested in GCP's specialized tools (like BigQuery and TensorFlow), Google Cloud Skills Boost is the best platform for hands-on training.

4. Coursera

- **What It Offers**: Online learning platform with courses from top universities and tech companies like Google, AWS, and IBM. Coursera provides certificates and career tracks for cloud roles like Cloud Engineer and Cloud Developer.
- **Ideal For**: People seeking industry-recognized credentials from companies like Google, AWS, and IBM.

- Key Features:
  - Offers Google's Cloud Engineer certificate and other cloud career tracks.
  - Courses from leading institutions like the University of Illinois and Duke University.
  - Industry-recognized certificates that can be shared on LinkedIn.
- Why It Matters: Coursera allows you to earn official certificates from big tech companies (like Google) and universities, giving you an edge when applying for cloud jobs.

5. Pluralsight
- What It Offers: A subscription-based platform with a library of cloud computing courses for AWS, Azure, and GCP. It also includes learning paths for DevOps, machine learning, and security.
- Ideal For: Developers, IT professionals, and DevOps engineers seeking technical skills and cloud certifications.
- Key Features:
  - Hands-on labs and practical exercises.
  - Certification prep for AWS, Azure, and GCP exams.
  - Skill IQ assessments that help users identify skill gaps.
- Why It Matters: Pluralsight focuses on technical skills and hands-on training, making it ideal for developers, DevOps engineers, and tech professionals who want to keep their skills sharp.

6. A Cloud Guru
- What It Offers: A platform with a focus on AWS, Azure, and GCP certifications. It provides hands-on sandbox environments for practicing cloud skills in a real-world setting.
- Ideal For: IT professionals and beginners preparing for AWS, Azure, or GCP certifications.
- Key Features:
  - Real cloud environments to practice tasks like deploying virtual machines or setting up S3 buckets.
  - Certification prep for AWS, Azure, and GCP exams.
  - Courses for other cloud concepts like cloud security and DevOps.
- Why It Matters: A Cloud Guru is one of the most well-known platforms for cloud learning, offering both hands-on practice and certification prep for all three major cloud providers.

B. Cloud Tools to Know

Learning cloud tools is essential for anyone pursuing a cloud computing career. These tools help with deployment, monitoring, automation, and security. Here's a list of the most important cloud tools and why you should know them.

1. Terraform
- What It Does: Infrastructure as Code (IaC) tool that allows users to define cloud infrastructure in code, enabling automated deployments.
- Use Case: Automate cloud infrastructure on AWS, Azure, and GCP.
- Why It Matters: It allows cloud engineers and DevOps professionals to create, change, and version control infrastructure just like application code.

2. Kubernetes
- What It Does: Container orchestration platform for managing, scaling, and automating containerized applications.
- Use Case: Deploy containerized apps using Docker and Kubernetes.
- Why It Matters: It's the industry standard for container management. Knowing Kubernetes is essential for roles like DevOps Engineer, Cloud Engineer, and Site Reliability Engineer (SRE).

3. Docker
- What It Does: Containerization platform that lets developers package apps and dependencies into portable containers.
- Use Case: Run containerized applications in Kubernetes, AWS, and Azure environments.
- Why It Matters: Docker enables portable, consistent application environments, making it easier to move apps between development, testing, and production.

4. AWS CloudFormation
- What It Does: Infrastructure as Code (IaC) tool that allows AWS users to define cloud infrastructure using YAML or JSON templates.
- Use Case: Automate the deployment of AWS services, like EC2, S3, and RDS.
- Why It Matters: It allows AWS users to automate infrastructure deployments, ensuring faster, repeatable deployments.

5. Ansible

- What It Does: IT automation tool used to configure systems, manage servers, and automate cloud tasks.
- Use Case: Automate server configuration, patching, and deployment.
- Why It Matters: It's one of the most popular automation tools for server management and cloud automation.

6. Jenkins

- What It Does: Continuous Integration/Continuous Delivery (CI/CD) tool that automates software builds, testing, and deployment.
- Use Case: Automate code deployment and testing for DevOps teams.
- Why It Matters: Jenkins enables faster, more efficient software releases and is a key tool in DevOps pipelines.

7. Prometheus

- What It Does: Open-source monitoring tool for collecting and analyzing system metrics.
- Use Case: Monitor system health, performance, and resource usage in cloud environments.
- Why It Matters: It helps DevOps teams and SREs ensure uptime, track performance, and respond to issues before they become critical.

8. AWS Lambda

- What It Does: Serverless compute service that lets you run code without managing servers.
- Use Case: Automate small tasks and run scripts in a serverless environment.
- Why It Matters: Serverless architecture reduces operational overhead, and learning AWS Lambda is essential for cloud-native development.

C. Recommended Books

- "Cloud Practitioner's Guide to AWS" – Ideal for beginners.
- "The Site Reliability Workbook" – DevOps, SRE, and Kubernetes workflows.
- "Infrastructure as Code" by Kief Morris – Learn to automate everything using IaC.

Conclusion:
Building a career in cloud computing offers limitless potential, but the path requires dedication. By earning relevant certifications, building hands-on experience, and developing a personal portfolio, you can future-proof your career. With roles like Cloud Engineer, AI Cloud Specialist, and Cloud Security Engineer in high demand, mastering the skills and tools in this book will set you on the path to success.

AI Insight:
"AI isn't just a skill to learn — it's a career multiplier. By mastering cloud computing with AI-driven tools, you can future-proof your path and secure your place in the cloud economy."

Chapter 35: Building a Cloud Strategy for Your Business

Building a cloud strategy is not just about moving data and applications to the cloud—it's about defining the business objectives, technical requirements, and operational processes needed to leverage cloud technology effectively. Without a clear strategy, companies face challenges like runaway costs, security vulnerabilities, and operational inefficiencies.

This chapter will guide you through the process of building a cloud strategy in three key parts:
1. Practical steps to develop and implement cloud strategies
2. Evaluating cloud providers and managing vendor lock-in
3. Tracking success and continuously optimizing your strategy

By the end of this chapter, you'll be equipped with the tools to create a future-proof cloud strategy for your business.

Practical Steps to Develop and Implement Cloud Strategies
A cloud strategy is a comprehensive plan that outlines how an organization will use cloud technology to meet its business goals. Whether you're migrating existing applications or building new cloud-native apps, having a formalized strategy is essential for success.

1. Assess Business Goals and Objectives
The first step is to define the role that cloud computing will play in achieving business goals. Every company has different goals, from reducing costs to scaling applications globally. Your strategy should support specific business outcomes.

Questions to Ask:
- What are the business drivers for adopting cloud? (Cost reduction? Speed to market? Innovation?)
- What key performance indicators (KPIs) will be used to measure success?
- Which departments, applications, or teams will be most impacted by this strategy?

Example:
If your company aims to improve customer experience through faster mobile apps, the cloud strategy should focus on serverless functions and low-latency edge computing.

2. Select the Right Cloud Deployment Model
Choosing the right cloud deployment model is one of the most important decisions a business can make when adopting cloud computing. The four main deployment models are Public Cloud, Private Cloud, Hybrid Cloud, and Multi-Cloud, each offering unique benefits and trade-offs. Here's an overview of these models to help you select the right one for your organization.

1. Public Cloud
- What It Is: A shared cloud infrastructure where multiple organizations use the same physical hardware, but their data and applications are isolated. Public cloud services are provided by third-party companies like AWS, Azure, and Google Cloud.
- Key Features:
  - On-demand access to compute, storage, and databases.
  - Pay-as-you-go pricing, meaning users only pay for what they consume.
  - Offers a wide range of services (like compute, storage, AI/ML tools, and serverless functions).
- Use Cases:
  - Startups and small businesses with limited budgets.
  - Businesses seeking to launch apps or prototypes quickly.
  - Companies looking to avoid the costs of managing physical hardware.
- Benefits:
  - Cost-effective and scalable, allowing businesses to start small and scale as needed.
  - Requires no hardware maintenance since it's managed by cloud providers.
  - Access to a broad range of services and AI tools like AWS SageMaker and Google Vertex AI.
- Drawbacks:
  - Limited control over infrastructure since it's managed by the provider.
  - May have issues with data privacy and compliance if data residency laws require data to remain in specific regions.

2. Private Cloud
- What It Is: A dedicated cloud environment that is exclusive to one organization. The organization owns and manages its cloud, giving it full control over resources and security. Private clouds can be hosted on-premises or at a third-party data center.
- Key Features:
  - Full control over data security, compliance, and infrastructure.

- o Used by industries with strict regulatory requirements (like healthcare, government, and finance).
  - o Customizable architecture tailored to business needs.

- Use Cases:
  - o Large enterprises and government agencies with strict security or compliance needs.
  - o Businesses managing sensitive customer data (like in healthcare and finance).
  - o Companies that already have a significant investment in on-premises data centers.
- Benefits:
  - o Higher security and privacy since the infrastructure is dedicated to a single organization.
  - o Provides the ability to customize the infrastructure to fit specific business needs.
  - o Full control of hardware, software, and network configurations.
- Drawbacks:
  - o High upfront costs for hardware, maintenance, and staffing.
  - o Limited scalability and flexibility compared to public cloud models.
  - o Requires in-house IT teams to manage the hardware and software, which can be costly.

3. Hybrid Cloud
- What It Is: A model that combines public and private clouds to allow data and applications to move between the two environments. Hybrid cloud enables businesses to run critical workloads on a private cloud while using the public cloud for scalability and additional resources.
- Key Features:
  - o Flexibility to move workloads between on-premises, private cloud, and public cloud.
  - o Combines the benefits of public and private clouds into a single, unified environment.
  - o Often managed using tools like Azure Arc or AWS Outposts.
- Use Cases:
  - o Companies with existing on-premises infrastructure but want access to public cloud scalability.
  - o Organizations that must comply with data privacy laws (like GDPR) by keeping certain data on-premises.
  - o Businesses running disaster recovery and backup systems using hybrid solutions.

- Benefits:
  - Data sovereignty and compliance are easier to achieve since businesses can keep sensitive data in private clouds.
  - Scalability of public cloud with the control of a private cloud.
  - Reduces downtime risks by having failover options in both public and private clouds.
- Drawbacks:
  - More complex management since it requires managing both on-premises and cloud-based infrastructure.
  - Higher costs compared to using public cloud alone.
  - Requires specialized skills and tools like Azure Arc, AWS Outposts, or VMware Cloud to manage hybrid workloads.

4. Multi-Cloud
- What It Is: The use of two or more cloud providers (like AWS, Azure, and Google Cloud) to avoid relying on a single provider. Multi-cloud enables businesses to choose the best cloud for specific workloads or to ensure vendor independence.
- Key Features:
  - Workloads distributed across multiple cloud providers (like AWS, Azure, and GCP).
  - Reduces the risk of vendor lock-in.
  - Often managed using multi-cloud management platforms like HashiCorp Terraform or CloudHealth.
- Use Cases:
  - Companies seeking to avoid vendor lock-in and maintain flexibility.
  - Businesses running apps on multiple clouds for redundancy and disaster recovery.
  - Enterprises that use specialized cloud services from multiple providers (e.g., AWS for compute, GCP for AI/ML, Azure for Microsoft tools).
- Benefits:
  - Avoids dependence on a single cloud provider, reducing risk from outages or price increases.
  - Offers access to the best services from each provider (like using AWS for EC2, GCP for BigQuery, and Azure for Active Directory).
  - Enables companies to use cloud-native features from multiple providers.

- Drawbacks:
  - Complex to manage since teams must monitor multiple providers, tools, and dashboards.
  - Data consistency can be a challenge since each provider may have its own formats and protocols.
  - Costs can increase due to duplicated tools and services across providers.

Which Cloud Deployment Model Should You Choose?
Your choice depends on business needs, compliance, and budget. Here's a quick guide on when to use each model:
- Choose Public Cloud if you want to save on upfront costs, access a large catalog of services, and need scalability and flexibility. Best for startups, small businesses, and SaaS companies.
- Choose Private Cloud if you have strict compliance needs (like healthcare and government) and need full control over data privacy and security. Best for large enterprises, financial services, and government agencies.
- Choose Hybrid Cloud if you want to retain on-premises infrastructure while using public cloud for burst capacity or backup. Best for businesses that need data sovereignty, disaster recovery, and hybrid app development.
- Choose Multi-Cloud if you want to avoid vendor lock-in or need to run different workloads on the best cloud for the task. Best for enterprises with global teams, redundancy needs, and multi-cloud disaster recovery plans.

Summary of Cloud Deployment Models
- Public Cloud: Shared infrastructure run by AWS, Azure, or GCP. Ideal for cost efficiency, scalability, and speed.
- Private Cloud: Dedicated cloud owned by a single organization. Best for security, data privacy, and regulatory compliance.
- Hybrid Cloud: Mix of public and private clouds. Best for flexibility, disaster recovery, and hybrid app development.
- Multi-Cloud: Uses multiple cloud providers (AWS, Azure, GCP) for flexibility, redundancy, and access to specialized services.

By selecting the right cloud deployment model for your business, you can optimize costs, improve agility, and ensure compliance. Whether you prioritize scalability (public cloud), data privacy (private cloud), or redundancy (multi-cloud), understanding the differences between these models is crucial to designing a successful cloud strategy.

Action Step:
Use AI-powered decision tools like AWS Migration Evaluator or Azure Migrate to assess which cloud model is best for your business.

3. Create a Cloud Governance Framework
Cloud governance defines the rules, policies, and controls that govern cloud usage. A well-defined framework ensures security, compliance, and cost efficiency. Without proper governance, teams may overspend or introduce security vulnerabilities.

Steps to Create a Governance Framework:
1. Define Cloud Access Control – Use IAM (Identity and Access Management) to restrict access to cloud resources.
2. Enforce Compliance Standards – Adopt compliance frameworks like GDPR, HIPAA, and ISO 27001.
3. Create a Cost Control Plan – Set spending limits and use tools like AWS Cost Explorer to track cloud bills.
4. Automation and Audits – Use AI-powered auditing tools like AWS Config to ensure compliance.

4. Identify Workloads and Application Priorities
Not every workload needs to be migrated to the cloud immediately. Identify which workloads to prioritize and plan application modernization where necessary. Some workloads are better suited for serverless or containerized microservices, while others may stay as virtual machines (VMs).

Questions to Ask:
- Which applications have the highest ROI when migrated to the cloud?
- Which applications require a complete re-architecting (e.g., moving to serverless or microservices)?
- Should we use the 6 Rs strategy (Rehost, Replatform, Refactor, etc.) for workload migration?

Action Step:
Create a list of all current applications, sort them by priority, and match them to the appropriate migration strategy.

5. Choose a Cloud Cost Management Strategy

One of the biggest challenges businesses face is cloud cost management. Without proper controls, cloud bills can spiral out of control. Your strategy should include cost allocation, usage tracking, and optimization.

Key Steps for Cost Management:
- Use AWS Cost Explorer or GCP Cost Management tools to identify cost spikes.
- Set budgets and alerts for spending limits.
- Implement auto-scaling to reduce unused resources.
- Use AI-driven cost optimization tools like CloudHealth to track and reduce spend.

Pro Tip:
Use serverless computing (like AWS Lambda) to avoid paying for idle resources.

6. Leverage AI-Driven Automation and Self-Healing Systems

AI-powered systems can automate key parts of your cloud strategy, from workload optimization to incident response.

Key Tools for AI-Driven Automation:
- AWS Auto Scaling – Automatically adjusts EC2 instances based on demand.
- AWS Fault Injection Simulator – Simulates cloud failures and helps design self-healing systems.
- Google Cloud AI Operations – Uses AI to analyze logs and predict failures.

Pro Tip:
By building self-healing cloud architectures, your systems can automatically recover from failures without human intervention.

7. Creating a Cloud Migration Roadmap

A cloud migration roadmap provides a clear, step-by-step approach for businesses to transition from on-premises infrastructure to the cloud while minimizing downtime, cost, and operational risk. The process typically includes six key phases: Assessment and Planning, Proof of Concept (PoC), Migration Preparation, Migration Execution, Testing and Validation, and Optimization and Continuous Improvement. It begins with assessing existing infrastructure, identifying migration priorities, and conducting a small-scale test migration (PoC) to validate the approach. Once the plan is refined, the preparation phase involves setting up backup systems, testing connectivity, and configuring rollback options. During execution, workloads are moved to the cloud in small phases using tools like AWS DMS or Azure Migrate to reduce risk. The migrated systems are then tested for performance, security, and data integrity.

After the migration is complete, businesses shift their focus to optimization and continuous improvement. This involves performance tuning, cost optimization, and security hardening. Teams use tools like AWS Cost Explorer, Azure Cost Management, and GCP Cost Insights to monitor and control expenses, while implementing security best practices like IAM policies and multi-factor authentication (MFA). Regular performance checks and system monitoring help maintain uptime, avoid bottlenecks, and ensure smooth day-to-day operations. By following this structured roadmap, businesses can successfully modernize their infrastructure, enabling scalability, agility, and long-term cost savings in the cloud.

8. Measure Success with Key Metrics
Define the metrics (KPIs) that will measure the success of your strategy. Your KPIs should be SMART (Specific, Measurable, Achievable, Relevant, Time-bound).

Example Cloud KPIs:
- Cloud Cost Savings – Track cost reductions before and after migration.
- Application Uptime – Measure the availability of key applications.
- Deployment Frequency – Track how often DevOps teams push updates.
- Incident Response Time – Measure how quickly issues are detected and resolved.

Action Step:
Use tools like AWS CloudWatch or Google Cloud Monitoring to track uptime, incident response times, and other key metrics.

Building a cloud strategy requires alignment between business goals, technical objectives, and operational controls. By following the steps outlined in this section, businesses can create a solid strategy that addresses governance, workload prioritization, cost management, and migration planning. With a clear roadmap in place, you'll avoid costly mistakes, reduce downtime, and set your organization up for long-term success in the cloud.

Tips for Optimization and Long-Term Efficiency
A strong cloud strategy isn't just about getting to the cloud — it's about staying optimized. Without the right controls, companies risk wasting resources, overspending, and underutilizing services. Achieving long-term efficiency requires a commitment to continuous improvement.

This section provides actionable tips for optimizing cloud performance, controlling costs, and achieving operational efficiency. By applying these principles, companies can make their cloud environment more agile, secure, and cost-effective.

1. Optimize Cloud Cost Management
Uncontrolled cloud costs are one of the biggest issues companies face after migration. By following FinOps (Financial Operations) principles, companies can maintain visibility into cloud spending and drive long-term cost efficiency.

A. Key Cost Optimization Strategies
- Rightsize Cloud Resources
  - Problem: Companies often over-provision VMs, containers, and storage.
  - Solution: Use AI-driven tools like AWS Compute Optimizer or Google Cloud Recommender to find underutilized VMs.
  - Action Step: Automatically downsize underutilized instances or switch to smaller instance types.
- Use Spot and Reserved Instances
  - Spot Instances: Leverage AWS or Azure spot instances for temporary workloads that don't require high availability.
  - Reserved Instances: Pre-purchase compute capacity at a discount (up to 75% savings).
  - Action Step: Identify non-critical workloads (like batch jobs) that can be offloaded to spot instances.
- Serverless Computing
  - Problem: Running VMs 24/7 costs money even when idle.
  - Solution: Replace VMs with serverless functions (AWS Lambda, Google Cloud Functions) to only pay for compute time.
  - Action Step: Refactor your apps into serverless workflows where possible.
- Automate Cost Alerts and Budgets
  - Action Step: Use AWS Budgets or GCP Cost Management to create spending alerts. Set usage limits and notify key stakeholders if usage exceeds targets.
  - AI Solution: AI cost monitoring tools like CloudHealth predict usage spikes before they happen.

B. Long-Term Cost Management Best Practices
- Use Cloud Cost Reports – Use AWS Cost and Usage Reports (CUR) to analyze past spending and predict future costs.
- Consolidate Billing Accounts – Merge multiple AWS or GCP billing accounts into a single account to maximize volume discounts.
- Use Savings Plans – AWS and Azure offer savings plans for long-term commitments, providing better discounts than on-demand rates.

2. Improve Performance and Scalability
Cloud performance optimization ensures low latency, fast response times, and seamless user experiences. By optimizing performance, companies can improve customer satisfaction and reduce downtime.

A. Scaling Best Practices
- Auto-Scaling and Elasticity
  - Use AWS Auto Scaling or Google Cloud Autoscaler to scale cloud instances up or down based on demand.
  - Enable scaling for stateless services, microservices, and serverless functions.
  - Pro Tip: Set custom scaling rules to prevent scaling "too late" during traffic spikes.
- Use Content Delivery Networks (CDNs)
  - CDNs cache static content like images and files closer to end users.
  - Example: Use AWS CloudFront or Azure CDN to cache static content in edge locations.
  - Pro Tip: Move large assets (like images or videos) to a CDN to reduce the load on primary servers.
- Horizontal Scaling (Scale Out)
  - Instead of "scaling up" (buying bigger machines), scale out by adding more servers to the workload.
  - Example: Break a monolithic app into microservices and scale each service independently.

B. Load Balancing and Traffic Optimization
- Use Load Balancers – Spread incoming traffic across multiple instances to prevent bottlenecks.
  - Tool: Use AWS Elastic Load Balancer (ELB), Azure Load Balancer, or Google Cloud Load Balancer.
  - Pro Tip: Set load balancers to use regional failover to maintain uptime.
- Route Traffic Using DNS Services
  - Use AWS Route 53 or Google Cloud DNS to send users to the fastest, closest data center.
  - Pro Tip: Configure DNS-based load balancing to handle large amounts of traffic during global launches.
- Proactive Scaling Using AI Predictions
  - AI models can predict future demand and pre-scale infrastructure accordingly.
  - Tool: Use AI models in AWS Predictive Scaling or Google Cloud's AI Operations to forecast usage spikes.

C. Storage Optimization
- Data Tiering
  - Use S3 Intelligent Tiering to automatically move objects to lower-cost storage tiers.
  - Archive older data using AWS Glacier or Azure Archive Storage for cost savings.
- Data Compression and Deduplication
  - Compress large files before storing them.
  - Pro Tip: Tools like AWS Storage Gateway and Azure Backup support built-in deduplication.

3. Increase Security and Compliance

Cloud security is a continuous process. Companies must stay ahead of threats by securing identities, encrypting data, and maintaining regulatory compliance.

A. Identity and Access Management (IAM)
- Principle of Least Privilege (PoLP)
  - Only grant the access users need and no more.
  - Action Step: Use AWS IAM roles and policies to restrict access.
- Multi-Factor Authentication (MFA)
  - Enable MFA on all AWS root accounts, service accounts, and privileged roles.
- Audit IAM Access Logs
  - Use AWS CloudTrail to see when users attempt to access resources they don't have permission for.

B. Encryption Best Practices
- Encrypt Data at Rest
  - Use AWS KMS or Azure Key Vault to encrypt data stored in S3, EBS, and RDS databases.
  - Pro Tip: Use automatic encryption for S3 buckets by default.
- Encrypt Data in Transit
  - Force HTTPS traffic only and encrypt API communications.
  - Tool: Use AWS Certificate Manager (ACM) to manage SSL/TLS certificates.

C. Compliance and Governance
- Use AI-Driven Compliance Tools
  - AWS Config monitors configuration drift and ensures compliance with standards like GDPR, HIPAA, and PCI-DSS.
  - Azure Policy enforces compliance at scale.
- Real-Time Threat Detection
  - Use AWS GuardDuty or Microsoft Defender for Cloud to detect abnormal behavior.
  - AI Tip: Use AI anomaly detection to spot unusual activity and stop attacks early.

4. Adopt Continuous Improvement and Automation
Cloud optimization is a continuous process. Companies that review and optimize monthly see the best results.

A. Review and Optimize Monthly
- Use Monthly Cloud Reviews
  - Schedule monthly meetings to review cloud usage reports.
  - Use AWS Cost and Usage Reports (CUR) to identify which teams are overspending.
- Run Postmortems After Outages
  - Use AWS Fault Injection Simulator to trigger controlled failures.
  - Conduct root cause analysis (RCA) after every incident.

B. Automate Wherever Possible
- Self-Healing Systems
  - Build systems that recover from failures automatically using AWS Auto Scaling and AWS Fault Injection Simulator.
- Auto-Tag Resources
  - Use AI tools to enforce tagging policies so you know which team owns each cloud resource.
- Automate Cost Optimization
  - Use AI cost optimization tools like CloudHealth or AWS Compute Optimizer to automatically resize instances.

Cloud optimization isn't a one-time effort. It's a continuous cycle of cost control, performance improvement, and automation. By following the tips in this section, companies can reduce costs, improve speed, and achieve higher uptime. Key tools like AWS Compute Optimizer, AWS Fault Injection Simulator, and Google Cloud Recommender ensure proactive automation and continuous optimization.

Aligning Cloud Goals with Business Objectives
A cloud strategy isn't just an IT initiative — it's a business strategy. For cloud adoption to be successful, it must be linked to measurable business outcomes like increased agility, cost reduction, and faster time to market. Without this alignment, cloud initiatives often lose focus, face resistance from stakeholders, and fail to deliver ROI.

This section explores how to align cloud goals with broader business objectives. It provides a step-by-step approach to ensuring that cloud investments support corporate goals, like improving customer experience, driving revenue growth, and enabling innovation.

1. Define Business Objectives and Link Them to Cloud Goals
The foundation of any successful cloud strategy starts with a clear understanding of the company's business objectives. Each cloud initiative should have a direct, measurable impact on these objectives. To create this alignment, you need to identify your company's key priorities and link them to cloud goals.

A business may aim to reduce operational costs, improve product delivery speed, or ensure better customer experiences. For example, if a company's primary goal is to reduce operational costs, the cloud goal might be to replace legacy infrastructure with a serverless architecture to eliminate the cost of running 24/7 servers. Similarly, if the company's goal is to enhance customer experience, the cloud goal may focus on multi-region app deployments to ensure fast response times for customers worldwide.

When setting these goals, it is important to follow the SMART goal framework — Specific, Measurable, Achievable, Relevant, and Time-bound. For example, instead of saying "improve system performance," a SMART goal might be "achieve a 20% reduction in API response time using AWS CloudFront within 90 days." This clear, quantifiable goal makes it easier to track progress and measure success.

One way to identify cloud goals is to conduct a business impact analysis (BIA). This approach ensures that each cloud objective directly supports a key business outcome. Companies might set goals like improving uptime, reducing total operating costs, or speeding up product delivery timelines. The key is to tie cloud goals directly to these outcomes so they can be clearly understood by stakeholders at all levels.

2. Engage Key Stakeholders and Define Roles
A successful cloud strategy requires support and engagement from multiple teams, not just IT. Cross-departmental collaboration ensures that business units, finance, and IT are all working toward the same objective. Without buy-in from key stakeholders, cloud initiatives risk delays, miscommunication, and funding issues.

To build alignment, it's important to define the roles of key players in the strategy. Executives, such as the CEO or CFO, focus on strategic alignment and business impact. Cloud architects handle technical design, and compliance teams ensure that regulatory requirements are met. DevOps engineers manage deployments and maintain uptime, while financial officers oversee the budget and ensure costs stay within limits.

To secure executive buy-in, it's essential to link cloud strategy to tangible business outcomes. Executives prioritize revenue growth, cost reduction, and customer experience, so frame the cloud strategy as a way to drive these goals forward. For example, instead of saying, "We'll use AWS Auto Scaling," say, "We'll reduce our operational costs by 30% by optimizing server usage with auto-scaling."

3. Measure and Report on Business Impact
After linking cloud goals to business objectives, it's crucial to track and report progress. Without this step, stakeholders may lose interest or question the value of the investment. Tracking progress ensures that your cloud initiatives stay relevant to business needs.

To measure success, use key performance indicators (KPIs). KPIs should be specific, actionable, and directly related to business outcomes. For example, if your business objective is to improve customer experience, one KPI might be average page load time. For a goal like reducing operating costs, a relevant KPI could be monthly cloud spend reduction.

When reporting KPIs, be sure to use clear, visual dashboards that non-technical stakeholders can understand. Tools like AWS Cost Explorer and Google Cloud Monitoring allow companies to visualize cloud usage, cost trends, and performance data. For example, you can show executives a dashboard that displays monthly cloud spending, uptime statistics, and system latency. This provides clear evidence of the value of your cloud strategy.

Tracking KPIs is a continuous process. Cloud usage and business needs evolve over time, so it's essential to review KPIs regularly. If your business objectives change, such as shifting from cost reduction to revenue growth, you may need to adjust which KPIs you track. Quarterly strategy review meetings are a great opportunity to assess the effectiveness of cloud initiatives and identify areas for improvement.

4. Continuous Alignment and Adaptation
Cloud strategies are never "set it and forget it." Business priorities, customer needs, and cloud technology evolve, and your strategy should evolve too. Continuous alignment ensures that cloud investments remain relevant and continue to provide value.

One of the most effective ways to maintain alignment is to conduct quarterly strategy reviews. These reviews bring together executives, technical leads, and finance stakeholders to discuss progress, challenges, and next steps. During the review, focus on three questions:
- Are we meeting our business objectives?
- Are we staying within budget?
- What new opportunities have emerged?

These reviews can also highlight areas where course corrections are needed. For example, if an application migration is taking longer than expected, the team may need to adopt a different approach, like switching from "Replatform" to "Rehost" under the 6 Rs strategy.

Cloud strategy reviews also ensure that cloud initiatives remain aligned with executive-level goals. If the company's priorities change — for instance, if there is a sudden need to reduce costs — the cloud strategy should shift accordingly. This might involve renegotiating reserved instance contracts, shutting down idle resources, or shifting to multi-cloud deployments.

5. Best Practices for Alignment
Achieving alignment between cloud goals and business objectives requires a clear, structured approach. Here are some best practices to follow:

Start with Business Objectives
- Before launching any cloud initiative, define the business objectives. Ask, "What does the business want to achieve?" Once you have that answer, define the cloud goals that support it. For example, if the objective is to improve customer experience, the cloud goal might be to reduce latency for end users by 20%.

Use SMART Goals

- SMART goals are the foundation of a successful strategy. Make sure each cloud goal is Specific, Measurable, Achievable, Relevant, and Time-bound. For example, instead of setting a vague goal like "Improve application performance," set a SMART goal like "Reduce page load time by 15% using CloudFront by Q4."

Assign Accountability

- Every cloud goal should have a single accountable owner. This could be a Cloud Architect, DevOps Lead, or Business Unit Manager. Having a clear owner ensures that someone is responsible for driving progress.

Leverage AI-Driven Tools for Alignment

- Use AI-driven analytics tools like AWS Compute Optimizer to identify cost savings, resource optimizations, and workload efficiencies. By providing predictive insights, these tools help companies make more informed, data-driven decisions that keep their cloud goals on track.

Build a Communication Plan

- Regularly update stakeholders on progress toward cloud goals. Use reports, dashboards, and performance scorecards to communicate business impact. Include metrics that matter to stakeholders, like cost savings, system uptime, and customer satisfaction improvements.

Review and Revise Quarterly

- Cloud initiatives aren't static. Review cloud goals and business objectives every quarter. If the company's business goals shift, adjust cloud strategy to maintain alignment. Quarterly reviews are a chance to identify "quick wins" and build momentum for the next quarter.

Aligning cloud goals with business objectives is a continuous process, not a one-time effort. It requires ongoing alignment between executives, technical teams, and finance stakeholders. Companies that master this process are more likely to see cloud investments deliver tangible results — from cost reduction and speed-to-market improvements to better customer experiences.

By following the steps outlined in this section, companies can achieve full alignment between cloud strategy and business goals. The result is a cloud environment that drives measurable value for the business, rather than being viewed as just an IT expense.

Conclusion:
Building a cloud strategy is more than just a technical exercise — it's a blueprint for business transformation. By aligning cloud initiatives with business objectives, organizations can achieve operational efficiency, cost savings, and customer satisfaction. Companies that adopt this approach move from "cloud for IT" to "cloud for business growth."

The journey to building a successful cloud strategy involves three key components:
1. Develop and Implement the Strategy – Define practical steps to prioritize workloads, choose the right cloud model, and establish a governance framework.
2. Optimize for Long-Term Efficiency – Control costs, improve performance, and leverage automation to drive continuous improvement.
3. Align Cloud Goals with Business Objectives – Ensure every cloud goal directly supports business priorities, from cost reduction to improved customer experience.

One of the most important lessons from this chapter is that cloud strategy is not static. Business needs evolve, and so must the strategy. By conducting quarterly reviews, updating goals, and maintaining strong stakeholder engagement, companies can stay ahead of changes and maintain alignment between cloud initiatives and business priorities.

To ensure success, leverage AI-driven tools for predictive insights, cost optimization, and performance tracking. AI tools like AWS Compute Optimizer, CloudHealth, and AWS Cost Explorer ensure that cloud goals remain relevant to business outcomes. AI also enables self-healing systems and intelligent workload distribution, allowing companies to achieve maximum uptime with minimal manual intervention.

Key Takeaways:
- A cloud strategy must be directly linked to key business outcomes like revenue growth, cost savings, and improved customer experience.
- Use the SMART goal framework to ensure cloud goals are specific, measurable, and time-bound.
- Engage key stakeholders (CFOs, CIOs, DevOps, and compliance teams) to secure buy-in and drive continuous improvement.

- Track key performance indicators (KPIs) like cost savings, application uptime, and system performance to prove ROI.
- Conduct quarterly strategy reviews to identify course corrections and adjust cloud goals as the business evolves.

Ultimately, a well-crafted cloud strategy is a growth engine for the business. It creates opportunities for faster innovation, operational agility, and cost efficiency. By leveraging AI tools and aligning cloud goals with business priorities, companies can ensure that their cloud investment is a driver of growth, not just an operational expense.

AI Insight:
"AI doesn't just follow strategy — it creates it. By using predictive insights, automated self-healing systems, and anomaly detection, AI helps businesses make smarter decisions about cloud goals, costs, and performance."

Chapter 36: Tools and Resources

In the world of cloud computing, having the right tools and resources can make the difference between struggling to keep up and thriving with confidence. Cloud platforms like AWS, Azure, and Google Cloud offer an abundance of services, but knowing which tools to use, how to use them, and how to stay ahead of emerging trends requires guidance.

This chapter provides a comprehensive toolkit for readers to continue their cloud journey. From essential tools to support cloud operations, to hands-on exercises that solidify learning, to career-enhancing certifications and study resources, this chapter ensures that you're fully equipped to succeed in the cloud computing landscape.

1. Interactive Exercises and Real-World Practice Labs
Cloud theory is important, but practical experience is critical. To truly master cloud concepts, you need hands-on practice with live cloud environments. This section introduces interactive exercises, practice labs, and sandbox environments that allow readers to apply their knowledge in real-world scenarios.

A. Interactive Exercises
These exercises cover essential concepts, from setting up virtual machines to configuring disaster recovery. Here's a selection of interactive exercises designed to reinforce the core skills taught in this book:
- Deploy a Virtual Machine (VM) in AWS, Azure, or GCP
  - Objective: Learn how to create, configure, and launch a virtual machine using the console.
  - Task: Spin up an EC2 instance in AWS, a Virtual Machine in Azure, or a Compute Engine VM in GCP.
  - Learning Outcome: Understand how to provision VMs, attach storage, and manage instance states (start, stop, reboot).
- Set Up IAM Roles and Policies
  - Objective: Create IAM roles for least-privilege access and enforce security best practices.
  - Task: Create a role for a "Developer" with restricted access to only certain S3 buckets.
  - Learning Outcome: Learn how to create and manage IAM roles, policies, and permissions for secure access.

- Build a Serverless Application Using AWS Lambda
  - Objective: Launch a serverless function using AWS Lambda.
  - Task: Write a simple Python function that processes data from an S3 bucket and logs it to CloudWatch.
  - Learning Outcome: Understand the principles of event-driven architecture and how to use AWS Lambda for serverless workflows.
- Automate Infrastructure Using Terraform
  - Objective: Use Infrastructure as Code (IaC) to automate cloud deployments.
  - Task: Write a Terraform script that deploys an EC2 instance with a security group and attached storage.
  - Learning Outcome: Learn the fundamentals of Infrastructure as Code (IaC) and how to use it for repeatable cloud deployments.
- Monitor and Scale a Cloud Application Using Auto-Scaling
  - Objective: Implement auto-scaling rules to ensure optimal performance during traffic spikes.
  - Task: Create an auto-scaling group for an EC2 instance, set triggers for scaling up/down, and test the configuration.
  - Learning Outcome: Learn to automate scaling based on traffic spikes and avoid over-provisioning resources.

B. Practice Labs and Sandbox Environments
- AWS Cloud Quest – Gamified interactive training where you complete tasks like launching EC2 instances, configuring Lambda, and managing IAM roles.
- Google Qwiklabs – Hands-on labs for Google Cloud with guided step-by-step activities for VM creation, Kubernetes setup, and app deployment.
- Microsoft Learn Sandbox – Azure's "sandbox" allows learners to explore the cloud environment and practice creating storage accounts, databases, and VMs.

Pro Tip: Take advantage of free-tier offerings from AWS, Azure, and Google Cloud to create a free, personal cloud environment. This allows you to build, experiment, and break things—without paying extra.

2. Essential Cloud Tools and AI-Driven Platforms
This section introduces the most essential cloud tools, platforms, and AI-driven solutions that will accelerate your cloud journey. These tools provide automation, security, cost control, and DevOps support.

A. Must-Know Cloud Tools
- AWS CloudFormation – Automate infrastructure as code (IaC) using YAML/JSON templates.
- Azure DevOps – Build CI/CD pipelines, automate deployments, and manage application releases.
- Terraform – Multi-cloud infrastructure automation tool that works across AWS, Azure, and GCP.
- Kubernetes – Orchestrate and manage containerized applications in the cloud.
- AWS Cost Explorer – Track and analyze cloud costs, usage trends, and cost forecasts.
- CloudHealth by VMware – AI-driven cost optimization and multi-cloud cost tracking platform.
- AWS Lambda – Serverless function service to create event-driven apps with zero infrastructure management.
- Google Cloud Deployment Manager – Automate and manage Google Cloud infrastructure as code.
- AWS Fault Injection Simulator – Simulate failures to test the resilience of cloud apps (chaos engineering).
- AWS GuardDuty – AI-driven security threat detection and anomaly detection in AWS environments.

B. AI-Driven Cloud Platforms
AI-driven platforms offer insights, automation, and decision support. These platforms use machine learning models to predict cost savings, suggest instance resizing, and detect anomalies.
- AWS Compute Optimizer – Recommends instance size adjustments to avoid over-provisioning.
- Azure Advisor – Offers cost-saving recommendations and performance improvements for Azure workloads.
- CloudHealth by VMware – Monitors multi-cloud spend, tracks usage, and recommends cost-saving actions.
- AWS Predictive Scaling – Uses AI to predict future demand and scale infrastructure in advance.
- Google Cloud Operations Suite (formerly Stackdriver) – Monitors app performance, collects logs, and detects anomalies using AI models.

3. Checklists, Templates, and Study Resources
This final section provides practical checklists, downloadable templates, and study resources to help readers master cloud computing concepts. From certification guides to cloud migration templates, this section ensures that readers have the resources they need to succeed.

A. Checklists
- Cloud Migration Checklist – Includes steps for planning, execution, testing, and validation of migrations.
- Security Compliance Checklist – Ensures compliance with GDPR, HIPAA, and PCI-DSS requirements.
- Cost Management Checklist – Tools and tasks to optimize cloud bills, reduce over-provisioning, and track usage.

B. Templates
- Cloud Strategy Template – Template to document your organization's cloud strategy, goals, and roadmap.
- Cloud Cost Optimization Plan – Pre-built template for controlling cloud costs and setting budget alerts.
- Cloud Incident Response Plan – Template for creating an incident response plan to manage cloud outages and security breaches.

C. Certification Resources
- AWS Certified Solutions Architect (Study Guide) – Step-by-step guide to passing the AWS Solutions Architect Associate exam.
- Microsoft Azure Fundamentals (AZ-900) – Certification study guide for Azure fundamentals.
- Google Cloud Professional Cloud Architect – Study path and practice questions for GCP's most sought-after certification.

D. Recommended Study Platforms
- A Cloud Guru – Comprehensive platform with certification courses for AWS, Azure, and GCP.
- Cloud Academy – Hands-on cloud training, certification prep, and career development.
- Linux Academy – Courses on cloud infrastructure, DevOps, and Linux.
- LinkedIn Learning – Cloud certification courses taught by industry experts.

Conclusion:
This chapter arms you with the most practical, hands-on tools for mastering cloud computing. From interactive labs and essential tools to certification resources and checklists, it offers everything you need to stay ahead in the cloud computing landscape.

Whether you're preparing for an AWS certification, improving cost efficiency, or launching your first cloud-native app, the resources in this chapter will support your journey every step of the way.

AI Insight:
"AI doesn't just teach you the cloud — it builds tools that make you a cloud expert. With AI-driven optimization tools and practice labs, your cloud skills will be sharper, your projects more successful, and your career more secure."

www.ingramcontent.com/pod-product-compliance
Lightning Source LLC
Chambersburg PA
CBHW060541200326
41521CB00007B/434